Advance praise for *Executive Coaching*

'*Executive Coaching* is just the right book for the services age. It's a high-quality Australian book, both in content and style of writing. The subject—how leaders can use coaching to enhance the performance and development of their people —applies wherever a high-performance culture is sought. Effective talent management is a major competitive opportunity—or threat!'
Meredith Hellicar, Chief Executive, Corrs Chambers Westgarth

'Attracting, developing and retaining the best people is probably the most sustainable competitive advantage that a business can have—that is why leading the war for talent is one of the key roles of today's CEOs. Written by someone who has many years of practising what he preaches in leading companies, including mine, I can recommend this book as providing practical and powerful advice to managers in the front line.'
David L.G. Hearn, Managing Director, Goodman Fielder

'All businesses in today's fast-changing corporate world are concerned about the development and retention of good people. Peter Stephenson's *Executive Coaching* addresses this concern, by providing a sound business tool for companies looking to introduce internal development programmes, or simply to understand the issue further.'
Peter Wilkinson, Chief Executive, David Jones

'It's an extremely difficult job as a CEO of a large company, particularly one undergoing major restructuring and cultural change. It's always tempting to take shortcuts and underestimate or under-attend to the human factor—a very necessary yet time-consuming alternative, in which most leaders need some help. *Executive Coaching* demonstrates how this can be done, practically and effectively.'
Dr Keith Barton, former Managing Director and CEO, James Hardie Industries

'Many business books focus on management principles for driving a company forward, while others focus on personal development so the reader can use the principles to rise above the crowd. Peter Stephenson's book is unusual in that its entire focus is on developing other people so that they can contribute at a much higher level, thereby ensuring both the individual's and the company's success.'
Nicholas R. McRae, Managing Director Australia/New Zealand, Reader's Digest

'With the business environment under constant change, there is a great and continuing need to ensure key people remain motivated and updated with the changing marketplace. *Executive Coaching* is one of the key planks in our company being able to provide this necessary support.'
Ross Brewer, Managing Director, P&O Maritime Services Pty Ltd

'Through a unique blend of practical management experience, human resource consultancy and an in-depth knowledge of all the relevant research, Peter Stephenson has in my experience added greatly to the career development of individuals and the management of talent by corporations.'
Ken Boag, Chief Operating Executive, Tower Corporation Holdings Limited

'Executive coaching offers probably the greatest opportunity for putting leadership into action and delivering outstanding business results through people. Peter Stephenson's book, *Executive Coaching*, provides leaders and managers the wherewithal for accomplishing this themselves.'
Paul Lilley, Chief Executive Officer, National Small Business, Westpac Banking Corporation

'Much of the training that organisations have invested in over the last 20 years has been totally ineffective and irrelevant. We have wasted our precious time and money on activities that have been unfocused, energy sapping and lifeless. It was the equivalent of giving somebody a new suit and sending them out in the pouring rain without an umbrella.

The recent emergence of coaching and mentoring for executive development is a positive step toward targeted, practical and timely learning strategies: learning that will make a real contribution to the bottom-line.'
John C. Reynolds, Group Executive—Human Resources and Public Affairs, Normandy Mining Limited

EXECUTIVE
COACHING

Dedicated to those fine Australian executives with whom I have been privileged to work and coach over the past ten years.

LEAD

DEVELOP

RETAIN

MOTIVATED

TALENTED

PEOPLE

EXECUTIVE
COACHING

PETER STEPHENSON

First published 2000

Pearson Education Australia
Unit 4, Level 2
14 Aquatic Drive
Frenchs Forest NSW 2086

Publisher: Nella Soeterboek
Project Editor: Carolyn Robson
Cover and internal design: Toni Hope-Caten
Typeset by The Type Group

Printed in Australia by Griffin Press

 2 3 4 5 04 03 02 01

National Library of Australia
Cataloguing-in-Publication Data

Stephenson, Peter.
Executive coaching: lead, develop, retain motivated talented people.

    Includes index.
    ISBN 1 74009 311 9.

    1. Executives – Training of. 2. Leadership. 3. Management –
    Study and teaching. I. Title

658.4092

An imprint of Pearson Education Australia

Table of Contents

About the author

Peter Stephenson is managing director of
The Stephenson Partnership which provides
executive coaching, career consulting and
mentoring to executives in top Australian
and international companies and the
public sector. Headquartered in Sydney, these
services are also provided through licensing
arrangements within companies—'coach-the-
coach'—and from licensed consultants who have been fully trained in The
Stephenson Partnership proprietary methodologies. A particularly fast-growth
area of the business entails on-line delivery of process and content, backed by
human interface. A veritable 'high tech–high touch' solution!

Peter has specialised in executive career consulting, coaching and mentoring
since 1990, although he first designed and marketed self-assessment processes
25 years ago.

He has worked in a number of company director positions in Australia,
Canada and the United Kingdom. He was NSW and ACT director of Davidson &
Associates, Australia's leading outplacement company; the founding managing
director of Deloitte Consulting Group; founding managing director of Hospital
Extension Services; director and general manager of Lucas Marine; and divisional
chief executive of a food group. He has extensive management consulting
experience in the South East Asia region, South Asia, Japan and the People's
Republic of China.

Peter has an exceptional understanding of the issues involved in
organisational change and their impact on executives and staff. He has worked
with many of Australia's top 100 companies on planning and implementing
change and on providing career consulting and coaching for directors and
executives.

Educated in the United Kingdom, Peter holds a postgraduate Diploma in Management Studies specialising in behavioural siences. He is a fellow of the Australian Institute of Company Directors and fellow of the Australian Institute of Management. He is the author of The Bulletproof Executive (HarperCollins, 1997) and of eight audio-cassette workbook programs on personal development and career success.

He can be contacted at The Stephenson Partnership in Sydney, New South Wales, Australia, http://www.thestephensonpartnership.com.au

Foreword

The background to *Executive Coaching* is nine years' empirical research by the author, Peter Stephenson, covering over 500 case studies of senior people and 70 organisational restructures.

Partway through this empirical research, emerging results were verified by an independent executive panel, leading to Stephenson's first book, *The Bulletproof Executive,* which was sold in Australia, the United States and the United Kingdom.

The Bulletproof Executive was effectively a survival guide for individual executives transitioning their way through their careers and included a range of key success factor guidelines. These guidelines are now used by The Stephenson Partnership in their executive coaching.

Readers of *The Bulletproof Executive* will recognise some of this material in *Executive Coaching*, which goes to the next stage and demonstrates how to use such guidelines, along with a broad range of other approaches and processes, in their own coaching applications.

Following on from Stephenson's initial empirical research, over the past 18 months, feedback on the topic of executive talent management has been sought from more than 150 executives including 15 focus group discussions. This has verified and amplified the following:

New executives don't always make it—some organisations often find it takes newly appointed executives nine months to get up to speed. Some perceive over 40% of them not to be up there within their first year, a significant proportion of whom leave within 20 months from starting in their new roles. At vast cost when you include hiring replacements.

No room for the 'controllersaurus'—many more established executives still operate as if in the industrial age and manage via top down 'controlling the what'. In today's information age, the knowledge era, neither customers nor staff will tolerate this. Superior results now come from 'creating the how' through enlightened leadership with a strong customer orientation. Adapt or move on is usually the message to executives.

Hire-and-fire, and jumping ship, alive and well—effectiveness as a leader is only part of the success equation; motivation through a sense of full alignment with the organisation is also vital for success. Yet the continuing practice of 'hire-and-fire' does little to build trust and commitment, let alone alignment. And so executives jump ship—often to the competition.

Huge executive wastage and unnecessary expense—the costs and missed opportunities caused by a talented executive resigning, along with replacement hiring, can run to many hundreds of thousands of dollars. As can the problems associated with underperforming executives, or those mismatched with their roles, usually left to sort it out for themselves. Similarly, the costs associated with dismissal and replacement hiring—still the preferred, yet costly, option for those executives seen as operating below par.

Results of change often dismal—two-thirds of company restructures and mergers do not yield sought-after bottomline improvements on time; less than 20% produce satisfactory outcomes; and one-third yield unsatisfactory levels of performance improvement, or it takes too long to achieve it. Also, 70% of organisations downsizing find no immediate increase in productivity and more than 50% fail to improve profitability the following year. These dismal results flow from the time taken for some executives to come to terms with, and adapt to change, creating a freeze-frame situation for those around them in their own progress (and the organisation's) through change.

Thus, it can be concluded that many executives cannot quite get a grip on these times of ambiguity, 'human resource-lean' enterprises, sudden and frequent bouts of change, or how to apply and live with 360° collaborative techniques.

And progressive organisations now know they have to do something significant to maximise the return on their investment in executives. Just like the professional golfer or rugby team, this can be achieved with a top coach using proven techniques. Also, executive coaching lessens the risks of losing motivated talent to the competition by aligning an individual's goals and plans with those of the organisation.

And so in 1998 Peter Stephenson put himself in the line of fire, by opening up in executive coaching in Sydney to help organisations and their executives attain quantum improvement in business performance. Called The Stephenson Partnership, their executive coaching, career consulting and mentoring, whether provided face-to-face, or in part on-line, makes and saves companies literally hundreds of thousands of dollars.

And now he has decided to share with all interested parties the approaches and processes which can be used for executives, and by executives, for:

➤ Halving the time it takes newly appointed executives and other key people to get up to speed and become 'profitable'. Similarly, at times of restructure or merger when executives and managers assume new roles or reporting relationships.

➤ Developing greater leverage and effect from leadership, teamwork, change management, interpersonal relations and communication.

➤ Attaining quantum improvements in the performance, motivation and effectiveness of established executives and key people, individually and in teams.

➤ Retaining motivated key people far longer.

➤ Re-aligning square pegs in round holes.

➤ Avoiding costly dismissals and replacement hiring.

Stephenson's approaches make sense. Improving executive effectiveness, say, by 10% to 20% or more, can have great leverage on teams and staff, and a profound impact on the bottomline. By comparison, the costs of dismissal and rehiring can run into many hundreds of thousands of dollars, as can the costs and missed opportunities of losing motivated talent to the competition. Often, a more than twentyfold return on the investment in coaching can be realised.

But buyer beware! There are many new so-called coaches coming into the market. Make sure they use coaching processes based on comprehensive empirical research and international best practice. To get results, they need to be delivered by senior business-oriented executives.

Peter Stephenson's armoury of proprietary processes comprises a database exceeding 1000 pages, a significant proportion of which are drawn from his earlier book, *The Bulletproof Executive*. This database represents his intellectual property, much of which he is now making available in this his second book, *Executive Coaching*.

His approaches are outcome focused and deliver short-term improvements and sustained long-term benefits. He has found that only selected tools and techniques in the hands of extensively trained and highly experienced business coaches will generate outstanding results. The coach who just 'wings it' is usually a waste of everyone's time and money.

In *Executive Coaching*, Peter Stephenson makes available much of what he has learned and practised with executives in some of the world's, and Australia's, leading corporations.

Where statistics are cited, these are all estimates based on Stephenson's empirical research over nine years and compared to a broad range of other input received from international sources, before final estimates are reached and presented.

Executive Coaching, while positioned at coaching at the executive level, is also relevant for coaching managers, senior professionals and supervisors. The intended readership audience is executives, managers, internal and external human resource consultants and others seeking to reap outstanding returns from every organisation's most valuable and yet variable resource, its people.

Chapter 1

SETTING THE SCENE FOR EXECUTIVE COACHING

66 Some organisations and their
leaders need to re-invent
themselves 99

INTRODUCTION

Having worked with more than 500 senior people as an executive coach, career consultant and mentor over the past nine years, I conclude that many of them still have a long way to go in getting the best out of their most valuable and variable resource—their staff. Many senior people need to reinvent themselves in terms of how they perform as leaders, and in the way they are motivated and create a motivational environment for others at work.

Of these, my first 300 case studies led to my book The *Bulletproof Executive*, my conclusions having been verified by an 85-member independent executive panel prior to its publication.

Since then, with the establishment of Australia's first dedicated executive coaching, career consulting and mentoring practice, The Stephenson Partnership, I have been able to advance my earlier findings and spell out the new rules of the executive game.

Any executive can identify with, and indeed lives and breathes, the era of economic rationalisation within which we all travel.

Whether it is a focus on bottomline and quarterly results, continuing cost reduction, flatter organisation structures, or change (not going away, just going faster), the impact on how we all feel and operate is profound. Many of us feel like expendable human assets, doing more at work, with less, faster! Whole-life balance issues abound. There is an erosion of employee trust, loyalty and commitment—even at the executive level.

And this is the era of executives being hired in profusion, being fired and jumping ship in profusion, at vast cost to the employer and with huge loss of valuable intellectual capital, which all seems to go unrecognised. It is all too easy to dismiss, replace, rehire and outplace, yet does this automatically lead to a more successful organisation? Probably not in many cases. But the market's financial analysts perceive such changes as the panacea and CEOs act accordingly.

And meanwhile, the greatest impact on corporate life into the 2000s accelerates unchecked, 'The Information Revolution!'—the era of knowledge.

THE INFORMATION REVOLUTION

It does not seem so long ago that we were all schooled in managing the 'factors of production', namely, land, labour, buildings, plant, equipment and raw materials. Indeed, many organisations are still in the industrial age where executives have tight control over these physical assets, the capital of the company.

However, with the insurgence of the personal computer and its linkage with advanced telecommunications, the door is open to assets over which executives have far less direct control. These are intellectual assets comprising customer and supplier information, processes, skills, experience, global alliances, patents and technology, along with an increasingly mobile and younger workforce with different mindsets to their forbears.

An example of this change in asset types, and the nature of the capital of the company, are airlines which own no planes. Their success depends on customer databases, landing rights and reservation systems which pop up first on the screen of the travel agent or on the Internet booking site.

Similarly, trucking companies which own no trucks, but which have captive customers locked into easily accessed and elegant scheduling and logistics systems connected to automated warehouses (which are also outsourced).

Finally, the sports shoe 'manufacturer' which, in fact, never manufactures a single shoe, its assets relating to product design and expertise in trade sales, distribution and consumer marketing, production being placed in the hands of the world's lowest cost plants wherever they might reside.

And so as we transition from the industrial age into the information age, the capital of the company changes from purely physical assets (over which the executive has tight control) towards intellectual assets (over which the executive has far less direct control), along with a vastly different workforce. And this is where the trouble can start!

The industrial age executive 'controlled the what' by managing the factors of production by conventional top-down management. A relatively simple command and control model accepted, albeit grudgingly, by the workforce of yesteryear.

The information age executive, on the other hand, can only 'create the how' by facilitating people and processes via enlightened leadership and with a strong customer orientation. A far more complex leadership and facilitation model expected by today's workers, who from early schooldays have been taught, it seems, to question almost everything.

The complexity is compounded as most organisations are in transition between these two so-called 'ages' and will likely retain one foot in each camp for many years to come. This means that executives need to develop within the leadership and facilitation paradigm, yet retain elements of the command and control paradigm, in other words increasingly create the how and yet continue to control some of the what, according to situations and priorities.

The final moving target is the organisation's expectations in terms of desirable management practices and leadership traits during this transition, compared to the executive or manager's perception of how they should act and behave. Clearly, opportunities abound for these expectations and perceptions to be poles apart, with some executives still stuck in command and control mode, and others earnest to win the popularity stakes in the feel-good, be nice to everyone, happy school of mismanagement.

All of this is happening and changing at such a pace, that it is indeed a 'revolution' we are experiencing, rather than evolution—an uncomfortable revolution it is for many. And caught up in the transition from 'controlling the what' to 'creating the how' is a range of key success factors for executives and managers, some very obvious, some hidden and which are described in Chapter 2—'Executive effectiveness: myths and realities'.

EXAMPLE

A top-performing and somewhat aggressive dealmaker was starting to alienate those around him, from whom he needed ongoing support and input. By learning to involve people and draw them out, rather than simply tell them what to do, he found the quality and quantity of their contributions increased and the workplace enhanced in terms of interpersonal relationships and cooperation.

ATTAINING NEW LEVELS OF EXECUTIVE EFFECTIVENESS

In the course of my work I meet many outstanding individuals in leadership and executive positions, but it begs the question what if they could really attain their full potential, for themselves and for the organisation? What might be the effect—if they could achieve maximum leverage through their staff, teams and budgets—on attaining financial and other results they do not currently aspire to?

I have found that most organisations, particularly at times of major change, fail to unlock the full potential of their most valuable and variable resource, their people. Many try a range of management approaches, which often turn out nothing more than half-baked, quick-fix solutions. I call them management 'mirages'.

Most organisations fail to address the key factor, that it all boils down to real leadership and teamwork in action, which needs to cascade powerfully through the organisation. This is the main opportunity facing most organisations today, and the challenge is how to make it really happen!

In this, I find that most conventional training, learning and development interventions provide new knowledge or self-awareness. The trouble is they do not make it happen, or they do not make it happen fast enough. Or they do not make it happen intensively or sustainably enough. This is because they often miss the point. They try to do it for leaders and executives, by encumbering them with largely unnecessary and ineffective processes, rather than emphasising content, in other words, focusing on how actually to lead and manage for high performance in teams and individually.

Leaders and executives can only do this for themselves, which is my approach, using my proven implementation processes which are based on extensive empirical and international research—the subject of this book.

With such input, leaders and executives can really attain new levels of effectiveness through high performance leadership, management and teamwork, and pass this down the organisation, and make this the culture: 'The way we do things around here!'

Reading and then using the contents of this book, can make this happen!

EMOTIONAL INTELLIGENCE

And in making it happen in this way, leaders and executives will be exhibiting and developing their emotional intelligence, which really is at the heart of leadership.

Why? Because emotional intelligence is about:

➤ recognising and dealing effectively with the way you think and feel, underpinning high levels of personal motivation, performance and self control;
➤ understanding how you are perceived by others and your impact on others;
➤ how to understand and handle other people and their feelings— the first step in inspiring and leading others towards positive goals;
➤ understanding and upholding universal values—walking the talk!

Emotional intelligence, therefore, requires great empathy and active listening skills, and a full understanding of, and how to deal with individual differences, often insufficiently practised by our leaders today.

EXAMPLE

I was called in at a time when the divisional general manager was at risk of alienating himself from his boss and derailing his career. Through executive coaching the divisional general manager became more aware of their differences in operating style and how to modify his behaviour to elicit a more favourable response. Also, their very different approaches once harmonised, led to greater synergy.

There is plenty of evidence to show that there is a strong correlation between emotional intelligence in the leaders, executives and managers within a company, and the delivery of superior business results.

Take the case of a major international fast moving consumer goods company. Divisional performance excelled where led by executives perceived to exhibit strong emotional intelligence, compared to divisional performance elsewhere.

It seems that all the attributes of the information age, collaborative and facilitative leaders exhibiting superior emotional intelligence, actually do generate superior results. Not that leaders should be soft or engage in the happy school of mismanagement. Rather, that they be able to leverage people and teams to the full, by treating them as human, rather than physical assets.

Which in a nutshell, is what this book is about!

KEYNOTE

➤ 'Doing more with less, faster' is here to stay!

➤ The Information Revolution requires 'creating the how' as well as 'controlling the what'.

➤ Many executives and managers pursue quick-fix solutions which invariably turn out as 'mirages'.

➤ They are also often encumbered with largely unnecessary and ineffective people processes.

➤ Executives have to lead and manage—processes can't.

➤ Emotional intelligence, which can be learned and applied, helps them do this.

Chapter 2

EXECUTIVE EFFECTIVENESS: MYTHS AND REALITIES

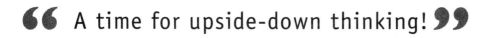 **A time for upside-down thinking!**

INTRODUCTION

Clearly, executives are caught in shifting sands as they confront unprecedented organisational change and complexity. And the journey through the sands, interspersed with periods of drought, memories of past safer havens, and glimpses of better conditions ahead, represents an opportunity for many, a challenge too, and for some, a threat.

This uncertain journey has caused many to search for props, frequently in the form of management fads, which often turn out to be mirages in the quest for executive and organisational success.

FIRST MIRAGE

The first mirage is that executive life is all about results. But results are a given these days and what actually separates successful executives from also-rans is how they behave, the degree to which they exhibit 'desirable' leadership traits, and how they manage and lead not only their direct reports but peers, senior colleagues, stakeholders and external contacts.

SECOND MIRAGE

The second mirage is that executive success is all about leadership. While leadership is a vital ingredient, success also depends on basic management and administrative competence in order to maximise the bottomline and shareholder returns. Success is also about motivation—no matter how skilled an executive may be as a leader or manager, without high levels of self-motivation at work, these skills will simply be underdeployed.

THIRD MIRAGE

The third mirage is that an organisation's success requires a team of stars at the executive level. While a team of stars clearly helps, what has an even more powerful effect is a star team. Developing teamwork through interpersonal relationships is at the heart of this, so that each team member harmonises, rather than competes with the other. This generates a powerfully synergistic effect, whereas the overly internally competitive team may eventually self-destruct.

FOURTH MIRAGE

The fourth mirage is that a new CEO or a new senior executive needs fresh blood, a new team, their own team—out with the old and in with the new! Coupled with this is the theme that people won't change and that the organisation is better off replacing apparently less than satisfactory performers and dispensing with their services.

Such loss of intellectual capital, the huge costs associated with 'fire-and-hire', the time and cost it takes for new people to get up to speed, and the erosion of employee trust and morale that this can cause, all suggest there must be a better way. And there is a better way. Starting at the top and cascading down throughout the organisation, executives and staff need to understand better what is expected of them at work and they need to be coached to help them generate great outcomes.

Just like the sports coach. The day of the executive spending more time coaching is now upon us, so that an organisation's most valuable and variable resource—its executives and staff—can continuously develop, remain motivated and stay with the organisation. A great way to position the organisation as an employer of choice!

FIFTH MIRAGE

The fifth mirage is that downsizing works. Invariably it doesn't! In fact, a range of studies show that two-thirds of organisations which downsize fail to attain their performance improvement objectives in terms of quantum and timeframe. There is a range of more graduated options than 'big bang' in downsizing, which if applied invariably generates better outcomes in the medium to longer term.

Such options include more attention to medium, if not longer term, staffing requirements and succession planning, natural attrition, early retirement, part-time work, job sharing, study leave, leave of absence, secondment and discretionary voluntary redundancy. But for now, 'big bang' seems to remain very much in vogue.

SIXTH MIRAGE

The sixth mirage is that executives and staff should now manage their own careers. This may be a natural reaction at times of organisational turbulence, in other words, for individuals to develop a sense of personal security in place of job security. However, if an organisation abdicates this responsibility to its staff, then one outcome may certainly be that the talent manages their way out of the organisation!

While I am not disputing the need for individuals to become more career resilient, I am not in favour of the career theme being abdicated to them. It would seem to make economic sense for line managers to put some energy and time into seeking greater career alignment for their staff—individual and organisational goals coinciding as far as possible—in order to generate a 'You win, I win, we all win together' outcome. The bottomline, therefore, is a degree of shared responsibility in career management to ensure, least of all, that the talent is nurtured and retained.

EXAMPLE

A senior operations executive reached a stage in her career when she felt she needed to move into a new position giving her greater commercial exposure, if necessary with a new company. Through career consulting she was able to determine an internal career path leading to major account management, which her company enthusiastically supported once she had demonstrated the mutual benefits potentially to be so derived.

SEVENTH MIRAGE

The seventh mirage is that an executive or indeed anyone in a company needs to conform and play it somewhat safe these days. But an organisation of clones is not going to go very far at all, and nor is the clone. Differences in terms of personal operating style and views on strategy and operations need to be encouraged, rather than scorned.

For this to happen the onus is on the organisation to create an environment which engenders motivation and thinking outside the square. And the onus is on the individual to communicate their ideas in a way whereby they are taken seriously and listened to, rather than too easily rejected. In this, personal selling and presentation skills clearly play important roles. As does a sense of personal confidence which can be developed through a greater understanding of self-image and career direction and destiny, no matter who the future employer might be.

EXAMPLE

A highly gifted and respected technical executive was seen lacking in leadership and administrative skills. Through executive coaching and career consulting I was able to help him and the organisation decide that he should concentrate on the leadership of innovation (where he could add great value), lessening the leadership of people emphasis. Professional consultative selling and influencing skills then formed the focus of his ongoing coaching and mentoring, greatly enhancing his personal impact.

EXECUTIVE SUCCESS FACTORS

Based on my research and experience over nearly a decade, 'controlling the what' continues to be a success factor (providing the control is subtle and facilitative, rather than autocratic) and focuses on the delivery of exceptional business results. This is the bottomline and a given, of course, but in today's fast-paced and constantly changing operational environment, doing more with less, faster, puts at risk even the basics of executive success, namely getting the job done well. Focusing on the primary drivers of business performance—leading, managing and developing talent and being alert to external trends and projections—all take on a new significance when executives are spread as thin as current cost structures dictate for the sake of competitiveness.

Moving more towards 'creating the how', a critical area is mastery in leading others in times of change. Change will not disappear, it will only accelerate! Adaptability, entrepreneurism (innovation balanced by risk management), resilience and, above all, open two-way communication are the base competencies on which change leadership mastery can be built, along with adopting restructuring 'best practice' and a consistent people emphasis.

Another mainly 'how'—and one of the most important—is executives fitting in and exhibiting personal chemistry which enables them to harmonise, not only with direct reports, but also with peers and senior colleagues. For this to happen their motivational needs (i.e. they may be material, structural, behavioural or emotional) must be satisfied by the organisation; they must exhibit appropriate leadership traits (the desirable balance between control and creativity, people and output); their operating style and team behaviour has to complement and add value to teamwork; and they also need to be in synchrony with the vagaries of organisational politics, power and influence.

The final 'how' is executives being perceived to be 'giving of their all' in their current roles, motivated and committed to the development of the business, not just going through the motions, but genuinely, even passionately aligned with their jobs, the organisation and its future. In this, the job, values and organisational fit are paramount, as is a clear sense of career direction, control and alignment with business strategy. This is a great way to enhance executive retention and reduce the risks and costs of losing talent.

And yet how many square pegs in round holes do you know, with the inevitable adverse impact on morale, motivation and performance?

THE MAIN DRIVERS OF SUCCESS

As we move down this list of 'what' and 'how' success factors, it is interesting to observe that the class of factor changes. The earlier factors are all about competence. The last factors are far more oriented towards motivation. And this spells out the two main drivers of effectiveness and success as an executive or manager: competence which is maximised through executive development; and motivation which is maximised through career and motivational alignment and a greater understanding of whole-life balance.

Executive development is well understood in corporate circles (even if inadequately attended to in many organisations in terms of attaining superlative outcomes).

Career and motivational alignment, along with whole-life balance, is less well understood and means that executives and managers as far as possible need to develop a clear and realistic sense of career direction and destiny. They then need to articulate this with the organisation, in order for them to be aligned with where the organisation is headed. This alignment process also addresses whole-life balance, not necessarily changing the balance, but enabling executives and managers to understand and better cope with balance issues.

The outcome? Not least of all a lighter, faster spring in the step of the executive and manager on the way to work and at work, in other words, a profound impact on motivation and performance.

The focus of this book is on the further development of competence via executive coaching and of motivation via career consulting. With each side of the success equation attended to, executive and manager effectiveness can be maximised and sustained.

IMPLICATIONS

Executive and organisational life grows more complex and the complexity is increasing. However, if through executive coaching and career coaching we are able to facilitate the main drivers of success in an executive or senior manager, then why cannot, and should not, executives and senior managers within organisations do this themselves? In other words coach their direct reports in the areas of both competence and motivation to help them become truly successful, and thereby make their own areas of the business and themselves successful.

Surely the essence of leadership must be to help your direct reports and other people in the organisation become successful, thereby leveraging on and sharing in their success? The leverage and organisational performance opportunities created outstrip all the management fads and can be nurtured and sustained as 'the way we do things around here'—part of the culture of the organisation.

'*Executive Coaching*' describes how executives and senior managers can accomplish this in most cases, leaving the tougher propositions, or when time is not permitting, for the professional external coach—but select them carefully!

KEYNOTE

- ➤ Make sure you are not seduced by fads, they invariably miss the point, and the main point is you!
- ➤ Don't be led astray by management mirages. The genuine oasis is your personal capacity to lead and manage, which is where the time and energy needs to be placed.
- ➤ Results are a given today. How you accomplish them is just as important. In this, motivation ranks as high as competence.
- ➤ The bottomline? Helping others become successful, and leveraging on and sharing in their success.

Chapter 3

TALENT MANAGEMENT

> 66 Look after the people, and the results will look after themselves! 99

INTRODUCTION

Based on my own empirical research in Australia over the past nine years, and third party surveys involving 1589 organisations, the attraction and retention of key people is a growing issue which may become a crucial success factor for companies competing successfully in the future.

Why do high performers leave? They leave for the following reasons:

➤ they feel underchallenged or undervalued;
➤ they see little opportunity for advancement;
➤ they do not receive enough recognition;
➤ they experience conflict;
➤ their roles dissatisfy them;
➤ they seek greater remuneration and benefits;
➤ they experience undue work pressure;
➤ they feel their work life is out of balance;
➤ they get poached.

While organisations endeavour to address such issues, and invariably try to apply golden handcuffs to key people, for many this still seems not to have the desired effect and the situation is deteriorating. The solution, in fact, starts with raising talent management to a boiling organisational imperative. This has to be the mindset, starting at the top.

Flowing from this is the relentless development of top talent, for example, placing people in new roles before they are ready. Providing great feedback. Recognising and attending to the size and scale of the retention problem by appointing 'talent-minders'. Managing the unsatisfactory performers out. And most importantly, providing coaching for continuing personal development and sense of career direction and attainment—an 'intrinsic' reward—generating the desired effect of: 'If I'm developing, I'll stay'. 'If I can achieve my career goals here, I'll stay.'

EXAMPLE
A technically/functionally gifted executive missed a promotion because of poorly developed leadership skills. It was feared he might leave. A process combining executive coaching and career consulting turned around his people skills and enabled him to re-align his career with the company. From that juncture he has continued to be a first-class contributor with a good future ahead of him.

Coaching is particularly important when key people are appointed to new roles or hired externally. It can hasten them up the learning curve to success and win their early loyalty. This can be achieved by addressing a range of critical success factors I have identified from research and experience relating to the assimilation of newly appointed executives. Coaching is also particularly important when the organisation is going through major change, including restructures and mergers. At such times external forces, including search companies, start raising doubts in the minds of the talent they target. They suggest greener pastures externally in place of organisational 'instability'—and the talent often gets poached.

Whenever coaching is offered—whether for personal development and/or career alignment with the organisation—it is in effect a statement that the organisation cares and that 'you are important to us'. As an extension of existing line management and human resources processes, it represents a powerful strategy for greater talent retention.

But firstly, how great or growing is the problem, and opportunity, in your own organisation? Why not review it? Quantify the costs of not attending further to talent retention, along with the financial benefits of so doing, and this may represent the start of an era which turns talent retention into a truly competitive advantage, rather than the threat which many organisations foresee.

WHY TALENT MANAGEMENT?

'Our number one problem is hiring, training and retaining employees', says the chief executive of an information technology and telecommunications company.

'We find it hard to attract highly talented people and we experience the loss of high performers, often to the competition', says the managing director of a major international corporation.

Time and again I hear such remarks and the situation seems to be deteriorating. There appears to be severe and worsening shortage of available key people, and in many industry sectors and job functions a war is looming for talent, which will likely become a crucial success factor for organisations competing successfully in the future.

Most companies in my experience are not well prepared to tackle this growing critical problem area, and even the apparently well-run companies are highly vulnerable. Indeed, even they seem to pay insufficient attention to the human factor, and continue to lead and manage their critical people more like physical assets than human assets.

And when you consider the costs of losing and replacing key people, it's really surprising that more executives do not pay greater attention to the subject of talent management. But then these costs often go unrecognised, as many financial management and reporting systems inadequately capture and categorise them—quite a few associated cost elements remain hidden.

First, there are the direct costs. These include the wasted training and development investment in the person resigning, potentially to a competitor's advantage. Then there is the search or recruitment fee for the replacement and the costs associated with the six to twelve month assimilation period of the new hire getting up to speed—some not making it, with the heavy associated induction turnover costs. And then there is the financial cost of the impact on business results during this whole process.

But it does not end there. There is a range of indirect costs during this process which include: the impact on morale and productivity of co-workers; the potential decline in sustained customer contact, relationships and service; the potential decline in quality; the potential impact on management succession; and the potential loss of competitive edge.

The all-up cost? About 12 months' gross compensation per leaver! Extrapolated, taking a population of say 200 key people, with an average gross compensation costs of $100 000, at 20% turnover, this equates to four million dollars annually!

CAUSES OF THE TALENT MANAGEMENT PROBLEM

What are the causes of the loss of talent?

Well, we have a strong economy in Australia along with most advanced economies, at a high point in its cycle. The demand for talented critical people is growing. The supply is in fact starting to decline through the '13/17 factor': a projected 13% to 17% reduction in those in their mid-thirties to mid-forties over the next 13 to 17 years.

Compounding this, leaders and managers still display an orientation towards just *results, results, results.* People come second. How long is it going to take before they realise optimal results come from putting *people, people, people* first. After all, the age-old definition of a manager is 'getting superior results through other people'. Why, after so long, is this still merely espoused in so many organisations, rather than put into action?

If you are a supervisor, manager or leader reading this, please remember and act accordingly—to your advantage and to the advantage of your organisation—that your key people deliver your results. Optimal results will only come about if you treat your vital people like valuable assets, and assets need to be continually maintained and developed in order to maximise ongoing returns from, and through them.

And then there are the problems associated with the larger organisation. A more complicated economy and company structure needs talent with advanced capabilities in: international business; leading in the multicultural environment; literacy in information technology and telecommunications; and, outward focused entrepreneurial competence.

It does not stop there. They need to be able to operate in wider, flatter spans of control where the number of direct reports and matrix reporting and communication lines are increasing.

This particularly causes increased stress and strain on middle management positions where there are higher standards imposed from above: increased responsibility for making decisions; wider spans of control; higher performance hurdles generally, along with tougher requirements for leading and managing; more direct reports; continuous shedding of staff; and higher expectations for technical know-how in order to understand, monitor and add value to what is going on at operational levels.

Clearly, middle management roles—squeezed from above and below—are causing increased pressure on jobholders, who themselves need ongoing maintenance and development, which they all too often appear not to get from their line managers.

DIFFERENT ORGANISATIONS' PROBLEMS AND OPPORTUNITIES

There are more large company problems! The growth in the availability of capital and more efficient financial markets have seen the advent of many more smaller and/or faster growth companies led by entrepreneurs who depend for their success upon the same motivated talent needed by larger companies. And that same motivated talent can find the smaller, fleeter-footed, faster growth companies more attractive places to work.

Why? Well, the job offer can be very different, very attractive, and certainly challenging! For example, the risks of a big established company failing are less. There is nothing guaranteed with the entrepreneurial outfit.

The big established company employee is beginning to realise that their employer may no longer offer predicability in career paths. The entrepreneur places no value on predicting career paths at all—'you can add value wherever you can contribute, provided it's what we need and where we are headed. That will build your career. But we won't even try to predict it!'

EXAMPLE

A financial expert became dissatisfied with being 'pigeonholed' as such, and was at risk of leaving the company. Through career consulting he was able to assess the transferability of his interests and capabilities into other functional areas. By demonstrating this potential, he was able to move to a strategic marketing role within the company. Since that time he has excelled and developed his career.

In the large company it is often difficult to be seen and recognised by top management unless you do well in a high impact, high visibility project or area of the company. In the entrepreneurial, particularly smaller environment, everyone knows who are making the major contributions.

Big established companies tend to offer high base salaries and staff may become eligible for options. In entrepreneurial and many smaller companies you *can* become seriously rich, but only if the company succeeds!

In big companies, management can be bureaucratic and even micro-managing. In entrepreneurial or smaller environments, management is usually far more freewheeling and hands-off. And so the job offer in smaller and more entrepreneurial companies can be very enticing to that same talent which larger more established organisations are often finding harder to attract and retain.

Much of my work is with larger organisations, although entrepreneurial and smaller environments are also beginning to understand and reap the returns to be achieved from executive coaching. Larger established company executives often ask how to offset the attraction and retention of talent challenge from the smaller and/or more entrepreneurial company.

Well, if you think about it, the larger more established environment in fact offers many benefits. The size and scale of an individual's impact can be far larger. There is often a readymade and greater depth and breadth of human resources for purposes of developing into new areas of business endeavour, and the capital resource base is stronger to support such endeavours. The larger more established organisational environment usually offers a greater choice of experiences for purposes of career development. Yes, the larger more established organisation can compete successfully for talent by understanding, promoting and using these competitive hiring and retention differentiations.

WHY DO HIGH PERFORMERS LEAVE?

Why do high performers leave their companies? They feel they are inappropriately valued. They see insufficient opportunities for career development. They do not believe themselves, their work or results are sufficiently recognised. They do not see eye-to-eye with their line manager. They find many elements of their job dissatisfying, or their organisation or work area lacking strategic vision or sense of purpose. They feel they are under-rewarded either in terms of salary or benefits.

Companies recognise much of this and try to respond accordingly: better remuneration, more responsibility, increased recognition, more development and training, better defined career development prospects and potential pathways, more flexible work arrangements, and more facilities at work (daycare, gym and so forth).

But for many organisations, all this still seems not be having the desired effect.

The symptoms may be being addressed, but the root of the problems (and opportunities) often go unattended. And they need to be attended to from the top. Unless talent management ascends the list of strategic priorities, the problems will remain largely unresolved and the opportunities unrealised.

TALENT MANAGEMENT STRATEGIES

Key people need personal attention, regularly. And to attract and retain critical people, the organisation needs to design and develop great employment propositions, in other words, why a bright, hard working and ambitious person would want to come and work for you, rather than for the leading or fastest growing company in your sector.

Yes, talent management starts with making it a boiling organisational imperative at the very top. This requires top people being directly involved in the hiring of key people, raising the hurdle heights for performance, being more explicit about expectations for results, monitoring, feedback and performance coaching.

Explicitness is also required at performance reviews when executives and managers really need to say it 'loud, and say it as it is' rather than tell the full story or complain to others after the performance review meeting.

And in all of this, people at the top of organisations need to be very clear as to who are the wealth developers, wealth sustainers, wealth investors, and wealth eroders.

WEALTH DEVELOPERS

The wealth developers are those who move with the flow and change with the times, whose performance is continually improving, who are seen as stars in their ascendancy, and who may be seen as successors to senior management, providing they are seen to have development potential (not just outstanding performance in their current roles).

WEALTH SUSTAINERS

The wealth sustainers are those who are hot on the heels of the wealth developers, and who display sufficient resilience to cope with the vagaries of organisational life and its ever increasing requirements for improved performance.

WEALTH INVESTORS

The wealth investors are those who have some way to go before becoming real assets, but who appear to offer the organisation potential. Clearly, these individuals are important targets for encouragement, development and training, for this potential to be realised. Perhaps they should be called investees, but they too are investing in their futures!

WEALTH ERODERS

And then we have the wealth eroders. They appear not to be able to keep pace with change, and even though their performance may be seen to be adequate, it's also often a real struggle to keep up. Clearly, the investment in development and training here may be questionable, as the returns will likely be sub-optimal.

And so the bottomline in talent management when it comes to segmenting the employee pool, according to their capacity to develop or erode wealth, is to focus on wealth developers, nurture wealth sustainers, develop wealth investors, and manage out wealth eroders via appropriate performance management processes.

Why the last recommendation? Well, measure the impact of a 10% to 20% below par performance on co-workers, direct reports, teams and budgets. The bottomline impact can be huge and adverse. And if you are managing them out, as you should be, make sure this is undertaken on a voluntary basis rather than involuntarily, in other words a dismissal. Executive coaching and career consulting can assist in this.

But if you see no other way than to fire the wealth eroders—and there are many other ways as addressed in Chapter 13—'A typical individual turnaround process', then be prepared to accept and suffer the consequences. The termination costs for senior people can often equate to six to eighteen months' gross remuneration.

MARKET SEGMENTATION AND THE ROLE OF COMPANY IMAGE

And so why would a talented person want to work with your organisation? In a nutshell, there are two main drivers. The first is your company's image as an employer. The second relates more to the work environment. Underpinning each of these drivers, of course, is appropriate and competitive salary and benefits.

The first driver, company image, has to start with a thorough understanding of the types of people who are attracted to your organisation and who tend to remain longer, motivated and productive.

Are they those who seek to attain career development opportunities in an environment perceived as successful? Are they those who are in it mainly for the money? Are they those who identify with the more intrinsic elements of what the company is trying to achieve and the challenges so created? Or are they those who are more interested in whole-life balance and who need flexibility in their work arrangements in order to accomplish this?

Organisations who are successful in talent management, for any given family of jobs, have identified the specific types of people they need to attract and retain, and the examples noted above are but some of the many combinations and possibilities.

Organisations less successful in talent management simply have not worked this out and take a shotgun approach to hiring and managing talent. The bottomline here is to work out who you are aiming for in terms of recruitment and retention, and to develop the company image as an employer, accordingly.

THE ROLE OF THE WORK ENVIRONMENT

Turning to the second driver, the work environment, the following factors can have a major impact on attracting and retaining motivated talent.

First, allow talented people more 'room to breathe' in their jobs. Out with micro-management and the 'controllersaurus' and in with breadth of role and scope of responsibility! Secondly, allow talent to grow in terms of decision-making responsibility and functional, technical or managerial leadership.

Next, don't overinvolve them in work which does not directly relate to the results which they seek to generate, for which they have been hired and for which they are being paid. Also, talented people often want a job role which creates challenge and 'stretch' but one which does not defeat them.

Other important ingredients for ensuring that the work environment attracts and retains talent are invariably variety and innovation—something new to work on, often—and, 'great' co-workers, be they line managers, peers or direct reports. Successful people breed, and help an organisation to retain, successful people.

Turning to the role of compensation in all of this, the golden rule is that money rarely motivates, but dissatisfies if it is inadequate. Nevertheless it usually needs to be highly competitive and ideally offer opportunities for longer term wealth generation for talent. Also, top performers need to earn considerably more than average performers, and know this is the case. Considerably more? Try 20% to 30%. Sounds expensive, but it is not if you work out the superb returns to be met from the extra investment.

The final ingredients relating to the work environment in the context of attracting and retaining talent, all relate to a highly proactive approach to talent development. This includes putting them in jobs before they are ready for them, treating and managing them as carefully as you would treat key customer accounts, moving wealth eroders out, and providing intrinsic rewards in the form of personalised coaching, career consulting and mentoring. So that the following ethos prevails: 'If I'm developing personally, I'll stay'. 'If I can further my career here, I'll stay.'

Such individual coaching input is particularly powerful with newly appointed vital people to help them hasten up the learning curve and generate fast-track results, lessening the risks associated with induction turnover. Also, when the organisation is going through restructure, merger or major change, coaching helps them adjust quickly if they are to be effective and timely change leaders of others, and more resistant to being poached.

And so in summary, the key ingredients in talent management appear to be:

➤ developing the organisation's image in the context of its values and culture;
➤ the fact that it is well managed;
➤ a place wherein exciting company challenges are pursued from a solid foundation of strong company performance and industry leadership; and
➤ a place wherein its cadre of key people represent outstanding talent.

It is also about the work environment which needs to offer freedom and autonomy, exciting challenges in its jobs, real potential for personal growth and career development, and line managers who are admired.

It is also for many about great remuneration which is being differentiated according to performance, those who perform enjoying high levels of total compensation. For others, it is about lifestyle.

HOW FURTHER TO IMPROVE TALENT MANAGEMENT

And so what might an organisation do to improve its talent management? Firstly, study the real causes and demographics of talented people who leave, and talented people who stay. This should then drive the further building and development of company image as an employer, and its work environment.

The outcome will likely suggest a fair and flexible culture which helps make motivated talent want to stay, work lives which feel rich and rewarding, a sense of ongoing personal and career development potential, an open two-way communicative and collegial environment, all backed by an appropriate reward system.

In other words, the ethos needs to be to treat key people as though they are volunteers who do not have to come to work, but who see the organisation as the type of place they want to go to, day after day—'A great place to work and grow!' But that great place to work and grow often needs to say goodbye to staff, and this is where all the other good work on talent management can come undone.

For example, I have come across many people whose dismissals—and the costs and trauma associated with them—potentially might never have happened, had some of the principles and practices in this book been adopted. The irony is that often such 'failures' end up working very satisfactorily and effectively for the competition, or are hired back later as contractors or consultants. Also, many organisations downsize only to find that six months later they are in hiring mode again!

The anatomy of a 'firing' often goes something like this. The individual's performance or fit becomes a concern and the boss perceives that 'things seem to be going a bit off the rails' without perhaps the boss or the individual really understanding the situation. Instead of talking about this in a constructive fashion, positions become polarised, two-way communication dries up, the situation goes from bad to worse, and … 'bang!' a dismissal is the outcome.

DISMISSAL AVOIDANCE

And so in addressing talent management, we need to examine possible dismissal avoidance strategies in more detail. To begin with, it is worth considering exactly what the more obvious reasons are for dismissals from the employer's perspective. Broadly speaking, employers categorise dismissals into four main groupings: economic, capability, self-motivation, and not fitting in.

ECONOMIC

In the recession of the early 1990s in Australia, and indeed since then, while largely undifferentiated organisations endeavour to compete on the basis of 'low cost', staff at all levels have been the target of an unprecedented volume of retrenchments. This has been exacerbated by international organisations seeking low-cost production and management, wherever this takes them worldwide. Economic rationalisation will continue into the foreseeable future for large and small organisations alike, as low cost continues for many to be the main competitive thrust—genuine 'differentiation' remaining an elusive competitive concept, let alone a reality, for so many companies.

Capability

This relates to whether or not an employee has the necessary experience, competencies and, in some cases, qualifications to be able to do the job. If the base capability is not there, the tenure of the employee is at extreme risk.

Self-motivation

Capability is one thing, but putting into practice what you can do, really depends on the level of self-motivation through job fit and the degree to which the 'atmospherics' of the organisation attend to the motivational needs of the individual.

Not fitting in

If an executive or manager has difficulty with an employee who, for whatever reason, seems to have a personal chemistry or fit problem with the people and the organisation, then a replacement is usually sought rather than time and effort spent in trying to resolve the problem. One reason is because not many senior people are equipped with the necessary skills to deal with personal chemistry and fit problems.

However, the economic justification for firing 'misfits' has always been, and remains, highly doubtful given all the costs associated with it. From a risk management perspective, how can you guarantee that a costly replacement will perform any better, particularly when you consider the inadequacies inherent in most hiring and selection procedures?

Alternatives to dismissal

In considering alternatives to economic reasons for dismissals, natural 'attrition', or natural labour turnover, can be a very cost-effective approach to staff reduction when economic reasons dictate this need. This cost effectiveness comes about from not having to pay separation packages, as a result of resignation rather than dismissal. Clearly this minimises the trauma often associated with dismissal which can be experienced not only by departees, but also by those senior executives having to dismiss them, as well as remaining executives, managers and staff who wonder when the axe may be wielded in their own directions. This is distracting, affects their morale and self-motivation, and results in lost productivity and lower job performance.

However, natural attrition may also have some drawbacks. This can include the wrong staff deciding to leave, in other words, the talent. Better performing employees are more readily employable elsewhere, rather than those considered to be of lesser potential, who find it harder to secure alternative employment. Unfortunately, therefore, at times of organisational difficulty or uncertainty, it is very often the talented employees that move on first.

Also people may move on of their own accord at the wrong time. With the rate and pace of change in the external environment creating the need for staff reductions, savings are often needed fast—or so it seems to the board of directors and CEO. Waiting for natural attrition may just take too long for them. However, if they researched the full costs of separation, lost motivation and productivity, and potentially adverse public and customer image at the time of major downsizings, they might be surprised to find that natural attrition can actually be a more cost-effective strategy.

But there is often more than meets the eye! Over the years many organisations have experienced the dreaded salary 'bracket creep', when salary bands at various levels—often fuelled by overzealous search and recruitment consultants whose fees are based on percentage of salary—have been soaring skywards, and this can be particularly costly at the senior staff level. The saving of removing, say, ten senior staff members, perhaps each with total annual compensation costs of $75 000 and not replacing them (but relying perhaps on a flattening of the organisation structure and redistribution of their job content), is $750 000 annually. Very tempting, even if the costs of removing them are high.

However, this may not be as cost-effective as it first may appear, as after their dismissals the new organisation structure can take a long time to recover and regain momentum, and really benefit from the savings. No small wonder some dismissed staff members find themselves back at the organisation working on contract, to help make this happen.

An alternative way to effect such savings, but at a reduced initial level, is to freeze the salaries of the employees in question, and even reduce their salaries following appropriate notice periods (having checked out the legal implications). But an across the board salary freeze or reduction may cause the talent to leave, and can damage morale and productivity over the longer term. Selective salary freezes or reductions may also be difficult to implement, but again need to be considered as options.

Indeed, the extent of this potential damage depends on how affected staff are managed at the time, and after they have been told about the change to their salary arrangements. For example, if they have been paid 'well over the top' as a result of salary bracket creep, then they are likely paid well over the external market rate. This can be confirmed by compensation specialists, recruiters and career consultants to whom access by affected staff should be encouraged, to check this out independently.

Other forms of pay cuts can also be used, for example, decreasing the base remuneration and increasing the incentive element which can be based on both organisational performance and personal results. Pay cuts can also be made in return for shares in the company.

Other strategies as alternatives to dismissal for economic reasons include early retirement, part-time work, job sharing, leave of absence, study leave, secondments to other organisations and voluntary redundancy.

EARLY RETIREMENT AND PART-TIME WORK

Offering incentives for early retirement can often be much more cost-effective than dismissals, as may be the opportunity to move to part-time work. There are countless numbers of staff perhaps in their fifties, who may have a partner working full- or part-time, whose children are working, and who have perhaps inherited some family assets. Such people might leap at the chance to work three or four days per week, or seriously consider the early retirement option. Retirement counselling of the type offered by career consultants often facilitates this option.

JOB SHARING

Taking the part-time strategy on a broader basis, this may create the opportunity for some jobs effectively to be shared. This job sharing strategy certainly may not fit some organisations, but may be suitable for the larger organisation with sizeable and homogeneous staff groups.

LEAVE OF ABSENCE

Leave of absence can also be offered, whether this be for study leave or a sabbatical. For example, when offered in one company employees retained their benefits and received government unemployment payments, and were 'rehired' when the fortunes of the company improved and they were needed again.

SECONDMENT

Another approach is secondment to suppliers and customers, sometimes on a salary-sharing basis between the two companies. This offers the seconded employee the opportunity to develop new skills and better understand the operations and needs of companies in the supply and distribution chain.

VOLUNTARY REDUNDANCY

Again, these approaches offer humane, dignified and sensitive treatment to those affected, as does the voluntary redundancy option which can be offered across the board or selectively. Across the board offers for voluntary redundancy may mean that the best employees—those more readily employable elsewhere—put their hands up and leave, denuding the organisation of talent.

Selective voluntary redundancy may take several forms including specific employees or areas of the organisation, or following a broader invitation for expressions of interest in voluntary redundancy with no guarantee it will be granted in each case. Selective offers may backfire, however, when those wishing to leave are in fact asked to stay and therefore feel penalised.

The story can go like this: 'You mean to tell me that you are letting others go with golden handshakes, who really have not performed well over the years, whereas in my case, and I'll remind you that all my performance appraisals have always been rated "excellent", my reward for this is that I don't get a golden handshake and I have to stay and work even harder as a result of fewer people remaining in the organisation … this is totally unfair!' Again, morale and performance can be adversely affected in such cases. Some companies have risk managed these situations successfully by granting loyalty bonuses to key staff after restructuring, when the organisation re-fires and attains new target levels of performance.

EXAMPLE

In one case I was called in to provide some career counselling to an employee, who after six months of being told his request for voluntary redundancy would likely be accepted, at the eleventh hour found his request was rejected. His reaction was to go on stress leave for two weeks and a resolve, on returning to work, to do the barest minimum 9.00 am to 5.00 pm. His objective was to trigger an involuntary redundancy at best, or a better work and home life balance at the very least! Even a small loyalty bonus might have eased this situation, and of course, he should never have been led to believe his request for voluntary redundancy would be granted in the first place.

However, voluntary redundancy certainly has its place, if carefully and sensitively planned and implemented, and has many advantages in the contexts of dismissal avoidance and enhancing sought-after employer status in the community.

In summary, because of the devastation layoffs create, there are a range of alternatives corporations should consider. When layoffs are unavoidable, I have found that advance notification, severance pay, extended benefits, retraining programs, career consulting and outplacement counselling help employees most, and also benefit the company.

OTHER ALTERNATIVES TO DISMISSAL

In considering alternatives to dismissals for reasons of capability, motivation and 'not fitting in', there are a broad range of alternatives. These include: internal redeployment; allowing resignation rather than dismissal; term contracts; proper use of performance appraisal processes; performance improvement programs; 'square-peg-in-round-hole' counselling; and mid-career counselling.

INTERNAL REDEPLOYMENT

Internal redeployment is a humane and sensitive approach, and for a broad range of reasons may be very appropriate to consider in many instances, and invariably is preferable to dismissal. These instances can include:

➤ When the 'atmospherics' in a certain part of the organisation do not attend to the motivational needs of the individual, be they material needs, structural needs, behavioural needs or emotional needs.

➤ When the individual exhibits leadership traits considered more desirable and relevant to other parts of the organisation.

➤ When the individual possesses a style which is considered to add greater value to a team elsewhere in the organisation, the individual perhaps being too much of a clone in the existing team, or too diametrically opposed to the current team leader in terms of operating style.

➤ Where current job fit is poor, in other words, the interests, values and motivational capabilities of the individual are not represented in the current job.

➤ Where career alignment is poor, for example, where an individual's career path aspirations are better met by the individual working elsewhere in the organisation.

➤ Where the individual operates in a staff management capacity, whereas a more functional or technical capacity may better suit the individual's strengths, or vice versa.

However, in reality, there may be limited opportunities for internal redeployment, as comparable level jobs may simply not be available (comparability means with the salary of the former job, at a reasonably nearby location, and requiring a comparable skill-set). As a result it may mean that the potential internal redeployee may well be eligible for a separation package instead of being redeployed.

Also, a major danger inherent in internal redeployment may be the 'dead-wood transfer' syndrome, where an individual who is perceived to have very poor capability, motivation or ability to fit in is transferred across to another area of the organisation as a problem for someone else to manage!

RESIGNATION RATHER THAN DISMISSAL

Allowing an individual to resign rather than be dismissed may enhance self-esteem and dignity on the part of the departee, albeit somewhat superficially. For some departees, it is what others discern which is important to them, and they may feel far better if they can be perceived as having resigned rather than as having been dismissed. From a re-employment perspective, a credible resignation is also better than a dismissal, but the emphasis has to be on the word 'credible'.

However, encouraging someone to resign rather than be dismissed may be fraught with legal dangers and can lead to cases of constructive dismissal and large payouts. Firstly, a strategy to offset these risks is to communicate to the individual at the termination interview that it is 'all over' and that the individual has to move on and find alternative employment.

Secondly, when it seems apparent the individual has accepted this information, be this at the first or subsequent meeting, and after a sufficient pause in the conversation allowing the dismissal message to really sink in, then to ask how the individual would like this information communicated to other parties within and outside the organisation. Invariably the conversation comes around to the concept of the departure being communicated as a resignation to other people, although the departee needs to understand clearly that this option is offered purely on the basis of meeting the best interests of the individual, and that the official behind the scenes 'line' remains that of the organisation terminating the individual's employment.

It might be unwise to offer this option, however, if the performance of the individual has been very poor and is recognised by employees or customers as such. Under these circumstances, and if a 'resignation' is allowed, there is a danger that management may be seen as lacking intestinal fortitude and as going for the soft option.

TERM CONTRACTS

Term contracts are becoming more popular in both public and private sectors, the term usually being between one and five years, although three years is often used. Such contracts offer the potential to sever the agreement if the employing organisation is less than inspired by the performance of the individual, and thus provide a cost-effective exit route, and an incentive for the individual to perform if seeking contract renewal.

However, term contracts may not always seem that attractive to new potential hires who perhaps favour the permanent employment option. The length of their terms can also pose problems if they underperform. Finally, payout arrangements can also prove costly, if the organisation needs to effect a termination prior to contract expiry.

FORMAL PERFORMANCE APPRAISAL PROCESSES

Formal performance appraisal processes are rarely correctly used. Firstly, the paperwork associated with them is often used subjectively and becomes no more than a 'happy sheet' to be completed every year. Secondly, when performance is assessed at being below satisfactory, this is often inadequately communicated to the appraisee, who does not always 'hear' bad news anyway. Thirdly, individual development needs often are poorly identified and development plans inadequately defined or implemented. Finally, if unsatisfactory performance is the case, formal warnings and supporting information are rarely adequately communicated or documented.

Yet the more objective use of performance appraisals and the real identification of, and attention to, development needs—let alone the correct application of formal warnings in extreme and adverse cases—offers a real alternative to dismissals, through rectification of performance problems before it becomes too late. The advantages of using these processes correctly include:

➤ The individual being appraised knows exactly what is expected.
➤ The person is given time and organisational support to develop their personal performance.

➤ There is an early warning of potential outcomes if unable or unwilling to develop.

➤ The individual can 'shape up' or 'ship out'—shipping out more often than not on a voluntary basis, usually knowing when the time is coming for this to happen, and with time to seek alternative employment.

However, until the executives and managers involved in the performance appraisal process become fully committed to the need for, and are adequately trained in, performance improvement counselling and coaching, and are prepared to invest the time, then it is unlikely that the full benefits of performance appraisal will be realised.

PERFORMANCE IMPROVEMENT PROGRAMS

Such is the case with performance improvement programs which can usefully be applied, following an unsatisfactory performance appraisal, or, at other times, when an individual's performance is perceived as being below satisfactory or deteriorating. Such programs are often given a timeframe, anything from three to six months, and indeed, have a start and end date with specific objectives, action plans and review dates which more often than not are monthly.

'SQUARE-PEG-IN-ROUND-HOLE' COUNSELLING

'Square-peg-in-round-hole' counselling applies to those individuals who seem, for one reason or another, to be in the wrong job or somehow misaligned, adversely impacting on their attitude, morale, or performance. It is also used when internal efforts to improve performance or fit issues have been exhausted, and dismissal is a real possibility. The orientation for such counselling can be 'career management', when an individual's career is perceived to be in crisis and when there is a need, somehow, to rekindle an individual's motivational fires to optimise their contribution to the organisation. This is an important role for the career consultant.

EXAMPLE

An executive found herself in a role which failed to meet her motivational needs. Considered talented, she was offered alternatives but it became apparent that there was also a poor organisational fit. Through career consulting she determined the time was opportune to leave the company and take a new career direction—far better than remain and allow her motivation and performance to continue to plateau.

Mid-career counselling

Mid-career counselling by an external specialist can also be usefully applied at that critical mid-career period for people in their early or mid-forties. Frequently I find such individuals promoted beyond their capabilities, in performance 'plateau', experiencing chemistry and fit problems, or indeed in mid-life crisis.

Whatever the cause, the notion of saving a valuable asset, where up to $1 million may have been invested in the development and training, say, of a 25-year service employee, simply makes sound business sense. Such counselling can be difficult to accomplish purely internally however, as both performance and fit issues can be very difficult to discuss, particularly with senior, long service and time-starved executives or managers, exacerbated by underdeveloped communication and counselling skills.

The role of career consulting in talent management

Such 'career consulting' exercises, whether with a square peg or mid-career orientation, usually commence with a consultant undertaking familiarisation and a preliminary assessment with the line manager responsible for the problem individual, with an HR executive also present. Symptoms and problems are addressed, the individual's career is reviewed and the strategy for introducing the external third party is jointly developed, in the context that the problem person needs to be in agreement and be committed to the career management program.

Once the program has been initiated, the early elements include self-assessment by the individual, with a personal, job and career focus. This can be complemented by confidential interviews with the individual's superior, peers, direct reports and sometimes customers, all with a job performance and future career options orientation. Fit issues, if indeed they exist, are usually uncovered in this interview process, as indeed are any other problems.

The desired outcome is to attain agreement with the individual regarding perceived problems and potential solutions which may entail clarifying any ambiguities or uncertainties; improving understanding of, and communication with, others in the organisation; and identification of other development needs and appropriate resources, whether this be for technical, functional, management or personal development.

Career consulting programs of this nature culminate in action planning and implementation. Action planning involves a mutually agreed development program using the organisation's internal development and training resources, wherever possible. Implementation of this is the responsibility of the individual, the line manager and the HR representative, in other words shared, with the external consultant appearing periodically for progress reviews and always available for hotline advice. At senior levels, the consultant can continue to be used effectively for ongoing coaching in the key development areas ascribed.

The bottomline of such career consulting programs is to achieve some sort of outcome, whether this be improved performance or fit in the present job, modifications to the present job or reporting relationships, or successful redeployment within or outside the organisation—the latter via resignation or joint agreement, rather than straight dismissal.

THE MAIN OPPORTUNITY

Apart from all these potential courses of action helping organisations manage their talented employees and avoid dismissals, there are direct financial savings related to separation packages, recruitment fees and the costs associated with new employee induction and assimilation.

However, the main opportunity for executives and managers deploying appropriate talent management (including dismissal avoidance) strategies is high levels of morale and performance, the further development of sought-after employer status by the organisation, and the attraction, retention and development of talented employees. This is the real opportunity. There is absolutely no reason why executives and managers cannot and should not prioritise talent management and dismissal avoidance principles and practices in their business operations. For those who do, the benefits are enormous.

The acid test is to ask yourself the following question. Who are more important, customers or employees? Your answer initially may be customers, but without motivated, productive staff, how can customer needs be fully met? The answer has to be both customers and employees—equal in importance.

And this is why talent management has to receive at least as much attention as the management of the customer base.

KEYNOTE

➤ Most organisations fail to realise that the attraction, development, motivation and retention of key people, if not now, will soon become their vital competitive strength or Achilles heel.

➤ The war for talent is looming, and most organisations are unprepared.

➤ Although money (an extrinsic reward) is treated as both magnet and anchor, intrinsic rewards in how people are led and encouraged to develop are far more potent.

➤ In this, perceiving key people as though they are volunteers is a thought-provoking way of evolving optimal employment and retention propositions, as is the practice of avoiding 'hire-and-fire', and together these lay the foundations of being perceived as an employer of choice.

Chapter 4

Where Executive Coaching

Adds Value

66 Executive coaching improves
executive effectiveness and the
bottomline, and works well,
appropriately applied, in a broad
range of scenarios **99**

Introduction

In any organisation, there exists a broad range of human capability, and coaching can
add value across this range. For example, coaching can be offered as a reward to top
performers, or as a means of retaining them longer in the organisation if they feel
they are continuing to develop. Coaching can also help them to attain an even
higher level of performance, or help groom them for promotion.

For those performing reasonably, coaching can help them further develop their
performance by enhancing their capabilities and/or helping them become more
motivationally aligned with the organisation. Motivational alignment can be
developed through coaching which takes a career development focus, seeing as an
outcome a greater coincidence between the goals of the organisation and the career
goals of the individual.

Coaching is also relevant to low performers, where performance turn-around can be obtained through coaching, or redeployment and transition to a more appropriate role within or outside the organisation.

For example, coaching can ensure faster, surer assimilation and job results for a newly appointed key person. For the more established contingent, coaching can further enhance their effectiveness.

At times of major organisational change, coaching can help individuals to develop their change leadership capabilities, and again attend to motivational alignment this could help prevent them getting poached or jumping ship at times of upheaval and uncertainty.

And in the case of a plateaued performance, perhaps of a longer serving person, coaching can help them to regenerate or allow them to come to the conclusion that they need to move on.

The life-cycle theme also applies to team coaching. New teams often need to fast-track their development. Team coaching is also highly applicable to those teams that may have become dysfunctional as a result of interpersonal, composition or process problems. Mature teams needing to regenerate can also benefit from team coaching.

SPECIFIC EXAMPLES WHERE COACHING ADDS VALUE

The following paragraphs represent some of the main ways by which executive coaching can add value in a range of frequently encountered scenarios.

NEWLY APPOINTED KEY PEOPLE

Some organisations often find it takes newly appointed key people, or those in new roles or reporting relationships after a restructure or merger, nine months to become 'profitable'. Some perceive over 40% of them not to be performing at their personal optimum within the first year in their new roles, a significant proportion of whom leave within 20 months.

Executive coaching helps them progress far more quickly and securely in their new roles, delivering results faster, also substantially lessening the risks associated with early turnover after the honeymoon period.

RETENTION OF TALENT

It is hard enough finding and developing talent, without then having to experience the costs and missed opportunities associated with their jumping ship. To help prevent this, organisations usually attend to *extrinsic* rewards by applying golden handcuffs, yet does this retain talented executives motivationally and ensure their ongoing commitment?

Through executive coaching, which is offered as an *intrinsic* reward, they become more motivationally aligned with the organisation, developing a strong sense of job, organisational and career fit. Why leave an organisation that is genuinely interested in helping you develop a greater sense of career alignment? For others, through executive coaching, they perceive the organisation as a source of enhanced opportunities for individualised personal development: 'So long as I'm growing, I'll stay!'

CHANGE LEADERSHIP

Studies and experience abound and verify that most restructures and mergers dissatisfy in terms of the degree and speed of performance improvement derived post-restructure. The common causes cited are morale and productivity. I take a different stance (based on my exposure to more than 70 restructures). The cause is invariably poor change leadership. Not that all executives do not know how to lead at times of change. More, that they themselves need to adjust to change quickly, if they are to be effective and timely change leaders of others.

I have identified six critical factors—executive assimilation, team synergy development, change leadership competencies, management of restructures, individual re-alignment and retention of talent—in which executive coaching can add value. The full power of change leadership can be quickly released and realised.

AFTER PERFORMANCE REVIEW OR 360° SURVEY

Many organisations have added 360° feedback of an individual's leadership, management or operating style—feedback from line manager, peers and direct reports (hence 360°)—to more conventional performance review processes.

All these valuable diagnostic processes are great at raising awareness of strengths and development needs, and in providing new knowledge about personal development priorities. However, clients tell us that they often fall short on developing the skills, capabilities and motivation needed to bring about real change in executive behaviour and habits. This takes time, effort and sustained input, which is why executive coaching is often selected as part of the solution.

EFFECTIVENESS OF ESTABLISHED EXECUTIVES

Many executives cannot quite get a grip on these times of ambiguity, human resource-lean enterprises, sudden and frequent bouts of change, or how to apply and live with 360° collaborative techniques. Executive coaching can help executives understand the new rules of the game and further develop their effectiveness in such areas as leadership, teamwork, change, interpersonal relations and communication.

FROM TECHNICAL OR FUNCTIONAL TO LEADERSHIP EXCELLENCE

We have all seen gifted, hard-driving technical or functional experts succeed well early on in their careers. And then something happens, such as a series of performance reviews focusing on the need to develop leadership skills and more collaborative behaviour, or even a missed promotion for the same reasons. It may be a case of the executive having been over-rewarded as a result of technical or functional excellence (so why change?), or simply having not dedicated sufficient priority, time or energy to interpersonal, leadership or related development requirements.

Whatever the cause, such people can find their technical or functional strengths, when overplayed, can become their Achilles heel. Executive coaching can help them shift their behaviour paradigm, and invariably you see early change and sustained results.

SENIOR EXECUTIVE MENTORING

It is often lonely at the top! And where can the CEO or senior executive go to get completely confidential and objective input? Executive coaching can come in where an objective, independent and highly experienced confidant can make all the difference as to how the executive performs, makes decisions, feels and is perceived to be operating.

Executive coaching can enable executives to tap into the highest level of intellectual capital available in such areas as leadership, interpersonal relationships, management of change, team development, and career and whole-life balance. While the coaching starts with an open agenda and is tailored to meet the executive's needs, outcomes also benefiting the organisation are invariably experienced.

NEW TEAMS

Change won't go away, it will only accelerate! And change creates new teams needing to get up to speed quickly and sustainably in order to yield benefits from the synergies and leverage they should create. Executive coaching with teams can optimise interpersonal relationships and executive teamwork through enhanced team processes and, in particular, a greater understanding of individual behavioural styles and how their differences can be harmonised to create a star team, rather than just a team of stars.

TEAMS NEEDING TO REGENERATE

Just as an organisation experiences different phases in its life-cycle—start up, early and secondary growth, adolescence/turbulence and maturity—so teams can experience similar phases. The last two are often a particular concern wherein the team needs to regenerate, if not reinvent itself. Adolescence/turbulence often coincides with interpersonal friction among team members. Maturity often coincides with 'meetings for the sake of meetings' and not a lot of creative output.

In such cases the executive coach can be called in as catalyst and facilitator to (1) identify, and (2) unjam the roadblocks—working closely with the team leader all the way, and maximising group and individual input. The team re-fires quickly and sustainably!

SQUARE PEGS IN ROUND HOLES

Continuing organisational change, let alone restructure, merger, acquisition or divestment, often leaves executives in roles and reporting relationships wherein their comfort levels, motivation, capability and performance deteriorate. Taken to the nth degree they react negatively, and this can degenerate to serious interpersonal issues. Executive coaching can help them and the organisation address any misalignment, work out the causes and implement appropriate solutions, invariably generating win-win outcomes.

DISMISSAL AVOIDANCE

As noted earlier, in today's knowledge era, superior results come from 'creating the how' through enlightened leadership with a strong customer orientation. Clearly, this largely supersedes industrial age top-down management 'controlling the what'. Whether this is the cause of an executive potentially derailing, or whether it is a straight performance or 'fit' issue, it makes sense to try to effect a turnaround through our input and save the inevitable costs and trauma associated with dismissal.

And if the executive concerned—through executive coaching—realises organisational expectations exceed personal capability, then it is better that they realise this themselves, rather than simply being told without their having recognised the warning signals. In this case mutual agreement to separate is a far better and often more cost-effective outcome.

INTERNAL OR EXTERNAL REDEPLOYMENT

Any executive in career transition needs to focus on the future and carefully define personal directions based on a clear understanding of self-image in the changing career environment. They would also be wise to look back and learn from the lessons of their past for purposes of building on their strengths and risk managing the resumption and progress of their careers, enhancing their ongoing effectiveness and success.

Executive coaching is geared towards individual needs and offers a new paradigm in cost-effective career transition support in: career planning and strategy development; lessons of the past; career attainment; successful assimilation into the new role; and independent business and portfolio careers.

PROFESSIONAL CONSULTATIVE SELLING

The key success factor for professional or business-to-business services firms is the attraction, development and retention of customers or clients. In my experience this is the discerning competitive characteristic which drives success, mediocrity or failure. And I believe, this is the one area where such firms fail to maximise their full potential!

Sales training courses are only the starting point in the journey to proficiency, let alone excellence: Building and applying new skills as if they are habits requires sustained effort and input over quite a considerable timeframe. This includes pre-brief, role play, test, de-brief and continuous improvement, under the watchful eye of a senior coach who has sufficient time, talent and technique to make the difference.

PROFESSIONAL PRESENTATIONS AND PUBLIC SPEAKING

Most executives, professionals and managers can find it quite stressful when they have to make a presentation to a group. Such apprehension is often caused by concerns about not being able to remember your lines, or making a fool of yourself, or giving a poor presentation, or failing to meet your objectives, but mainly from inadequate training and preparation.

Yes, the secret to making successful speeches is to be both trained and prepared, particularly in the art of presentation delivery which is 80% of the group communication success formula. And through coaching in professional presentations and public speaking, the presentation delivery of employees can become outstanding.

These examples where executive coaching can play a major role represent but a small proportion of the possibilities and benefits to be gained.

Later, we will examine some of these examples—'applications' of coaching—in greater detail.

KEYNOTE

➤ Executive coaching works well in the case of new hires, established staff, staff entering some form of transition, and with teams.

➤ To be effective, both organisational and individual needs and sought outcomes need to be clearly articulated and vigorously pursued.

➤ Coaching is not a warm and fuzzy 'talk-fest'—it's about improving effectiveness and the retention of motivated talent.

➤ In summary, coaching adds genuine value to that most vital yet variable resource of the organisation—its people.

Chapter 5

Economic Benefits of Executive Coaching

66 Where else can you get a more than 20-fold return on your investment in 18 months? 99

Introduction

In this era of flatter organisational structures with matrix communication and reporting lines, and where change won't go away, it will only accelerate—no wonder attention to the human factor can come second.

It's often hard to find the time to coach those executives and key people who really need help, let alone the higher performers, where every unit of coaching in fact provides the best return.

And return on investment, as well as making available the necessary time and capability, is why an increasing number of organisations use executive coaches, whether appointed internally or sourced externally.

For example, halving the time for a newly appointed executive to get up to speed can, in effect, save 20% of their first year's cost of employment. It can also improve their personal leverage on their team and staff, and the budgets for which they are responsible, by one-third in the first 12 months. The quantification of all this can run into hundreds of thousands of dollars.

As can the quantification of the personal leverage generated by even a 10% improvement in the effectiveness or motivation of an established executive, or a team. Particularly at times of organisational change, restructuring or merger.

And then it comes to the retention of motivated talent, or at the other end of the spectrum, the avoidance of a dismissal. In each case the costs and other benefits are even more obvious, and again can run into hundreds of thousands of dollars (particularly when you cost in the hiring and assimilation of a replacement).

I have been able to develop a methodology whereby the costs and financial benefits of any executive coaching assignment can be examined at the outset, invariably generating a strong business case.

The starting point is the identification of needs and sought outcomes, and by the coach and line manager examining a case together, they can soon identify whether the ends justify the means.

NEEDS AND SOUGHT OUTCOMES

In identifying needs and sought outcomes, the coach needs to assess whether the coaching process is targeted at newly appointed executives, established executives, executives potentially in career transition, or when the organisation is experiencing dramatic change and when change leadership is the priority.

The next step is to see where the organisation is, compared with Australian and international performance experience benchmarks, by firstly understanding these benchmarks and then probing the organisation in terms of needs and sought outcomes compared with them.

NEWLY APPOINTED EXECUTIVES

In the case of newly appointed executives, the experience benchmarks suggest that some organisations often find it takes newly appointed executives nine months to become 'profitable'. Some perceive over 40% of newly appointed executives not to be performing at their optimum within the first year, a significant proportion of whom leave within 20 months from starting in their new roles.

Therefore the coach might investigate as follows:

➤ 'Has your organisation been satisfied with how long it takes newly appointed executives to get up to speed?'
➤ 'Would you like them to progress more quickly and securely in their new roles, delivering results faster?'

➤ 'Would you like to lessen the risks associated with executive turnover after the honeymoon period?'

ESTABLISHED EXECUTIVES

In the case of established executives, the experience benchmarks suggest that many executives still live in the industrial age and manage via top down 'controlling the what'. In today's information age, the knowledge era, superior results come from 'creating the how' through enlightened leadership with a strong customer orientation. Effectiveness as a leader is only part of the success equation; motivation through a sense of full alignment with the organisation is also a prerequisite for success.

Therefore the coach might inquire if your organisation is satisfied with the level of effectiveness of each of your executives:

➤ 'In the pursuit of continuous improvement in results?'
➤ 'In such areas as leadership, teamwork, interpersonal relationships and communication?' and
➤ 'In their motivational alignment with the organisation?'

EXECUTIVES POTENTIALLY IN CAREER TRANSITION

In the case of executives potentially in career transition, the experience benchmarks suggest that the costs and missed opportunities caused by a talented executive resigning, along with replacement hiring, can run to many hundreds of thousands of dollars. As can the problems associated with underperforming executives, or those mismatched with their roles. Similarly, the costs associated with dismissal and replacement hiring.

Therefore the coach might ask:

➤ 'Is the organisation satisfied with its ability to retain executive talent?'
➤ 'Are there any executive square pegs in round holes?'
➤ 'Is there a need for any executives to reconsider their career directions or options, including redeployment?'

CHANGE LEADERSHIP

In the case of change leadership at times of restructure or merger, the experience benchmarks suggest that two-thirds of restructures (including mergers) do not yield sought-after bottomline improvements on time, less than 20% produce satisfactory outcomes and one-third yield unsatisfactory levels of performance improvement or the time taken to achieve it. Seventy per cent of organisations downsizing find no immediate increase in productivity and more than 50% fail to improve profitability the year after.

Therefore the coach might ask the following questions:

➤ 'Is the organisation satisfied with how long it takes executives in new roles or reporting relationships after restructuring to get up to speed?'

➤ 'Are newly constituted executive teams galvanising quickly, yielding the much needed synergy and leverage they can produce?'

➤ 'Do each of your executives demonstrate capability in the change leadership competence areas of adaptability, entrepreneurism (innovation balanced by risk management), resilience and open, two-way communication?'

➤ 'Has or will restructuring leave any executives in new roles or reporting relationships demotivated, performing poorly or with a sense that they have lost out or that their future promotional prospects are limited?'

➤ 'At times of major change does it concern you that some of your key people will be poached?'

ECONOMIC BENEFITS

We do not lay claim, nor should the coach, to having all the answers on the economic benefits of the following examples, as they are always organisational and case specific. Therefore treat the following as a checklist of thought-prompters, which can be used as a basis for review within the context of the organisation and its specific needs and sought outcomes.

PROFIT POTENTIAL OF A NEWLY APPOINTED EXECUTIVE GETTING UP TO SPEED FASTER

Some organisations find it takes nine months for a newly appointed executive to attain a level of effectiveness comparable to an established peer, that is, to become 'profitable'. Accomplishing this four to five months faster would impact favourably on business results, and might effectively 'save' four to five months' gross compensation (or a significant proportion thereof). Early success also lessens the risks of early, costly executive turnover.

COSTS OF A NEWLY APPOINTED EXECUTIVE NOT MAKING THE GRADE FAST ENOUGH

Separation package, legal costs, outplacement fee, search fees for replacement, impact on business results during the replacement's assimilation period, costs associated with replacement getting up to speed (not least of all, as some organisations experience, an average of 40% of gross compensation, for a nine month period, the initial 'productivity factor', for example 30% of annual gross compensation).

DOLLAR POTENTIAL OF INCREASING EXECUTIVE/TEAM EFFECTIVENESS

This is hard to quantify, but could a 15% increase in effectiveness and/or in an executive's motivation at work, have an extra 15% leverage on performance through their team or staff, and/or on budgets within executive control, for example a 15% performance improvement or cost reduction?

COSTS OF LOSS OF EXECUTIVE TALENT

Search fees for replacement, impact on business results during the replacement's assimilation period, costs associated with replacement getting up to speed, in the case of a high flier joining the competition, profit potential to competitor (equates cost to organisation?).

COSTS ASSOCIATED WITH AN EXECUTIVE SQUARE PEG IN A ROUND HOLE

This is hard to quantify, but if executive effectiveness and/or motivational alignment were reduced by 20%, then could this have a 20% adverse impact on performance through their team or staff, and/or on budgets within executive control, for example 20% performance reduction or cost increase?

COSTS OF AN EXECUTIVE DISMISSAL

Separation package, legal costs, outplacement fee, search fees for replacement, impact on business results during the replacement's assimilation period, costs associated with replacement getting up to speed.

INDIRECT ECONOMIC IMPACTS

Morale, staff absenteeism and turnover, wasted development and training, customer interface continuity, reputation, attractiveness as employer of choice for hiring new talent, executives leaving favourably disposed to the organisation, in other words as 'allies'.

The bottomline regarding economic benefits is that executive coaching as we have defined it, invariably yields a more than 20-fold return in the investment in it, within an 18-month period.

Where else can organisations attain such a return? If you know, please tell me!

KEYNOTE

➤ If you can't quantify the bottomline effect of any intervention, why bother?

➤ Many organisations do not seek to capture management information which quantifies the full effect of human effectiveness or staff retention/loss.

➤ With a little probing and analysis, measures and benchmarks can be developed and used to assess the economic benefits/costs of undertaking a coaching intervention, or not!

Chapter 6

CORE COACHING PROCESSES

66 The tailored application of core processes underpins coaching effectiveness and efficiency 99

INTRODUCTION

This chapter describes core coaching processes common to many coaching programs.

Subsequent chapters then describe specific programs in terms of both sequence and content, along with any additional processes specific to a particular program.

DIFFERENCES BETWEEN COUNSELLING AND COACHING

Counselling can be defined as a process entailing support, encouragement, questioning and listening by an executive to help an individual define and work through personal problems or organisational changes which affect job motivation or performance.

Coaching is a similar process but also entails guidelines, examples, role plays, pre-briefings and debriefings by the executive to train and orient an individual to the realities and demands of work and to help remove any barriers to optimum work performance or behaviour.

Counselling and coaching share many of the same characteristics. At times they may seem to overlap. However, as a guide, use *counselling* when there are personal problems or organisational changes affecting job performance or motivation. Use coaching when there is a lack of skill or knowledge about job responsibilities, or about desirable leadership, in-team or interpersonal behaviour.

PRINCIPLES OF COACHING

You should always be exceptionally well prepared for each coaching session and clear about the ground to be covered and the outcomes sought.

But the key to coaching is to put the onus on the individual to make decisions and concentrate on what they are doing development-wise, rather than you having to tell them what to do or how to do it. Indeed, the ideal coaching approach combines the following phases: the individual determines development areas, strategies, tactics and so forth with the coach's help and guidelines; the coach previews implementation steps via discussion, rehearsal, role play or other approaches; the individual then tests or implements modified practices or behaviours in the workplace; the coach then debriefs by discussing how the implementation went; and back to the first and subsequent phases of the same sequence, in other words, a continuous sequence.

In approaching coaching sessions the following points need careful consideration. What is your role as coach? Judge, counsellor, supporter, manager, adviser? Clearly, at times you will be a counsellor when the individual needs a facilitator to unravel and manage an issue. Never be a manager or a judge! And yes, plenty of support and advice, but be careful of your paradigm versus the paradigm of the individual when it comes to straight advice—better to be the supporter and through a questioning approach encourage the individual to determine appropriate outcomes.

Indeed coaching is not telling or teaching, it relies heavily on questioning and feedback and, in fact, creating an environment wherein the individual can learn. In this coaching relies heavily on the formula given to us by the Almighty—namely we have two ears and one mouth and must use them in this proportion at all times!

How long should a coaching session be? I recommend one to one and a half hour sessions in a neutral meeting room or office (for confidentiality, greater session impact and fewer interruptions).

Other critical ingredients for coaching include: handing out relevant guidelines for subsequent discussion (at the next meeting); summarising; paraphrasing; active listening (nodding in agreement); pausing; provision of clear, direct feedback; embracing praise, support and challenge.

The oldest and still the most powerful coaching tactic for fostering critical thinking is questioning. Through questioning, we focus on getting individuals to work out appropriate solutions, rather than provide the answers. The coach emulates an inquiring mind by continually probing into the subject with questions.

Coaches can question goals and purposes. They can delve into the nature of the question, problem, or issue that is on the table. They can inquire whether or not the individual has relevant data and information. They can consider alternative interpretations of the data and information. They can analyse key concepts and ideas. They can question assumptions being made. They can ask individuals to draw out the implications and consequences of what they are saying. Coaches can consider alternative points of view. These, however, represent a small proportion of the total potential for using questions as a coach.

In summary, a coach needs to keep the meeting focused; keep the discussion relevant to the work setting; stimulate the session with probing questions; periodically summarise what has (and has not) been dealt with or resolved; and draw the individual deeply into the dialogue.

INTRODUCING COACHING TO LINE MANAGERS

In order to introduce coaching to line managers and executives in a way which attracts their interest and influences them to use it as a development tool, the coach needs to emphasise the bottomline impact of coaching. The story line may go something like this:

'In this era of flatter organisational structures with matrix communication and reporting lines, and where change won't go away, it will only accelerate—no wonder attention to the human factor can come second.

It's often hard to find the time to coach those key people who really need help, let alone the higher performers, where every unit of coaching in fact provides the best return.

And return on investment, as well as making available the necessary time and capability, is what coaching is all about.

For example, halving the time for a newly appointed key person to get up to speed can, in effect, save 20% of their first year's cost of employment. It can also improve their personal leverage on their team and staff, and the budgets for which they are responsible by one-third in the first 12 months. The quantification of all this can run into hundreds of thousands of dollars.

As can the quantification of the personal leverage generated by even a 10% improvement in the effectiveness or motivation of an established key person, or a team. Particularly at times of organisational change, restructuring or merger.

And then it comes to the retention of motivated talent, or at the other end of the spectrum the avoidance of a dismissal. In each case the costs and other benefits are even more obvious, and again can run into hundreds of thousands of dollars (particularly when you cost in the hiring and assimilation of a replacement).

I'd like to go over a methodology whereby the costs and financial benefits of any coaching assignment can be examined at the outset, invariably generating a strong business case.

The starting point is the identification of needs and sought outcomes, and by examining a case together we can soon identify whether the ends justify the means'.

The way is then clear for the coach to use the methodology relating to the economic benefits of coaching, as described in Chapter 5–'Economic benefits of executive coaching', which represents a powerful and convincing approach for the introduction of coaching.

INTRODUCING THE COACH TO THE COACHEE

The next step is for the individual's line manager to introduce the subject of coaching to the individual themself. The following statements can be used effectively for this.

'Coaching is positive, an opportunity, a statement that we value you and are interested in supporting you in your further development as a key person in this organisation.'

Suggest an informal meeting with the coach 'to see if you think it will be worthwhile—you decide'. This maximises ownership of the process by the individual. 'Let me know how your meeting goes and assuming you wish to proceed, the three or four of us (manager, individual, HR executive as appropriate, coach) should get together briefly to agree on what we jointly seek to achieve and how any of us can assist in this.'

Coaching is confidential. The coach will not reveal content of the program to anyone. However, the individual is expected to communicate with their line manager about forward-looking personal development or career plans resulting from the process, and their manager can help with implementation through ongoing feedback. The coach will occasionally touch base with the line manager noting where the individual is, in the process *not* the content.

Coaching is time efficient. It will fit in with the individual's schedules and priorities. However, weekly one to one-and-a-half hour meetings may be needed initially to get some early traction in the process. The process can last three to six months, tapering, and the individual may remain in touch with the coach for a year or longer.

NEEDS ANALYSIS

In order to determine a line manager's needs for coaching with one of their direct reports, or, in order to determine the needs directly from the individual, clearly a questioning approach is an appropriate entry point. This may usefully take the following sequence: background and current status; things which are going well at the organisation, department or individual level; things which lend themselves to improvement; the downside if such improvements are not attained; the upside of their attainment; and the resultant needs for coaching, defined as specifically as possible.

Once the needs have been specified, the coach then should describe how coaching can add value in helping the individual attain these needs. The previous section on introducing the coach can be used as a guideline for this, and if the themes therein have been used for purposes of introducing the coach, then the coach repeating them is powerfully reinforcing.

In concluding needs analysis there should be a 'triangular' meeting attended by the coachee, coach, line manager and possibly HR executive, in order to agree on the way forward and the outcomes sought.

CAREER REVIEW

The career review is somewhat like a selection interview and focuses on qualifications, experience, competencies (technical, functional or managerial) and achievements—the results the individual has been able to attain and the actions taken to accomplish them, which in themselves reveal much about skills and other personal traits.

In summarising at the end of this review, the following questions can be usefully deployed: How satisfied are you with your career and its progress to date?; What have been the high points of your career?; What have been the low points?; What job position(s) have you enjoyed the most?; What job position(s) have you enjoyed the least?

What have been your greatest achievements?; What does this tell others and you about your greatest capabilities, skills and other personal traits?; Which of the above are transferable to other job roles, occupations or business sectors?; Specifically what types of jobs (different to my current or most recent job) might they match?;

What have been your greatest setbacks or failures?; What does this tell others and you about your areas of least strength?; What does this suggest in terms of personal development opportunities and priorities?; and

On reading your résumé, how might a headhunter describe you in a few lines of text to a client? Now summarise very briefly your own self-assessment of your track record, if it is different to the above.

ROLE REVIEW

If there is a job specification, ask the individual to go over it.

Whether there is a job specification or not, use the following as a checklist:

➤ *A brief outline.* The history of the organisation (or the individual's part of the organisation), its development and growth, should be given.

➤ *Its products and services.* The volume in relation to the industry and its competitors.

➤ *The markets.* For the products and services, the methods of distribution, sales turnover and profitability.

➤ *Centres and methods of operation.* Locations, and the number of people employed both in total and within the department or function concerned.

➤ *Position title and purpose.* A straightforward, simple statement of what needs to be done and the objectives to be achieved.

➤ *Relationships.* The main reporting and working relationships should be indicated. These will cover internal and external contacts, committees, boards and all relationships in a 360° sense.

➤ *Dimensions.* What often determines the size or seniority of the position are the number of people reporting to the individual, the size of the budgets they control and the volume of business and profitability that they will be expected to generate. If the individual sits on boards or committees or is a representative on outside bodies, then this also gives an indication of the size and nature of the position. If they are expected to travel abroad then the expected percentage of their time they will be travelling should be noted.

➤ *Accountabilities*. This should describe the individual's tasks and the areas where they have sole responsibility or accountability for results. It should include their own key result areas with standards and a time scale where possible, and also those of their direct reports. The main decisions taken by them, or delegated, or referred elsewhere should also be recorded.

➤ *Controls*. The controls and communications relating directly to the individual's main result areas should be indicated, listing their importance and effectiveness, number, method and frequency.

➤ *Attainment of objectives*. These should define the principal objectives to be achieved and set out priorities and timeframes. Note should be made of the resources required and the support necessary from superiors or colleagues to achieve these objectives. They should be quantified as far as possible.

➤ *Other expectations, activities and milestones*. Listed here should be a complete assessment of all other requirements during the next 12 months, with dates for completion and other relevant criteria, including needs and opportunities for development and training.

REVIEW OF PREVIOUS FEEDBACK

A key element of coaching is to leverage off existing management and human resources processes which have already been used with an individual. For example, the following processes, psychological assessment, performance review or appraisal, diagnostic tests or checklists used as part of training, 360° surveys and so forth.

In some instances, the coach may be unfamiliar with such processes but this does not matter. Rather, the coach should ask the individual what they have been able to conclude from the results of such processes and, if necessary, go over the relevant paperwork with the coachee, but always putting the onus on the individual to explain and draw down the most significant implications for development or career direction.

And do not ignore the strengths-side of the equation. Indeed, focus initially on the strengths of the individual as articulated through previous feedback. Later, address 'development opportunities' rather than 'weaknesses', as this has a far more positive effect.

SDOT ANALYSIS AND DEVELOPMENT PRIORITIES

SDOT is the acronym for Strengths, Development Needs, Opportunities and Threats. SDOT analysis therefore 'rounds off' earlier discussions by summarising an individual's strengths, perceived development needs, other future opportunities and possible threats on the horizon.

From this, either in the existing job or future career context, with the coach's help the individual can focus on the top two or three development priorities for themselves, for example:

➤ 'I need to listen more and talk less at meetings.'
➤ 'I need to spend more time working one-on-one with my direct reports.'
➤ 'I need to praise in public more, and reserve criticism for one-on-one private discussion.'
➤ 'I need to make myself more accessible.'

SELF-MANAGEMENT OF DEVELOPMENT

In converting development priorities into implementation, take each priority one at a time; the following sequence is a powerful way to attain some early progress.

The coach needs to help the individual answer the following questions. What did I do recently which required use of the competencies I am trying to develop? What went well? What could have gone better? What can I do differently next time to improve my performance? What are the main points I wish to improve on? How should I improve on them? When can I try out these improvements?

The coachee then needs to try out these improvements when the situation allows this, modifying them to meet the prevailing needs.

Other tips for this include: seeking feedback from others—line manager, peers, direct reports; accepting criticism with an open mind and feeding this back into the process; and continuous improvement rather than improvement then plateau (then taper?).

360° SURVEYS

Multi-level or 360° surveys have become very popular in organisations as a means of helping individuals understand how their work practices, behaviour and other elements of competence is perceived by others, compared with their own self-perception. The key is to convert newfound self-awareness from such surveys into appropriate development actions, often the missing link, and where coaching can add great value.

Indeed, 360° surveys are often used early in the coaching process for diagnosis and analysis. However, such surveys should not be treated as a straight scorecard of the individual's performance, rather, they are developmental tools indicating the individual's 'preferred' self-positioning in the various competency areas versus the 'perceptions' by others of the individual's behaviour in these areas.

In other words, 'what you see' is not always 'what you get' from either perspective. We've all heard of the stern troop commander with the heart of gold, or executives who believe themselves to be approachable and 'open', but whose staff avoid them.

There is a need for caution in the following areas:

➤ The individual may have a far higher opinion of their performance in certain competency areas compared to the perceptions of others—it is not a simple black and white situation as the individual may be trying to perform well in such areas but they simply may not be coming across in this way (often as a result of work pressures, time constraints, conflicting priorities and so forth ... 'I really do care about people, but I simply don't have time to show it!').

➤ Bias or subjectivity by survey respondents, who for whatever reason, may not be scoring the survey fairly, can distort results, harmfully and distressingly.

➤ Bias by the individual (but limited when they understand that only they will see the results and that they don't have to show the results to their line manager).

➤ Bias by the line manager who presumes the way the individual behaves with them is the way they behave with their direct reports or peers.

➤ Bias by the line manager who may be closer to understanding organisational requirements or perspectives on, say, leadership behaviour than the individual, or who may simply not know the individual well enough, or who may be overly influenced by the line manager/direct report power relationship.

➤ Bias by peers who may not be that close to the individual or who may feel they are competing with them.

➤ Bias by direct reports who see their participation in the survey as a chance to 'score a few points', 'get their own back' and so forth.

The best way to use survey results is to help the individual draw their own interpretations and conclusions and develop their own personal development themes with the coach's help, rather than simply transfer raw findings and commentary to the action plans. The coach's understanding of the person's job specification and business plan, along with interview findings, coupled with the coach's own experience in organisational life will help the coach enable the individual to do this.

THIRD PARTY INTERVIEWS

Third party interviews are an excellent way to help an individual diagnose and self-prescribe competence and career development priorities. They need to be undertaken confidentially by the coach, who later provides aggregate feedback in a way whereby the precise source of feedback remains anonymous.

The third party interviews need to be positioned in a positive light, both for the coachee and the interview respondents, the earlier section on introducing the coach can be usefully used as a guideline in this regard.

Typical questions may include:

➤ How long and in what capacities have you known the individual?
➤ How would you describe him/her as an executive?
➤ How would you describe him/her as a person?
➤ Strengths?
➤ Technical and functional development opportunities?
➤ Behavioural and interpersonal development opportunities?
➤ Current job fit?
➤ Organisational fit?
➤ Looking ahead, how would you see their career progressing in the organisation?
➤ Roles ahead and timeframes?

PSYCHOLOGICAL ASSESSMENT

I have found psychological assessment advantageous when an individual rejects the notion of undertaking a 360° survey or third party interviews, and yet where additional diagnostic feedback is required. Also, when through the counselling process the coach feels that there are hidden or significant issues connected to personality which need to be better understood by the individual in order to help them move forward in their development.

However, many individuals are sceptical or reluctant to undertake full psychological assessment and, since in coaching we advocate concentrating on behaviour rather than personality, with diagnostic feedback being available in a variety of forms, we perceive psychological assessment solely as an option.

When it is advantageous to conduct it, I advocate top, full-time practising organisational or industrial psychologists who will select appropriate instruments according to needs.

Coaching meetings, progress reporting and closure

In preparing for planning and conducting coaching meetings the following sequence can be adopted:

➤ Counselling mode: an informal and questioning opening approach to see how things are going with the coachee—see the earlier section on counselling.
➤ Meeting objectives and outcomes: what the coach and individual might seek to attain in the meeting.
➤ Review general progress since last meeting.
➤ Pre- or debrief one or more self-management of development process sequences as discussed earlier.
➤ Agree on next meeting date.
➤ Action items between now and then (individual and possibly coach).
➤ Meeting summary and wrap-up.
➤ What the next meeting is intended to cover.

Progress review sessions are held periodically between individual, line manager, sometimes the human resources executive and the coach. The individual usually leads the discussion. It is wise for the individual and coach to plan these sessions in advance by using the following checklist:

➤ Meeting outcomes and impact we are trying to leave with line manager and HR executive?
➤ Areas we need to concentrate on at the meeting?
➤ Areas we need to avoid at the meeting?
➤ Any other aspects line manager and HR executive might like to discuss?
➤ Agreed next steps?

The coach's role is to support the coachee in progress reporting, and while the coach will tend to leave content to the coachee to describe, the coach will often allude to the process undertaken and note the current stage within the process.

Turning to the closure meeting at the end of the coaching program, the following sequence is often undertaken:

➤ The coach to recap on outcomes sought and work program.

➤ The individual to recap on progress made.

➤ The individual asks their line manager and HR executive for verification of progress and any views regarding future development areas.

➤ The coach asks if all parties are satisfied with the outcomes. If not, the coach establishes what still needs to be undertaken and achieved.

A TYPICAL COACHING SEQUENCE SUMMARISED

Typically, in most coaching sequences—and a broad range is described in Chapters 8–16—four phases represent the classic work program: situation assessment, fact finding, early wins and sustainable development.

SITUATION ASSESSMENT

In situation assessment, we attain organisational and individual perspectives which are aligned and agreed. From the earlier sections in this chapter, the following are usually included: introducing coaching to line managers, introducing coach to the coachee, and needs analysis.

FACT FINDING

Regarding fact finding, the following elements are undertaken in an appropriate sequence according to needs: career review, role review, review of previous feedback, SDOT analysis, 360° surveys, third party interviews and psychological assessment.

An important consideration in fact finding is that the various selected diagnostic processes should be deployed sequentially over a timeframe in order to develop some momentum and sustainability in identifying and pursuing personal development priorities.

EARLY WINS

Early wins in terms of identifying a need for some form of changed behaviour, and then implementing it in the work environment are important in the context of building confidence in the process and a thirst for more wins. Also, through perceptions from those working with the individual that some beneficial change is occurring quickly and noticeably. Development priorities following SDOT analysis, along with self-management of development represent the key enabling elements for early wins.

SUSTAINABLE DEVELOPMENT

Sustainable development comes about through ongoing counselling, coaching meetings, progress reporting and closure. And sustainable development continues after closure, particularly if the line manager—through their involvement in the coaching program even if they have not been enacting the role of formal coach (it is preferable they do enact the role!)—continues as a more effective day-to-day informal coach, after the formal coaching program has run its course.

In this the learning should be that every line manager operates continuously as a coach, which is by far the most powerful way to maximise the potential of the people in the organisation.

KEYNOTE

➤ The core 'coaching' processes include:

counselling

coaching

introducing coaching to line managers

introducing the coach to the coachee

needs analysis

career review

role review

review of previous feedback

SDOT analysis

development priorities

self-management of development

360° surveys

third party interviews

psychological assessment

coaching meetings

progress reporting

closure

typical sequencing.

➤ They can be tailored to a broad range of scenarios and ensure both coaching effectiveness and efficiency.

Chapter 7

A Typical Executive Coaching Process

❝ Building and sustaining the effectiveness and success of key people, individually and in teams **❞**

Introduction

The focus of executive coaching addresses executive development needs, either by way of intervention when there is a problem or crisis or as part of the general executive development process.

It is effective in helping close the gap between current job requirements and an individual's performance, stress levels or 'fit'; assisting executives to lead major change; development of executives in present and for future roles; learning from lessons of the past; and, for fast-track and secure induction of new hires.

Executive coaching is conducted typically over three to six months or longer. It can be offered to concentrate on executive development in such areas as: interpersonal relationships and communication; leading, managing and developing talent; focusing on the primary drivers of business performance; becoming more proactive regarding customers, external trends and projections; change-agent competencies; organisational restructuring; applying a consistent people emphasis; teamwork; politics, power and influence; professional consultative selling; and, professional presentations and public speaking.

Executive coaching offers an opportunity to both the organisation and the executive to define and address specific development needs confidentially, and in a way which can help executives change their behaviour and the way they operate, and sustain such changes.

Typically there are three stages, the first entailing analysis of the executive's role and reporting relationships, and of any previous performance evaluations and other diagnostic feedback. From this, initial development priorities can be established, tested and pursued.

Additionally, a multi-level survey in full or in part can be used to complement the organisation's existing human resources and performance management processes. The coach can also conduct associated third party interviews to verify and amplify previous findings.

The second stage entails further action planning though the confirmation and more comprehensive definition of executive development needs. Objectives, executive development strategies and action plans are then agreed and presented by the participant to their senior line and human resources executives, with the help of the coach.

The final stage is implementation, involving use as appropriate of the organisation's executive development resources, as well as periodic executive coaching and hotline advice.

I always encourage regular feedback to/from the individual's senior line and HR executives by the participant with the help of the coach, with utmost respect for confidentiality. In this way, opportunities are also created for senior line executives to be drawn in as internal coaches.

A TYPICAL COACHING PROCESS IN MORE DETAIL

In describing a typical process I will include reference to the core coaching processes in Chapter 6, and these include introducing coaching to line managers, introducing the coach to the coachee, needs analysis, career review, role review, review of previous feedback and so forth.

In introducing coaching to the line manager, quite apart from the economic benefits argument (Chapter 5—'Economic benefits of executive coaching') and core introductory process described in Chapter 6—'Core coaching processes', I also find the sports analogy a useful one, in other words, that top sportspeople attain optimum performance through coaching. Compare this to the executive paradigm, so often encountered, that in making it to the ranks of executive leadership 'one has made it' and continuing personal and professional development is something that may get attended to if the individual has the time and interest!

Through needs analysis with the line manager and sometimes HR executive you need to be able to crystallise it down to what the true development needs are (rather than the symptoms) and the outcomes sought. And in this, be very careful about timeframes. Any effective executive coaching should render some early gains, but coaching input needs to be there for several months if not longer. This is because effectively in helping an individual change their work practices, behaviour or competencies, they are having to change habits which can be a superhuman task only accomplished with perseverance and continuing input.

When introducing the coach to the coachee there is often some anxiety both by the line manager and HR executive as to how the coachee will accept coaching. Frankly, I have rarely encountered any problem. Providing the earlier guidelines are used and a positive approach taken, there should be little, if any resistance. Indeed, the opposite usually applies and the coachee welcomes it when they understand how coaching works.

When coaching is first used in an organisation or particular area, try using this as an introductory mechanism. Namely, that the organisation wishes to pilot coaching—test it out—and the particular individual potentially to be coached is invited to help the organisation do this. This approach rarely fails to generate the desired outcome!

The further needs analysis undertaken with the coachee can be quite illuminating and reveal the other side of the story, yet invariably there is a high degree of coincidence between the line manager and the coachee's story lines. If there are any differences in story lines, it is usually degree rather than context. In the worst case scenario however—and any coach needs to be aware that they will almost certainly encounter this—the line manager has neither informed the coachee about performance expectations nor provided feedback.

This is where the 'triangular' meeting between all parties, the next step in the process, is particularly important. The coach often needs to prepare the line manager to be candid about their perceptions of needs and sought outcomes at the triangular meeting. The coach also needs to alert the coachee that they may receive some 'robust' feedback at this meeting which they usually find most interesting and accept positively, now that they know they have a coaching program and a coach to advise and make real headway in personal development.

The first coaching meeting, or meetings depending upon needs, cover career review, to provide background, role review to provide context, review of previous feedback to provide initial diagnosis and SDOT analysis and development priorities to crystallise everything into an initial action plan designed to generate some early progress—'early wins'. Use of the self-management of development process (again Chapter 6—'Core coaching processes') is an invaluable aid for this. Two to three, perhaps four meetings usually suffice to complete these initial stages, but if more are needed, it is worthwhile the investment of time.

Turning to further diagnosis, an appropriate 360° survey can be a powerful feedback mechanism. There are many available 'off the shelf' or they can be purpose designed. I use my own proprietary Adeptus Process® multi-level survey material which assesses management practices, motivational delegation, leadership of change, operating style, leadership traits, public speaking and presentations, in-team behaviour, and a range of other job and people related success factors.

In fact, all these factors relate to my findings regarding the success factors in 300 case studies of executives and senior people with whom I worked professionally over a five-year period. My findings were tested on, and verified by, an independent panel of 85 top executives, and published in my book *The Bulletproof Executive*.

To their advantage, coachees can immediately access guidelines in my book as they come out of the survey process, having prioritised two to three key development areas. Indeed, each of the 32 topics in the survey is cross-indexed to relevant chapters in this text. Rather than assume that each success factor area is of equal relevance to the coachee in their particular role in the organisation, survey results and targeted development areas are always addressed in the context of what the organisation expects and seeks. Even if the organisation has not articulated this as standard practice—by way of example, specified sought leadership competencies, the coachee can usually determine appropriate development areas through discussion with their line manager and HR executive against which they can compare survey results. Such discussions are really worthwhile and add great value to the whole coaching process in the context of further aligning it with organisational needs and expectations.

INTERPERSONAL RELATIONSHIPS

One development area often targeted is interpersonal relations. For this, the 'gurus' have developed countless surveys and models depicting differing personal styles, behaviour or personality. Drawing on much of this thinking and on my own empirical research, I have been able to produce a survey element within my proprietary Adeptus Process®—a suite of survey and diagnostic material used in coaching which bridges conventional wisdom with my practical experience. Firstly, it provides some primary guidelines on behaviour, secondly enables the observer to determine their own and others' operating styles quickly and precisely, and finally can be used in improving interpersonal relationships.

EXAMPLE

Visualise two very different individuals. The first is operations manager in an airline catering and food service organisation in London. She is described by her colleagues as being highly 'hands-on' and action-oriented. She talks a lot to her staff, actively giving them instructions as they go about their work. She seems preoccupied with results and displays a strong output orientation. She exhibits highly 'proactive' behaviour.

The second is the employee relations manager in the sales and service centre of a major consumer electronics manufacturer in San Francisco. He is seen to be 'hands-off', believing that line managers and supervisors need to be the primary interface with hourly paid employees. He appears to be calm in nature, he is an excellent and 'active' listener, and is regarded as extremely friendly and approachable by all. He evaluates situations with care and with special consideration of the human factor. He exhibits highly 'receptive' behaviour.

Most of us are in fact a mixture of 'proactiveness' and 'receptiveness' in the way we behave. Indeed, there are several different operating styles which blend proactiveness and receptiveness together.

➤ *High proactiveness and low receptiveness.* This is somewhat like the first example, but perhaps not to her extreme. The label I give to this style is commander/doer, the key characteristics being hands-on, action, talking, results, and above all, an output-orientation.

Commander/doers both direct others, often quite forcefully, and are people of action. They are always on the go and can never sit still. They put a lot of effort into things and like to keep on the move. They can be very energetic and they find it hard to relax. They take a down-to-earth attitude, relying on commonsense approaches. They prefer tangible, concrete objects rather than 'airy-fairy' ideas or feelings. They learn by doing rather than by reading. Also, they are confident in meeting new circumstances or strange situations alone. Commander/doers are happy to rely on their own capabilities in any environment or in tackling any matter.

➤ *High receptiveness and low proactiveness.* This is somewhat like the second example, but perhaps not to his extreme. The label I give to this style is empathiser/humanist, the key characteristics being hands-off, reflective, listening, and above all, a people-orientation.

The empathiser/humanist is able to understand other people, their ideas, attitudes or behaviour and is affected in mood or behaviour by others—what people say or do. People of this style enjoy listening to others, are cooperative, and enjoy their company. Empathiser/humanists allow and encourage others to have their say; they believe in majority decisions, but not to the disadvantage of minorities. Also, they dislike unduly forcing or asserting themselves over other people.

➤ *High proactiveness and high receptiveness.* This is a combination of styles in the direction of both of the above examples. The label I give to this style is responder/initiator, the key characteristics being a capacity both to get involved and stand aside, to act and to be reflective, to talk and to listen, and to seek tangible results but also to be oriented towards people.

The responder/initiator tends to exhibit good levels of both proactive and receptive behaviour. Indeed, people with this style of behaviour usually display great enthusiasm in working with others, being both active listeners and enthusiastic talkers. They sell themselves well and are usually good presenters.

➤ *Low proactiveness and low receptiveness.* The label I give to this style is evaluator/detailer, the key characteristics being neither particularly hands-on, nor overly action-orientated, nor an active responder nor initiator. Such people tend to remain alone or detached rather than engage in too much group or individual interaction—they tend to stay out of the limelight. They are often non-committal, yet invariably factual and analytical, in fact classic planners and detailers.

In this regard, the evaluator/detailer takes a lot of care over things; is painstaking in doing things; sometimes is seen as cautious; likes to do a job well; and, does not like sloppiness or a casual approach. People with this style take a consistently steady approach to all situations, are unflappable, are neither easily aroused or stimulated nor provoked, and are often thought of as cold and unemotional. Evaluator/detailers tackle things in a controlled way, are quite happy with their own company, and are self-sufficient.

➤ *A mixture of low and high proactiveness and low and high receptiveness.* This is the idea generator, who is a combination of the previous four styles, and is able to nimbly dart from one operating style to another operating style, often exhibiting extremes of behaviour and flashes of inspiration and creativity, seeing 'endless possibilities'.

Idea generators are very concerned with the 'big picture', knowledge and theory, often forgetting practical application. However, they do jump in and apply themselves enthusiastically when committed to a course of action. People of this operating style usually are interested in the future and the longer term, perhaps more than the 'here and now'. Idea generators often change their minds, or courses of action and enjoy variety.

Idea generators also have a preference for 'doing their own thing'; they do not always agree with or conform to other people, their wishes, ideas, attitudes or behaviour; and, they enjoy freedom of choice.

➤ *A mixture of a reasonable degree of proactiveness and a reasonable degree of receptiveness.* This is the all-rounder, who seldom if ever shows extremes of any type of behaviour, exhibiting more of a balanced, yet flexible style. All-rounders often represent the stabilising factor in teams and can make good chairpersons. They can help the team reach consensus and are able to compromise. While not usually being seen as the life and soul of the party, they are usually quite popular and their opinions are often sought. They usually give others a fair hearing.

All-rounders are well able to identify with all the other styles and converse with them easily, providing extremes in behaviour are not evident, which can cause them some difficulties. Indeed, when others are exhibiting extremes in behaviour, all-rounders often act as moderators.

One way of assessing your own and other people's operating styles is first to gauge the degree of proactiveness and receptiveness of the person in mind, in terms of the way that person behaves. How proactive and how receptive are they? This approach may lead you to operating style definition more easily. Also, anyone can display a combination of operating styles, but will usually exhibit a main style, perhaps along with a subordinate style.

Operating styles can also vary depending upon circumstances, for example, the main style of an individual working under stressful conditions may be very different to their style at home under more relaxed conditions. Clearly, for our purposes we need to concentrate on the work situation.

In communicating well with others and in seeking to develop good interpersonal relations, you first need to be clear about your own operating style—the way you come across:

➤ *The commander/doer* often speaks rapidly and enthusiastically and usually exudes an air of confidence and a down-to-earth attitude. However, when over-utilising these positive attributes, commander/doers can speak or progress too quickly, and can appear to be somewhat short-sighted and too keen on action, rather than on taking longer term or bigger picture scenarios into consideration. They can also at times be overly blunt and disinterested in social niceties.

➤ *If you are a responder/initiator or all-rounder*, this suggests you have behavioural flexibility and that you should find it quite easy to adapt your operating style to meet the needs of others. The only caveat here is that all-rounders may come across as being a little flat or uninspiring at times.

➤ *The empathiser/humanist* probably reads the other party or audience well and empathises with them. They usually come across in a friendly and courteous manner and often seek involvement of others through their use of questions, comments and examples. However, when over-utilising these positive attributes, empathiser/humanists may become swayed by the mood and views of the other party and even lose control. They also may harp too long on the historical perspective—'the way we used to do things'—and appear not to come to the point too quickly. They may also be too anxious to please.

➤ *Evaluator/detailers* often speak with accuracy and clarity and achieve their objectives in the time allocated. However, an over-utilisation of these positive attributes may include a preference for being too dogmatic and a failure to empathise with the other party. They can sometimes come across as dull and monotonous, and preoccupied with content rather than how they come across.

➤ *Idea generators* can often speak with plenty of creativity and bright ideas. However, when over-utilising these positive attributes they can be hard to follow or understand and may be too theoretical. They can also be poor time managers, and have difficulty in emphasising the main point or ending their discussions with impact. They may also fail to read the other party or audience accurately, being more concerned with their own discussion content.

In order to enhance interpersonal relations, you have to take this thinking further and vary your approach and operating style, depending on the other party. This is quite natural. We don't act the same way with different kinds of people we meet or different family members; we are constantly adjusting our style, depending on the response we get. By understanding different operating styles, with practice anyone can adjust their style to elicit the most positive response from others. Individuals tend to prefer people whom they perceive to be most like themselves.

We all have enough facets to our personalities to downplay some traits and emphasise others in a particular situation, without appearing phoney. By identifying the operating styles of the other party, you can adapt your own style in order to gain the most favourable reaction and response. The research for this is best undertaken in advance:

➤ *The responder/initiator*. These people are assertive, enthusiastic, expressive and make quick decisions. They listen to you, but also tend to want to have their say. You need to 'engage' in communication with these individuals to be most effective.

➤ *The commander/doer*. These people are assertive, goal-orientated, impatient for results, and decisive. They dislike inaction or beating about the bush and prefer it if you stick to business, talk facts and come to the point quickly.

➤ *The empathiser/humanist*. This type of person is warm and friendly, but a little hesitant to take risks and makes decisions very carefully. Here you will be more successful if you show interest and support, and provide reassurance rather than pressure.

➤ *The evaluator/detailer*. This person is very organised, precise, analytical and cautious. There is a dislike of sloppiness, failure to provide concrete facts and evidence or a disregard for rules and regulations. You will increase your chances of success with this person if you are on time, provide full details, and allow sufficient time to verify facts and make careful decisions.

➤ *The all-rounder*. This person has a flexible style and can get on with anyone providing they don't show extremes in behaviour. Showing versatility in your own style, but using moderation throughout your interaction, will have the best impact on the all-rounder.

➤ *The idea generator.* This person also has a flexible style but shows extremes and sometimes even inconsistencies in behaviour. Idea generators need to be enthused and excited by both the content and delivery of your interaction to have the greatest effect on how they perceive you. They tend to fly off in several directions at once and so need to be kept on track. Summarising your key points at the end of your discussion will be effective with these individuals.

This operating style methodology serves as a highly effective coaching frame of reference for discussion with and use by coachees.

LEADERSHIP

Another development area often targeted is leadership, and the following methodology can be used powerfully by coach and coachee.

Many organisations have not yet reached the point where they can specify *desirable* leadership traits in a manner by which individuals can pursue them effectively for purposes of personal development. However, this does not prevent organisations from reacting negatively when *undesirable* traits are being exhibited!

These can be as basic as executives and managers being too production (rather than customer) oriented; too autocratic; not supporting equal employment or promotion; exhibiting racism, sexism, harassment or discrimination; being involved in unfair dismissal; making preferential appointments; not engaging in adequate two-way communication; and not being prepared to delegate or change.

What seems to be lacking in many organisations today is a simple conceptual model or framework which can be understood and applied by individuals and organisations in their identification, pursuit and adoption of ideal or desirable leadership traits. I will now demonstrate a model I use—which also forms part of the Adeptus Process® multi-level survey—which first describes people displaying desirable and perhaps less desirable leadership traits. You be the judge as to whether their traits are desirable or undesirable!

CASE STUDY

The first example is a senior executive responsible for a significant sports footwear production plant and distributorship in Kuala Lumpur, Malaysia. He is well qualified having both an MBA and a degree in economics. He believes he is a specialist in sports footwear, emphasises low-cost production and tight centralised control. He also personally gets involved in the detail of operations which he has divided into three strategic business units. He excels at administration, has good local knowledge and perspective, always conforms with head office and expects his subordinates to operate by the rule book.

Although market demands change quite rapidly—sports footwear now being predominantly fashion items—he believes in the 'continuation of the status quo': develop and update the product according to customer needs, but produce and distribute it conventionally. Clearly, he is production-driven. When confronted by operational problems, he personally gets involved in solving them and he is seen as a logical problem-solver. I call this first example the production controller.

CASE STUDY

In the second example the executive runs the French operations of a high-tech office equipment company in Paris. She is seen as being very considerate of her 3400 staff, displaying a caring attitude and relying very much on natural attrition rather than retrenchment for downsizing as the organisation flexes its way into the 2000s. The firm pays its staff quite well and has the best employee sickness benefits, health insurance and personal disability and lifecover in its industry.

However, the executive in this case is also considered autocratic. She believes in discipline (she doesn't always seem to trust her staff), tight control and firm directive management. She has taken great pains to develop a formal and hierarchical organisation structure, where jobs, reporting relationships, accountabilities and authority are all very clearly defined and rigidly adhered to. While she seeks to communicate with staff, she relies heavily on selectively 'transmitting' information top-down, but the opportunities and processes for her 'receiving' information bottom-up are less evident.

As an individual she is fiercely competitive with her peers, and she is often thought to be too self-promotional, putting herself rather than her team first when she visits her superiors in Japan for quarterly business reviews. I call this second example the benevolent autocrat.

CASE STUDY

Our third example works in London, United Kingdom and is a senior executive in the publishing industry. He has lived in several countries and this seems to have equipped him with a global perspective and knowledge. He is considered by his industry peers to be a non-conformist, taking a highly customer-centred and entrepreneurial approach to the strategic development of his publishing 'mini-empire'. Although at the same time he understands, commits to, and deploys the core competencies of his organisation as much as possible.

Taking a flexible approach and believing in decentralised control, he and his team quickly respond to change and are considered to be pioneers and pathfinders in their industry. Personally, he is financially astute, uses a lot of initiative, and is perceived to be a creative problem-solver with broad-based general management capabilities. I call this third example the visionary strategist.

CASE STUDY

Our final example runs a software development company in Vancouver. She is considered to be a natural and inspirational leader of people, be they employees or customers. Being both customer-oriented and empowering her employees, she has a track record of unparalleled software development success in her field, being the 'first to market' with true innovation, only accomplished by defining customer needs and by relying on a committed team to convert concepts into real solutions.

When questioned at an industry conference about leadership styles, she emphasised her beliefs in flat organisational hierarchies, open two-way communication, learning, people development and the need for leaders to relate well to both groups of people and individuals.

An article on her company in a business periodical reported an interview with several of her staff. They said she was trusting of employees, unstructured, certainly not directive, and always seemed to put the customer and her team first, rather than herself. They also applauded her creativity—her capacity to think outside the square—and her ability to enthuse others in innovative approaches and solutions. I call this fourth example the inspirational leader.

Four very different sets of leadership traits and in each case, very successful people! Which traits are more desirable, and which are less desirable? What are the common threads in each subset of traits? Of course, the degree of desirability or undesirability is defined by the orientation and perception of the beholder. Some of us do not trust staff, others believe in firm discipline, while others believe in more of a hands-off or creative style.

Similarly with organisations, some companies have a culture wherein the production controller would be perceived as exhibiting highly desirable leadership traits, whereas other organisations may prefer the traits exhibited by the visionary strategist. Yet other organisations, particularly the larger and more decentralised, may identify well with a blend of three or even four different subsets of traits. Invariably, flexibility is sought in most executives and managers, rather than rigidity.

In the ideal setting, both individuals and their organisations must come to some agreement on what they mean by desirable leadership traits for executives, managers and other key people to be successful. To enable this to happen, they need to develop a common language to describe this other 'make or break' area of leadership success.

Two dimensions together define the major categories of leadership traits in the examples we have cited. The first dimension relates to the degree of people orientation versus the degree of output orientation. Clearly, some leaders are highly oriented towards output, tasks and production, whereas others are more oriented towards people, be they employees or customers. Some leaders are a blend of the two, or verge towards one orientation or the other.

The second dimension relates to the degree of control versus the degree of creativity. Again, some leaders are very dominant—they often seek to be in control or impose controls on others, and they are likely to be intensive in their approach. Other leaders think much more outside the square and are more interested in a hands-off and creative environment.

By comparing these two sets of dimensions we can evolve the following four leadership trait groupings:

➤ High emphasis on output and control: the *production controller*.
➤ High emphasis on control and people: the *benevolent autocrat*.
➤ High emphasis on people and creativity: the *inspirational leader*.
➤ High emphasis on creativity and output: the *visionary strategist*.

Increasingly, it seems desirable leadership traits are perceived by employers as a dual orientation towards people and creativity. This is because many organisations have been through a period of unprecedented restructuring and downsizing—managing the costs—when a production and control mentality was highly relevant.

In this current economic climate of low inflation and high competition, many of these same organisations are seeking to regenerate and grow, perhaps into entirely new profitable areas, or by being very different to their competitors. This will only come about through an increased orientation towards people (both employees and customers) and creative approaches.

If there is a gap between what is sought by the organisation and the coachee's traits in their current role, then the alternatives the coach might suggest for the coachee to consider, are:

➤ Ignore it. Hope that the gap will go unrecognised. However, in today's smaller and flatter organisational structures, every single cog has to be moving in harmony with every other cog. In the heavy machinery of old bureaucratic structures the occasional rusty cog could survive unnoticed, but today, every rusty cog is exposed and vulnerable.

➤ Attack it. Refuse to change and buck the trend, but beware! Organisations rather than individuals usually win out.

➤ Change the organisation. Try to change organisational requirements for leadership traits more towards your own traits, but how movable are mountains!

➤ Change your attitude. View the problem as an opportunity rather than a threat.

➤ Change your traits. Try to get your traits to coincide more with the expectations of your organisation.

➤ Retreat. Move to another part of the organisation or remove yourself altogether from the organisation.

MOTIVATIONAL DELEGATION

Other development areas often targeted in executive coaching are delegation and motivation.

I believe that effective delegation is probably one of the most important management functions in running large organisations. All the other functional areas of planning, organising, monitoring and so forth can only be effective if the manager is a capable delegator.

I see delegation as a four step approach: decide what needs to be delegated (and in this context 'more' rather than 'less' can and should be delegated in most cases); decide to whom the responsibility for such activities should be delegated; explain the reasons for and objectives of the delegated responsibility; and, provide sufficient resources and authority for the responsibility to be carried through and for the required activities to be accomplished.

Based on my experience, some of the rules for effective delegation include:

➤ Only delegate if you are prepared to take some risks, which can be minimised through effective monitoring.

➤ Only delegate when you are prepared to put in sufficient time and effort to make delegation work successfully.

➤ Delegate in those areas where you are conducting activities which do not use your greatest competencies and capabilities.

➤ Delegate to save time that can be used on activities which cannot be undertaken by direct reports.

➤ Delegate only when you have confidence in your direct reports to assume delegated responsibilities and accomplish required activities.

➤ Delegate to improve the involvement of your direct reports, which can enhance their motivation and personal performance.

➤ Delegate in order to develop your direct reports for increased responsibilities.

➤ Provide sufficient authority to the direct report to whom you are delegating and define the parameters of this authority.

➤ Establish priorities and deadlines for completion of tasks and for progress reports.

➤ Relinquish sufficient control for your direct reports to buy ownership of your delegation and to have freedom to act.

In my experience as a senior executive, manager and administrator, effective delegation throughout the organisation frees up the bottlenecks and allows executives and managers to concentrate on higher level matters, for which after all, they are being paid. Providing these guidelines are followed at all levels, the organisation can move forward with greater involvement, commitment, speed and effect.

Turning to an individual's capacity to create a motivational environment within which others can work and flourish, the following key points in an individual developing as a 'motivator' are important:

➤ Selecting and developing staff on the basis of a strong work ethic and high personal standards in terms of results.

➤ Establishing challenging jobs which in themselves create satisfaction, enjoyment and self-motivation.

➤ Developing an external image and internal identity of the organisation based on clearly articulated values, principles, mission and goals, with which employees can identify enthusiastically and in which they can visualise their own success.

➤ Encouraging employees to be involved in goal-setting (which buys their ownership of such goals and enhances their self-esteem), offering freedom to, and support in accomplishing such goals, especially where their own goals coincide with the goals of the organisation.

➤ Creating a positive, active, and mutually involving working environment, with a sense of dynamism, progression and 'change for the best', a commitment to excellence and winning, and encouraging a sense of self-direction and empowerment.

➤ Also creating an environment where personal power (which is earned) and influence (which is also earned) prevail, rather than formal authority (which is often mandated).

➤ Praising in public, and counselling and taking action for poor performance in private, at the time such performance is recognised, and with consistency in terms of application across all direct reports.

➤ Meeting the motivational needs of each individual as far as possible be they material (remuneration, safety and security), structural (degree and type of structure, bureaucracy and systems), behavioural (management style and interpersonal relationships), or, emotional (trust, social, self-esteem and self-realisation).

➤ Creating an environment where the executive or manager's style is based on integrity, is more democratic than autocratic, is consultative, participative and delegating.

Over the years I have examined the principal causes of success and failure by executives and managers in the area of management practices, and I have been able to consolidate my findings into one new core competence for effective staff management: motivational delegation.

Motivational delegation embraces both the individual delegating to direct reports effectively and creating a motivational environment, and when these two factors are combined, they have a powerful leadership and leverage effect on people.

Indeed, comparing delegation and motivation together, as I do through the Adeptus Process® multi-level survey and follow-up guidelines, the following cluster of characteristics can be described:

➤ Strong motivator and strong delegator suggests the motivational delegator—the optimal staff manager.

➤ Strong motivator and weak delegator suggests the sub-maximiser delegator—fails to realise the potential for great team results.

➤ Weak motivator and weak delegator suggests the blocker delegator—clogs the machinery and output of management and staff.

➤ Weak motivator and strong delegator suggests the bureaucratic delegator— delegation by mandate to an unenthusiastic audience.

GROOMING PEOPLE FOR TOP ROLES

In providing executive coaching to help groom people for top roles, the coach needs to work firstly with the organisation to gain an understanding of, or help them develop their own criteria in terms of ideal leadership competencies sought. With a specific participating executive or key person in mind, the coach also needs to ascertain from their senior line executive—often the CEO—their perceived strengths and development opportunities against such criteria.

The coach then meets the participating individual, being introduced on the basis of promise rather than threat! The coach asks them about their self-perception of strengths and development opportunities, which are later discussed and ratified between CEO, human resources director (if involved), the participating executive and the coach.

The coach then moves forward either on an executive coaching path or possibly an executive mentoring program (see Chapter 11—'A typical executive mentoring process'). Coaching is more structured compared with the way a coach undertakes mentoring. Coaching offers an opportunity to both the organisation and the individual to define and address specific development needs confidentially, and in a way which can help individuals change their behaviour and the way they operate, and sustain such changes.

In keeping with other executive coaching programs, and by way of reminder, typically there are several coaching elements. The first entails analysis of the individual's role and reporting relationships, and of any previous performance evaluations and other diagnostic feedback. From this, initial development priorities can be established, tested and pursued. Additionally, coaches can use multi-level surveys to complement the organisation's existing human resources and performance management processes. The coach can also conduct associated third party interviews to verify and amplify previous findings.

The second element entails further action planning through the confirmation and more comprehensive definition of individual development needs. Objectives, individual development strategies and action plans are then agreed and presented by the individual to their senior line executive, with the help of the coach. The final element is ongoing implementation, involving use as appropriate, of the organisation's personal and professional development resources, as well as periodic ongoing executive coaching and hotline advice.

The coach should encourage regular feedback to/from the individual's senior line individual by the participant with the help of the coach, with utmost respect for confidentiality. In this way, opportunities are also created for senior line executives to be drawn in as internal coaches.

As with all coaching programs, the coach always needs to tailor the approach to meet precise needs, and invariably the organisation and the individual are joint beneficiaries as new levels of leadership effectiveness and potential are realised.

What makes an outstanding leader?

Nine years' Australian empirical research working with well over 500 senior people, my own survey of the leadership competencies sought within a range of leading international corporations, along with third party international studies on the subject, suggest the following top criteria. I use these criteria as a guideline for diagnosis, action planning and implementation when the coaching focus is grooming people for top roles:

➤ *Helicopter perspective*: rises above day-to-day operational routine and sees and understands the bigger picture; sees and exploits the linkages between areas or issues of significance; is capable of detailed analysis, makes decisions and solves problems in their wider context; and, is intuitive and instinctive.

➤ *Strategic perspective*: focuses on external trends and projections relating to relevant aspects of international affairs, the economy, government, society, markets, customers, consumers, suppliers, technology and competitors; thinks outside the square; and, pursues opportunities for innovation and new paradigms.

➤ *Inspirational leadership*: develops vision; articulates the vision; inspires others to participate; and, supports, values, and empowers them in their progress towards attaining the vision.

➤ *Developing others*: helps others identify and attain development needs in the context of attaining the vision; inspires continuous learning; prioritises coaching; and, acts as role model through continuous self-development.

➤ *Teamwork*: works cooperatively with direct reports, peers and other teams; dual focus (i.e. on team priorities as well as on functional priorities); displays cross-functional rather than just silo perspective; synchronises diverse capabilities and operating styles of team members to optimise synergy; and operates efficient team processes.

➤ *Advanced team leadership*: in leading/facilitating their team of direct reports, ensures members operate flexibly between both as a functional group and a mutually accountable and committed leadership team, selecting times and events judiciously for operating as a leadership team (i.e. where real opportunities exist for collective input and a cross-functional orientation); and, as a functional group, where a functional orientation and strong overall single leader prevails.

➤ *Influencing*: sees situations from others' points of view; has a flexible approach in dealing with people; 'pulls' them persuasively and convincingly, rather than 'pushes'; listens as much as talks in communication; assertive and a strong negotiator when needed, but seeks win-win; continuously maintains, develops and leverages off strong internal and external networks; and, uses politics, power and influence positively.

➤ *Commanding*: when the going gets tough, or the magnitude or urgency of tasks at hand require, can take a firm stance and call others to required action, even if this creates resistance or unpopularity; and, in this displays courage and gets the required results.

➤ *Managing ambiguity*: copes well with ambiguity, risk, and diverse and complex tasks; sustains the morale and productivity of others in times of change and uncertainty; controls the controllables rather than wastes time on matters outside your control; and, displays a sixth sense of what might be around the corner and pre-empts/adapts accordingly.

➤ *Leveraging diverse knowledge*: in response to the information age, the era of knowledge, 'creates the how' by facilitating people and processes via enlightened leadership with a strong customer orientation; rather than simply 'controls the what' by managing via conventional top-down management; and in this, understands, adapts to, and leverages diversity in gender, ethnic background and age (e.g. generation Xers (in their twenties and early thirties) and Yers (just entering the workforce), independent, self-directed and resourceful, often sceptical of authority and institutions, their first loyalty being to themselves and their own careers).

➤ *Efficiency and effectiveness*: maximises efficient deployment and use of all resources through appropriate practices, processes and procedures; benchmarks internally and externally; helps others establish, monitor and develop their performance against agreed expectations; and recognises individual and team contributions as well as provides candid corrective feedback.

➤ *Decision-making*: engages in systematic analysis yet retains broad perspective; reviews alternatives; thinks creatively; involves others in decision-making; learns from lessons of the past; makes sound, timely decisions; and, exhibits sound commercial judgement.

➤ *Achieving results*: understands and pursues their primary business objective, supporting objectives and main drivers of primary objective; in this, displays energy, a sense of urgency, tenacity, initiative and adaptability; enlists appropriate organisational support; and, aligns others, gaining their commitment to achieve sought outcomes.

Performance review, 360° feedback ... what next?

In many organisations I find executives well equipped with a variety of performance review tools, 360° feedback surveys, leadership course manuals and related materials. These invariably suggest or even prescribe a range of personal and professional development opportunities. Such material can be invaluable for additional self-awareness and the acquisition of new knowledge (i.e. about leadership).

However, back in the day-to-day executive's world, it is all too easy for such new insights and good intentions to slip down the priority list and not get the attention they deserve. This is why I am often called in to assist executives convert what they have learned into practical application.

In this I act as an extension to the follow-up input provided internally, where available time to do this is often too short and intermittent. Particularly when you consider that changing, for example, leadership behaviour, may represent as great a challenge for the individual as changing habits. This usually requires sustained effort over quite a long timeframe to lessen the risks associated with reverting to type when under pressure.

And this is the type and duration of effort which can be supported by executive coaching. The fact the work is in confidence and should have no political agenda, means the coach can also become a confidant and mentor in assisting executives achieve their personal and professional development goals.

In this, is the coach seen as a promise or threat? Because the work is, in effect, for and with the executives being coached, coaches are invariably seen by them as a positive and supportive resource from the outset. And increasingly, executive coaches are being used by many organisations.

Progressive organisations now realise that performance reviews and 360° surveys are only the starting point in building and sustaining the effectiveness of their key people.

EXAMPLE

A successful executive received executive coaching to develop further her 360° leadership skills. As a result, she is now in a position where promotion is likely to occur within the next 18 months.

CONTINUING AND CONCLUDING THE TYPICAL COACHING PROCESS

As mentioned earlier, the provision of guidelines to coachees as they identify areas for personal development helps them 'think outside the square' in selecting, testing and implementing new approaches.

Indeed, by providing guidelines, be they from print, audio, video or PC sources (and a myriad exist!), discussing alternatives with the coach and then using the self-management of development process described in Chapter 6—'Core coaching processes', represents a powerful way to attain some traction in personal development.

Continuing feedback is an added stimulus and often a further eye opener, as can be the feedback from third party interviews which are usefully undertaken after a 360° survey in order to verify and amplify findings to date. Although Chapter 6 describes the typical questions to be included in such interviews, always add or substitute topics which have come forward from previous diagnosis as needing further attention and insights.

Quite apart from regular and ongoing progress meetings between coachee and their line manager (with and without coach and HR executive), following the interviews and the subsequent feedback session to coachee, the time is ripe for a more comprehensive 'mid-program' progress meeting between all parties. Here, the coach typically opens by reminding everyone of the process undertaken and the stage reached in the process. The coachee then describes forward looking positive action plans along with their perceived self-progress. Perceived economic and other benefits should also form part of the agenda.

Inevitably the line manager is drawn into this discussion, more often than not with positive commentary on how they perceive progress. The coach can also seize the opportunity of asking the coachee at this meeting what 'any of us can do to help further' in the development process, paving the way for the line manager to become more, rather than less involved, as the program continues.

And the program does need to continue in order to see sustained development rather than revertion to earlier type. Remember, much of the development work being undertaken by the coachee is akin to changing habits, and old habits die hard!

Thus you often experience the need for coaching—having taken perhaps three to six months to this point—needing to continue for perhaps another three to six months. The style of coaching may change over this latter period, becoming more on-the-job issues based, with the coach being more of a mentor in their approach.

What is crucial however, and needs to be reinforced at the closure meeting, is the ongoing relationship of the line manager and coachee, the manager more and more assuming the ongoing coaching mantle, as the initial third party coach transitions away. All this assumes that the initial coach was a third party, and of course this need not be, and in most cases perhaps should not be the case. Far better the line manager is the coach from the outset!

EXAMPLE

The CEO of a newly restructured management group, comprising 15 senior executives, engaged on an executive coaching program with an emphasis on how to coach his direct reports and others. Heading a professional services firm, he realised that its people-intensive nature required emphasis on the continuing development of executives and staff for the organisation itself to be able to develop successfully and prosper.

KEYNOTE

➤ Executive coaching can have a broad range of applications.
➤ Often, the focus is leadership development or improving interpersonal relationships.
➤ Also, more effective delegation into a motivational environment frees up the delegator to concentrate on higher level priorities, and which allows delegates to develop.
➤ And finally, coaching is used in grooming people for top roles, which requires a range of special competencies which can be developed through coaching.
➤ The use of core coaching processes and case specific guidelines create a potent cocktail which brings about beneficial change.

Chapter 8

A TYPICAL CAREER CONSULTING PROCESS

66 Retaining motivated talent and maximising individual and organisational alignment **99**

INTRODUCTION

The object of career consulting is to help executives further develop their self-motivation through a greater sense of personal career direction and control, and, wherever possible, by aligning their personal career goals with corporate goals. This results in the executive becoming more confident, career resilient and productive, enabling them to 'give of their all' and operate proactively in their work environment.

Career consulting is used:

➤ for input to succession planning;
➤ for turning around an individual's motivation;
➤ for executive re-alignment at times of restructure or merger;
➤ for helping prevent the resignation and loss of talent;
➤ for mature executives considering the last chapters of their careers.

The process usually commences with the consultant undertaking familiarisation with the executive's line manager and human resources executive. The executive's career is reviewed and the strategy for introducing the external third party (the consultant) is jointly developed. This is in the context that the executive needs to be committed to the career consulting program, with the assurance that confidentiality will be strictly maintained.

Once the program has been initiated, the early elements include a review of the executive's role and reporting relationships followed by an examination of previous performance evaluations and any other existing diagnostic feedback. Career evaluation then follows, potentially using a range of assessment techniques. The consultant's role is to act as a sounding board, confidant and devil's advocate— ensuring realistic career expectations at all times.

Third party interviews are also conducted by the consultant to help verify and amplify the executive's self-image within the career environment and further reality-check career directions. Opportunities for executive development are also highlighted.

The outcome may include:

➤ the clarification of any ambiguities or uncertainties regarding the present role and career directions;

➤ improved understanding of, and communication with, others in the organisation about career matters;

➤ opportunities for further career alignment with the organisation;

➤ assessment of shorter and longer term career development options within, or in some cases outside, the organisation;

➤ the identification of executive development needs and possible resources, including the consultant potentially acting as coach.

Career consulting processes of this nature culminate in action planning and implementation. This entails, wherever possible, a mutually agreed emphasis on career alignment with the organisation, and appropriate individual and organisational development plans. To ensure alignment occurs, or that other sought-after outcomes are being pursued and attained, regular ongoing career consulting and development coaching is provided. Progress feedback sessions by the executive are also conducted, with the consultant's help, offering an opportunity for the senior line executive to be drawn in as an internal coach.

CASE STUDY

This is the story of a bright, ambitious, well-qualified and aggressive young executive who worked and developed her career successfully in a technical/functional environment.

All was going well and the executive was rewarded both financially and with successive promotions for achieving great results. And then an otherwise impeccable track record was put into question when the executive missed out on a promotion, on account of being too aggressive (overplaying her strengths) and of not having developed as a well-rounded collaborative leader. The executive's natural reaction was to resign—the competition had already made overtures.

I was called in urgently to provide executive coaching and career consulting in an endeavour to retain this valuable talent and help her develop appropriate leadership skills. After some initial cynicism, the 'penny dropped' and the executive began to modify her behaviour with direct reports, peers and senior colleagues, and to identify career directions and options within the existing organisation.

The executive remains within the same organisation today, her career having flourished, and she now being considered an effective leader.

CASE STUDY

The next story is very similar, but with two differences. Firstly, the executive was of mature years. Secondly, the outcome of my work was for their role to be changed to significantly lessen the management element. But again, there is a happy ending to the story.

The executive delivers even more impressive bottomline results—unfettered from the shackles of what was a sizeable staff and administration management role—and experiences less work-related stress as a result. The executive will most likely stay with the organisation until retirement.

The courageous player in this latter case was the CEO, who eventually agreed that the organisation needed to 'flex' to accommodate this rare talent, and to tailor the role to capitalise on the individual's indisputable strengths. So there we have two very different, yet highly satisfying and successful outcomes for each organisation, executive and executive coach. And 'successful outcomes' is what executive coaching and career consulting is all about.

A TYPICAL CAREER CONSULTING PROCESS IN MORE DETAIL

In describing a typical career consulting process I will include reference to the core coaching processes in Chapter 6—introducing coaching to line managers, needs analysis, and so forth. Because the sequencing is also very comparable to a typical executive coaching process, I will concentrate on the main differences to this process rather than become overly repetitive.

Therefore, the commencement of the program is very similar to the foregoing process with appropriate modifications to place the process in the career idiom. Early stages include: introducing coaching to line managers (here I am using the term coaching generically, in other words to cover career consulting also). Introducing the coach to the coachee. Needs analysis. Review of previous feedback. SDOT analysis and development priorities (development here referring to personal development within the general sense of initial thoughts and themes relating to career development).

In place of a new 360° survey however, the career consultant takes the individual through a full career planning process. Elements of my own process are described in this chapter. This process usually entails three to six meetings in order to do it justice, and to allow for plenty of homework and thinking/reflecting time by the individual. As is the case with any planning and strategy development exercise, you cannot force an outcome—it has to evolve, and this can take some time. Forced outcomes are invariably fallacious.

As I go through the process with an individual I always remind them that we are trying to pursue 'career alignment' with the organisation as far as is possible. I often start off by recapping what is happening in the career environment and why executives and managers should be considering career alignment as one of the main planks in their human resources development processes.

In the career environment today we see many smaller flatter organisations, fewer middle management positions, apparently fewer promotional opportunities, and continuing organisational change. It is no small wonder that staff view their future careers with uncertainty. In many cases their commitment to the organisation, let alone trust, has been eroded, with a significant impact on their job performance.

However, help is now at hand! Not only can the theme of career alignment provide more clarity about an individual's future, a greater sense of control over your own destiny, and thereby improved morale, but it should also be a fundamental element of performance management, and is often the 'missing link'.

Conventional performance management systems start with what the organisation seeks in terms of skills, competencies, aptitudes and so forth, which through performance appraisal leads to the identification of individual training and development needs. This is primarily an organisation-centred approach to performance management—so often seen in organisations today—but so often failing to take full account of the interests, values, capabilities and preferences of the individual. In fact, the employee-centred approach, often the missing link in performance management systems, takes great account of what the individual seeks, leading to implications for organisational development, training, management succession and so on.

The 'bottomline' is that when both approaches are applied in an organisation, there becomes a greater degree of 'coincidence' between organisational and individual goals, leading to enhanced organisational and individual performance. Naturally, the greater the degree of coincidence the better. As executives and managers, therefore, what are we trying to achieve through greater career alignment?

Firstly, we are trying to attain improved morale and sense of personal control and destiny by each individual. Secondly, we are seeking improved job performance and individual 'value' to the organisation in the case of each employee. Next, we are trying to redefine career progress: central (expanding the existing job) and horizontal progress (job rotation at the same level), as well as vertical progress (promotion) for which the potential is now much reduced in today's flatter organisations. Finally, by concentrating on individuals and their careers, we are attempting to develop a sense of personal security in lieu of job security, or an ethos of lifetime 'employability' possibly with several employers, rather than 'life employment' with one employer. In fact, we are trying to help individuals attain personal commitment to an outcome, which can include staying and progressing within the organisation (for most employees), moving to another part of the organisation, or leaving the organisation voluntarily and developing your career elsewhere (perhaps for a small number of employees who cannot see their own futures coinciding with the future of the organisation).

In endeavouring to maximise career alignment for their staff, executives and managers really need to help their employees in their understanding and apply relevant areas of career thinking, as follows:

➤ *Job fit*. People need to be able to identify their main occupational interests, motivational capabilities and values and ensure they are represented in current and future jobs. If they are not, then the job parameters need to be altered, or the individual needs to change to a job offering a better match with these criteria in order to maximise self-motivation and personal effectiveness.

➤ *Strategic directions of the organisation.* People need to be clear about the future directions of the organisation, in order to maximise the alignment of organisational and personal goals. These future directions need to be specific enough to be converted into the outlook for organisational structure, roles and required competencies. However, in most cases, such specification may be difficult to attain, and so individuals need to be encouraged to sell themselves, network and develop informal alliances within the organisation and find out for themselves where, when and how organisational developments may coincide with their own plans for their career development.

➤ *Chemistry and fit.* Whether it relates to the team setting, to desirable leadership traits, to motivational needs, or to politics, power and influence, the organisation needs to monitor individual chemistry and fit. Where difficulties are perceived to exist, assist individuals in this vital area, which may require helping them to modify their behaviour, reporting relationships or team composition.

➤ *Performance appraisal and improvement programs.* Such programs need to give an equal emphasis to the goals of the organisation and to the goals of the individual, in order to optimise career alignment, job performance and the value of the individual to the organisation.

If all these areas are prioritised, and appropriate development initiatives undertaken as the need arises, the career alignment of individuals and the organisation will be enhanced substantially. The benefits of this include:

➤ Individuals feeling more in control of their careers and less vulnerable to the vagaries of organisational life.

➤ Talented individuals being less likely to leave the organisation for 'pastures greener' and more likely to stay, contribute and develop.

➤ Helping those who may feel themselves or be perceived as being on a 'performance plateau'—uplifting their performance levels.

➤ Helping staff become more motivationally aligned to the organisation (particularly at times of organisational change and restructuring).

➤ Individuals becoming more aligned to the organisation in terms of job fit, organisational fit, career goals, commitment and personal chemistry.

➤ In achieving these outcomes, the role of the line manager to whom the individual reports must not be underestimated or avoided. By providing them with the language and thinking behind career alignment, they will be able to enter into constructive dialogue with their direct reports, maximising their tenure as motivated contributors and minimising the chances of the loss of talent. In other words, the best career consultant is often the individual's line manager!

KEY AREAS IN CAREER PLANNING

My career planning process has several key areas which I find particularly valuable in career consulting: career planning overview; self-image; job fit; the career environment; career stages; and alternatives to seeking and attaining straight promotion.

CAREER PLANNING OVERVIEW

In addressing the first of these—career planning overview—one should begin with self-image, derived from honest self and career assessment. The coachee should also try to get feedback from as many sources as possible in order to reality-check and finalise this self-image. I will examine self-image in greater detail shortly.

Derived from this self-image and a study of the career environment, the individual engaging in career planning needs to come up with a list of activity choices—jobs or activities which they would like to be involved in in the medium to longer term (i.e. not necessarily their next job, but taking a longer term perspective). These form their preliminary career goals. They should be as specific as possible. For example, 'move sideways to a new job position' or 'move up to a higher executive level' are too vague. 'Attaining a divisional finance director position within three to five years' is much better.

Defining your job opportunities comes next. The individual needs to decide which shorter term job positions, relating and leading to their career goals, are available to them. They will need to do some research here to find out which desired job opportunities may be available within their own job or organisation, and which are only available externally. They need to draw on their own experience, and on the experiences of others, as well as on relevant articles, professional publications and other desk and library research.

Next, you need to analyse the demands of the new jobs picked out for consideration. What kind of capabilities, operating styles and so forth are required for fulfilling these new jobs? This issue needs to be examined in three ways: the demands of the new jobs as the individual sees them; the demands of the new jobs as viewed by others in their organisation or contact network; and the demands of the new jobs as viewed by people who are actually performing them now, perhaps elsewhere. These three views may differ, and will need to be reconciled somehow, in order to arrive at a realistic assessment of your ideal new job position.

Next comes matching the new job demands with your own self-image. The individual will either need to develop the skills and attributes necessary to grow into the new job role, or may have to abandon it in favour of something with a better match to their self-image.

If the individual has identified areas of mismatch and conflict, either their career goals must be adjusted, their values and priorities reconsidered, or their skills and capabilities in certain areas upgraded, in other words development or change. In some cases, external factors, such as organisational policies or the attitudes of family and friends, may be causing the conflict. Sometimes these external blocks can be changed, but often they cannot. In the latter case, the individual needs to accept this as a reality, and find other ways of satisfying their career goals, or adjust their goals accordingly.

Now comes formulating career objectives and strategies. These are both the specific career objectives based on earlier elements of the career planning process, and the methods and actions needed to achieve these objectives.

Commitment to performance comes next. You should set performance standards for yourself, and monitor progress towards your career objectives. You need to make these standards specific and measurable, such as 'improve my presentation skills noticeably by using computer graphics, to the extent that I become leader of the key account presentation team within six months'. Try to make this performance commitment to those who have some stake in it—your chairman or CEO, or your partner.

Establishing specific performance standards will serve as a basis on which to provide necessary feedback. The individual needs to seek feedback from those around them at work, and take heed of their response as to how they are progressing, and integrate it into their store of experience. Also, they need to use it to modify their career development strategies or their self-image.

Finally, you always need to ensure you update and pursue an ongoing program of self-development, and not just rely on the employer for development and training— the responsibility is the individual's!

SELF-IMAGE

Now for a more detailed review of self-image, which accounts for 80% of the career planning process. Imagine you yourself are going through the process of better understanding self-image as you read the following.

Whatever way you look at it, planning and managing your career in the 2000s is going to require far more knowledge, skills, courage and determination than has ever been demanded of individuals before. We are living in extraordinary times and this demands extraordinary methods of dealing with the career situations executives find themselves in. Taking stock of your career is the first step and in so doing, you need to undertake some self and career assessment covering a range of elements of the career mix. In short these include:

➤ *Your track record.* Here your career assessment needs to include your qualifications, experience, competencies in the world of work (i.e. technical, functional or managerial) and your achievements (the results you have been able to attain and the actions you have taken to accomplish them, which in themselves tell you and others a lot about your skills and other personal traits).

➤ *Your interests, motivational capabilities, job requirements, values and whole-life balance.* Ideally work in a job or career environment which accommodates your interests, motivational capabilities, job requirements, values and whole-life balance. Job fit now and ahead is essential in order to maximise job satisfaction, self-motivation and personal performance.

➤ *Your operating style.* Commanding and doing, responding and initiating, empathising, evaluating and detailing, generating ideas, facilitating and chairing. What this means in terms of job fit and existing or future team make-up, needs to be assessed.

➤ *Your management capabilities and leadership traits.* Address the requirements and expectations of your employer regarding both management capabilities and desirable leadership traits to help propel the organisation into the future. In this context leadership traits include controlling output and/or people, creative strategy development, visionary leadership, leading according to situations, priorities and team capabilities.

➤ *Your atmospheric needs.* Be very clear about your needs to maximise your self-motivation, in other words the way you ideally need to be compensated, your preferred type of organisation structure, your preferred management style by others in the organisation, your motivational needs in terms of interpersonal relationships and trust, and your needs for a sense of personal achievement—all in order to maximise your self-motivation and personal effectiveness.

All of the above are the ingredients of taking stock of your career, and in fact represent your career self-image which is the focal point on which further career planning is based.

However, many people focus on what they want in their careers, where they want to be and how much money they want to make, without taking the time to really look at where they are now, and what they have to work with. What is the point of planning a journey, checking the road map, knowing where you are headed and when you expect to arrive, if you neglect to tune up your engine and make sure you have enough petrol, oil, or air in the tyres to get you there? All the enthusiasm in the world won't get you to your destination, without first taking stock of where you are now, and what you will need, to get you to where you want to be. We seldom take time and effort to examine ourselves in such depth, and the experience and self-knowledge gained in doing this, is well worth the effort.

In addressing the second key area of the career planning process—interests, motivational capabilities and career areas, we need to examine 'job fit'.

JOB FIT

Job fit is a prerequisite for job satisfaction, self-motivation and personal performance. When in place, job fit creates a situation where you look forward to going to work and are perceived to be 'giving of your all' rather than coasting or 'going through the motions' at work. Selection of job fit is critical for those considering career planning or changing their jobs.

It is interesting to note that of those hundreds of key people with whom I have worked on career transition programs, about half eventually change industry sector, one-third change job function and about one-quarter eventually go into some form of business for themselves (often contracting or counselling). In so doing, job fit is an essential success factor and ensuring this occurs requires considerable forethought, as well as self- and job analysis.

One of the most demanding challenges relating to this is the plight of 'generalists' who have been leaving organisations in their droves, owing to flatter, more competitive structures, as well as personal computers replacing people in the monitoring of human performance. Such generalists often need to dig deep into their minds to work out their interests and transferable skills and where they are ideally headed jobwise (which may be unlikely to be to other generalist positions, some of which have disappeared). For them, therefore, it is all about selecting job fit—'what type of job will suit me best?'

Job fit depends on two very different components: the nature of the work itself, and the fit with certain personal characteristics. When these two components match each other, this generates outstanding fit, self-motivation and personal performance. The personal characteristics representing one side of the job fit formula include occupational interests and motivational capabilities. The nature of work representing the other side of the formula is described in the form of 12 discrete career areas.

The main occupational interest areas can be summarised as follows. (Note that these are interests, and not necessarily capabilities, which are summarised later.)

➤ *Scientific*: an interest in facts, particularly relating to the natural sciences; a desire to work out how things occur, why they occur and what results from them; an interest in finding things out, perhaps by using laboratory techniques or doing research; and, analytical and investigatory activities.

➤ *Social*: an interest in people rather than things; an interest in listening to other people and a genuine concern for their troubles and problems; and, an interest in supplying services which others need and will be happy to receive.

➤ *Persuasive*: an interest in meeting and convincing people, and promoting your ideas, beliefs, projects or sales; an interest in influencing people in some way, their attitudes or behaviour; and an enjoyment in persuading people via discussion, debate or argument.

➤ *Literary*: an enjoyment of writing and words; an interest in any activity that needs the use of imaginative verbal descriptions; a love of books, reading or reciting; and, an interest in writing or speaking originally and imaginatively.

➤ *Artistic*: an enjoyment of visual art, design or drama; an interest in colour and artistic activities with a desire to create something of imagination or beauty; and, a keen interest in your surroundings or in some aspect of design.

➤ *Clerical*: an interest in administration, office or clerical work, often based on a routine requiring accuracy and precision; and, an interest in recording and filing, coding and classifying, where detailed numerate, scientific or technical knowledge may not be needed to any great degree.

➤ *Practical*: a liking of being 'good with your hands'; an interest in repairing and making things; a preference for learning by doing rather than by reading; a liking for working with tools and materials rather than with words; and, an interest in constructing or building things.

➤ *Musical*: an enjoyment of, or interest in, any type of music, playing musical instruments or singing; an enjoyment of listening to people play music; and, a love of going to musical concerts, films or shows.

➤ *Computational*: an interest in working with figures; an interest in dealing with numbers and mathematical problems and concepts; an interest in using mental arithmetic or formulae; and, an interest in proving or disproving things with figures.

➤ *Outside*: an interest in being or working outside, sometimes involving considerable physical activity and/or travel; a dislike of having to work inside the whole time and of routine work or regularity; and, an interest in animals, in growing crops or plants, or in moving from place to place.

➤ *Technical*: an interest in work which entails dealing with anything technical, such as machines, engines, tools, computers, or electrical and electronic equipment; a preference for operating anything technical; and, an interest in how and why technical items work.

➤ *Medical*: an interest in medical and biological subjects; an interest in healing and caring for sick people; a desire to investigate the causes and relieve the effects of illness and disease; and, an interest in various aspects of mental or physical health.

Clearly, some interests relate more to certain career areas than to others, and your major occupational interests need to be represented in your job to enhance self-motivation and personal performance.

Motivational capabilities are those capabilities which you enjoy using—whether you are born with them or whether you develop them through learning and application. They also form part of personal characteristics and one side of the job fit formula. They can be summarised as follows:

➤ *Memory*: an ability to remember, to retain things in your mind and to recall things from the past; and, a good memory perhaps is better at remembering certain things, for example, faces rather than names.

➤ *Verbal comprehension*: an ability to understand accurately the meaning of words — both written and spoken; an ability to read and understand 'difficult' books or reports, and to differentiate between words with closely similar meanings; and, having an extensive vocabulary.

➤ *Numeracy*: an ability to understand and express ideas by way of numbers; an ability to understand mathematical concepts and numerical problems; and, an ability to understand statistical tables, gambling or betting 'odds', or technical data.

➤ *Spatial ability*: an ability to see and understand shapes or objects in more than one dimension; an ability to understand complicated diagrams or technical drawings in three dimensions; a good sense of direction; and, good at puzzles where you fit or disentangle complicated objects and shapes.

➤ *Perception*: an ability to perceive or notice things in detail, or to understand situations; and, an ability to notice quickly if something is wrong, or to pick up important details or information which others can miss.

➤ *Fluency*: an ability to express your views or meaning in the correct spoken words; a good communicator with an ability to argue or persuade; well able to make your meaning clear in discussion; and, good self-expression.

➤ *Reasoning ability*: an ability to reason, to progress from the known to the unknown by using logic and drawing conclusions; an ability to solve problems, to see when people contradict themselves in a discussion or argument; and, to resolve complex matters through logical reasoning.

➤ *Creativity*: an ability to produce a stream of new, useful or creative ideas; an ability to be inventive or creative and think of more than one way of looking at a problem or answering a question; and, being good at art or design, or at creative problem-solving, or at computer graphics.

➤ *Social ability*: an ability to get on well with other people from a wide range of backgrounds, beliefs or views; an ability to get other people to accept your views, to trust, confide in you and to do things for you; and, a capacity to mix with anyone socially.

➤ *Clerical speed and accuracy*: an ability to be quick and accurate with anything clerical such as spotting typing mistakes, filing, cross-checking columns of figures, note-taking etc.; and, good at clerical activities, typically undertaken in administration.

As with occupational interests, some motivational capabilities relate more to certain career areas than to others, and again they need to be represented in your job if your self-motivation and personal performance are to be maximised.

As noted earlier, 12 major career areas represent the other side of the job fit formula. Each career area relates more to certain occupational interests and motivational capabilities than to others. While these career areas represent an open field of choice for people at the start of their careers, it is surprising how people can make career changes later in their careers in order to maximise job fit and other criteria.

➤ *Practical careers* are for practically minded individuals who like to work with their hands, and this can often include outdoor work. This type of work often suits people who have a spatial ability. Typical careers include: the armed services; manufacturing and distribution; building, civil engineering and land services; agriculture, horticulture, forestry and parks, fisheries; clothing industry; and, metal and printing industries.

➤ *Technical careers* are for practical and technical individuals, sometimes with outside and/or medical interests and an interest in science. They often require a good memory, a capacity for thinking spatially—in three dimensions—and sometimes numeracy. Perception and reasoning ability are also often required. Relevant career areas include: health and hospital services; science; engineering; management services; media services; metal and printing industries; building, civil engineering and land services; and, agriculture, horticulture, forestry and fisheries.

➤ *Analytical careers* are for the computational and sometimes clerical-minded individual. Abilities include memory, numeracy, spatial, perception, reasoning and sometimes clerical speed and accuracy—often a details person. Analytical career areas can be found in a range of business sectors and are often located in the management services functional area of organisations.

➤ *Scientific careers* are for the scientifically and in some instances social welfare or computational-minded individual, sometimes with medical interests. Ability requirements often include a good memory, numeracy, spatial, perception, reasoning and creativity. Career areas include science and health and hospital services.

➤ *Creative careers* are for the literary, or artistic, or musical individual, sometimes with persuasive or practical interests, often with spatial ability, perception, creativity, and in some cases verbal comprehension, fluency or social ability. Career areas include: creative art; fashion and design; entertainment and recreation; and, media and publications.

➤ *Careers in design* include artistic, technical and sometimes practical or computational interests. Requirements often include a good memory, spatial ability, perception, reasoning, creativity and sometimes numeracy. Career areas include: creative art; fashion and design; technical design; media and publications; and, building, architecture, civil engineering and land services.

➤ *People-oriented careers* are for the individual who has social welfare and sometimes persuasive, practical or medical interests. Perception, fluency, reasoning and social abilities are often key requirements. Relevant career areas include: teaching and cultural activities; catering and personal services; health and hospital services; social work; human resources management; and, transport, travel and materials handling.

➤ *Managerial careers* are for the more persuasive and sometimes social welfare-oriented individual who often has good perception, fluency, reasoning and social ability. Career areas include: the armed services; management and administration; inspection; security and protective services; and, transport, travel and materials handling.

➤ *Enterprising careers* are for the individual who is persuasive and sometimes social welfare-oriented. The individual is perceptive, fluent, has good reasoning ability, is social, and is sometimes spatial and creative. Career areas usually include a marketing orientation in a wide variety of different businesses and sectors.

➤ *Entrepreneurial careers* often are for the 'entrepreneur' who is a persuasive and practical individual and is perceptive, has good reasoning abilities and is sometimes fluent or creative. Careers include independent business and sales.

➤ *Administrative careers* are often for the individual with clerical and sometimes social welfare and computational interests, and often require a good memory, verbal comprehension, perception, reasoning ability, clerical speed and accuracy, and now and then numeracy and social abilities. Careers in administration can be found across a wide range of business areas.

➤ *Professional services careers* often suit individuals with persuasive and sometimes clerical and computational interests and often require a good memory, verbal comprehension, perception, fluency, reasoning, social ability and sometimes numeracy. Typical career areas include: law; finance and accounting; and, management or business consultancy.

Clearly, some career areas relate more to certain occupational interests and motivational capabilities than to others, and ideally your existing or new job will offer a good match in this regard.

In summary, a high level of job fit should enhance the prospects of an individual feeling self-motivated in the work they do, and improve their personal performance. A low level of job fit will have the reverse effect and if this is the case, they need to consider their options.

Based on my work with executives and other key people, I am amazed by how many people have been in jobs and work environments which do not fully accommodate their interests or motivational capabilities. Not only does this often mean that through lack of self-motivation they fail to perform at their personal best, but it also means that a large proportion of their lives—vital people working some 100 000 hours in their careers—is unfulfilled. The worst case scenario is that they become 'square pegs in round holes'.

'SQUARE PEGS IN ROUND HOLES'

Given the average CEO tenure in any given role is approximately three-and-a-half years, and the related fact that wave after wave of organisational change sweeps up the shores of corporate Australia, no small wonder many executives feel they are swimming against the tide in roles for which they are not entirely suited.

And if job fit or motivational needs are not satisfied, then morale and performance are invariably adversely affected—not only for the executive in question—but also through a negative leverage effect on those working for them and with them. The cumulative adverse impact of all this can run into hundreds of thousands of dollars which should flow to the bottomline. What is often needed, yet invariably not provided, is the 'good oil' of helping the executive and the organisation come to terms with the misfit situation, and work out a win-win solution.

Perhaps the executive needs to change their expectations, attitude or behaviour. Perhaps the role can be modified to maximise fit and motivation. Perhaps it is simply a case of recognising that the requirements of the job are at variance with the capabilities of the executive. But rather than allow the situation to deteriorate until it becomes unsalvageable—again, potentially a very high cost outcome—I advocate positive intervention by an appropriately experienced executive coach. Coaching can often help the executive address the situation comprehensively and logically, with a view then to entering into meaningful dialogue with their manager and HR executive, leading to a work-out rather than walk-away situation.

There is no mystique to the role of the coach in this. Needs analysis, situation review, third party feedback, confidential confidant and sounding board, Australian empirical research, all play a part in developing new depths of insights in both the individual and within the organisation, as to the issues as well as the prospective solutions. And in implementing the solution, the role of the coach is to facilitate a successful outcome.

The process usually entails a combination of executive coaching (relating to the capability-side of the equation) and career consulting (relating to job fit, career and motivational alignment). It is powerful. It invariably delivers results.

One of the most exciting parts of the professional work of the career consultant is to help individuals re-align themselves in this context and to see them self-motivated and performing at their personal optimum. As well as reaping the rewards of greater job satisfaction, improved personal performance and enhanced remuneration, at the same time they are seen to be contributing more fully to their organisations.

THE CAREER ENVIRONMENT

Turning to the second topic area I find particularly valuable in career consulting—the career environment and career stages—it is important to help the coachee examine some of the work trends over the next decade.

➤ *Information technology and telecommunications (IT & T)*. IT & T will have a greater and greater impact upon our personal and work lives. There is no stemming the tide and people who are serious about future career growth and opportunities will do well to learn how IT & T can and will affect their careers and adjust accordingly.

➤ *Ageing workforce, fewer younger executives*. As the baby boomers age, there will be a shortage of younger people coming through, creating employment opportunities for older executives and managers who wish to keep working, although not necessarily in senior positions.

➤ *Regular job changes*. Executive mobility among jobs and organisations is increasing as people look not only for more money but also for opportunities to learn and grow in their careers.

➤ *Greater utilisation of talent*. Executive, managerial and professional talent existing within an organisation is often greatly underutilised. As we move into the 2000s, every individual has to count in these leaner, keener organisations.

➤ *End of life-long employment with, and loyalty to one employer*. Individuals will stay only as long as they are meeting their personal career goals. This does not mean they do not commit themselves fully to the job at hand while they are there.

➤ *High level of restructures, mergers, acquisitions and divestments.* The search for increased efficiencies and profits by these means will continue, with their resulting shuffle in executive and management ranks.

➤ *Dual-career marriages.* As more and more women enter the executive world it can no longer be assumed that either partner will give up a lucrative career to follow the other. Offers of promotion and transfer will increasingly be evaluated in terms of each career and decisions to accept or refuse made on this basis.

➤ *Higher educated executives.* Higher education will be appreciated and rewarded even more, with masters and doctorate degrees becoming more common in executive suites. Psychologists and others interested in the utilisation of human resources will be more in evidence.

➤ *Flexible work arrangements.* Today's fairly rigid work schedules will increasingly be replaced by part-time, project and contract arrangements to take advantage of high-level skills and know-how as and when needed.

➤ *Leisure time.* The time demands of work may or may not decrease owing to technological innovation and more efficient work methods, leaving more or less time for non-work pursuits. The jury is divided!

➤ *Continuing emphasis on productivity.* Executives and managers even now have to be more efficient and productive than before, for less money. This is in response to the need to keep costs down and efficiency up, enhancing but not guaranteeing individual job security and advancement.

Some individuals are discouraged by the rate and acceleration of the changes taking place around us. Is there any point in planning ahead very far, and why invest time and effort in a career if it will not even exist five or ten years from now? The answer is 'yes'—it is worth the planning and effort. We all need to feel productive in a job we enjoy and to feel that we have a future. So we must know ourselves well, plan for what we want and go after it with enthusiasm.

The real key as individuals build their careers is to keep a very wary eye on what is happening around themselves and expect to be making continual adjustments to keep pace with new developments in their fields and to take advantage of the vast range of opportunities as they arise. In considering the career environment and the outlook for the future, the following represent useful discussion areas relating to careers and the future:

➤ *Information technology and telecommunications.* The rapid growth of technology is having, and will continue to have, a dramatic impact on career development. In fact, it has been predicted that some 50% of the jobs that will exist 15 years from now have not yet been invented.

Here are some specific questions to consider:

– What new kinds of businesses and executive and managerial jobs will the new technologies create?
– Where will future career opportunities relating to technology lie?
– Which jobs will experience technology-driven growth in the years ahead?
– Which jobs will experience technology-driven decline?

➤ *The economy and business.* In looking at the economic and business environment, you are basically looking at those factors which influence the demand for your own capabilities, the supply of these capabilities from yourself and others, and the competition for jobs requiring these capabilities in the economy. The relationship between supply and demand drives price, and in this case salary levels!

Also, keep in mind that people with highly specialised expertise in one area may find the market for their capabilities more limited than for those with expertise that is more generally applicable. However, do not underestimate the potential of selecting a specialisation for which you believe there will be demand well into the future, and then becoming one of the best at it.

EXAMPLE

The caveat here, however, and by way of example, is an individual with a high degree of expertise in, say, aerospace engineering. That person will not have the same range of career options as someone with accounting, legal, or general management expertise, which is more easily transferable among different organisations and industries. But on the other hand, there are a lot of unemployed general managers.

Too many people ignore the fact that there are economic and business cycles when planning their career. In good times the tendency is to reap the benefits of your sought-after capabilities with little concern for the future. Then, if the hard times hit, and the demand for these capabilities falls off, there is a struggle to develop new capabilities that should have been developed earlier in anticipation of a downturn or change in the cycle.

This all takes its toll, in time, money and frustration. Economic and business cycles and variation in demand for certain skills and capabilities are a fact of life. Prepare yourself accordingly!

And so economic and business variables in the environment can certainly affect career development. Some questions to ask and answer here are:

– Which parts of the economy and businesses are likely to expand or contract over the next decade?
– What will be the impact of globalisation in this context—local businesses investing overseas and overseas business investing here or elsewhere?
– What kinds of skills, abilities and personal characteristics are in demand today, and what kinds will be in demand in the years ahead?
– Will they remain in demand over the short- or long-term?
– Which areas of the economy or business are likely to use your capabilities the most?
– Is the demand for your capabilities cyclical or fairly consistent?
– What are the costs of upgrading your capabilities or developing new ones?
– What are the potential returns on time and money used in such upgrading and development?

➤ *Government and politics.* In developing a career plan, it is becoming increasingly necessary to take into account governmental, political and legal implications. The various levels of government are affecting our lives to an ever-increasing degree. For example, tax legislation has a great influence on personal lifestyles. It also can affect such career decisions as whether or not to start up your own business.

Also, individuals are now seeking satisfaction and self-fulfilment in their careers, rather than just financial security. These aspirations decrease somewhat in a recession, but the underlying need for job satisfaction is still there, and can affect the morale and productivity of employees who are forced to remain in jobs they dislike.

Question areas promoting good and relevant discussion can relate to the likely impact of government and politics on the career of the individual engaged in career consulting.

➤ *Social demography.* Environmental shifts in social demographic attitudes, behaviours and values must be taken into account in career planning. Understanding these trends puts us in a far better position to take advantage of potential career opportunities.

For example, increasing career opportunities for women and minority groups can affect the career strategies of people outside these groups. Increasing competition for executive positions is a reality, and no longer limited to the 'chosen few' in any organisation. Organisations today are just as likely to bring in talent from outside to fill these positions as they are to promote from within.

Also, individuals no longer feel an obligation to remain with one organisation for most of their careers. There is a growing restlessness, as people switch employers and even careers, if their needs are not being met. Concern for self-development encompassing all aspects of your life means that people are no longer willing to sacrifice everything for the demands of the job. Mid-life career switches, allowing individuals to develop a new set of talents and interests are becoming common, and a future trend may be a complete career change every ten years or so.

The ageing population along with smaller families also offers opportunities and threats: opportunities, given time, for the continuing employment of mature executives, although not necessarily in top positions; threats, as many individuals in the ranks of the baby boomers currently experience when being cast out of organisations to make way for younger, more up-to-date and less expensive human resources. All of these social trends affect your career, but can be seen as opportunities, rather than threats, with careful career planning.

The likely impact of social demography on the career of the individual engaged in career consulting can also form the basis of an important and relevant discussion.

CAREER STAGES

Moving on to career stages, career strategies need different pointers at different ages. I will now briefly trace through the career journey from the 20-year-old to the 60-year-old employee, to see how young, middle-aged and senior people may regard their jobs, their careers, and the people they work with.

Many young people today, unlike the 'flower children' of the 1960s, are highly ambitious and career-orientated. They are pursuing undergraduate and graduate degrees in droves. Many are holding down jobs during the day and taking courses at night to upgrade their knowledge and skills and thus further their careers. More than any other age groups, people in their early twenties are anxious to get a job that will allow them to use their talents and educational background. Unfortunately, they must sometimes lower their expectations, at least when starting out on their career path.

People in their early twenties tend to be impatient with incompetence and are disappointed with what appears to them to be a lack of professionalism and a rigid outlook displayed by some older people at work, which may or may not be a valid opinion.

Here is some advice for those in this age group: learn your job thoroughly, particularly the base (and sometimes more boring) elements, and get to understand the organisational structure in your work environment. Do your share of the dirty work, work hard, but seek help when it is needed. Communicate, get feedback, and develop career focus and goals. Be prepared to bide your time, as it may take a while to get where you want to be. Don't job hop, but be prepared to move on in order to gain experience elsewhere.

People in their late twenties and early thirties are on the move more than any other age group. They are determined to find positions that will propel them to success. As a result, it is not unusual to find people in this age group making two or three job changes within a ten-year period. This involves a certain degree of risk, but they can afford to take such risks, at least until they hit the really heavy financial responsibilities in their forties or fifties. In this age group people are, however, more careful and deliberate about job changes than people in their twenties.

People in their late twenties and early thirties become impatient with a job that does not allow them to get ahead fast enough. This period is also characterised by complete career shifts as values and goals are re-examined. Many people continue or complete their formal education at this age through full-time or part-time study. Concurrent with this, if they manage to find a satisfying and well-paid position they tend to settle down for the long haul, at least until their market worth changes drastically.

People in this age group like to be creative, utilise their talents, influence the organisation's direction and work with other motivated people. The main causes of job dissatisfaction at this age are lack of support from top management, lack of direction, poor communication, organisational politics and interpersonal problems. Many in this group switch jobs if they do not like or respect their manager or top management, or if they can find a position elsewhere offering a better chance for growth and success.

Some tips for people in this age group include understanding the informal network in organisations and building relationships. Delegate properly and develop yourself to be able to fill the job above yours. Develop your direct reports also. Keep your sense of humour and stay physically fit, up-to-date, decisive, and honest. Make contributions and above all, be seen to get results.

Many people in their late thirties and early forties are restless and looking for a chance to move up or on in their careers. They realise that there will be fewer and fewer opportunities later. Their approach to changing jobs is more cautious, as they can no longer afford to take great risks, but they still often seek positions with more money or prestige. However, people in this age group feel that they can no longer switch jobs as often as before, as potential employers may look suspiciously at job hoppers of this age group. They realise that their work record and reputation will be on the line more than when they were younger.

Many in this group feel that it is impossible for them to move perhaps because they lack a formal education, or fear a loss of financial security. Some may have been with the same organisation for 20 years or so in a speciality field, and feel trapped. Most have become fairly competent at their work, however, and have learned how to utilise the political network to get ahead. They value good communication skills, good health, a competent staff, teamwork and the ability to give praise and recognition where it is due.

Some tips for people in their late thirties and early forties include developing a sense of personal security by ensuring that your skills and capabilities will remain in demand. If necessary, retrain or acquire new skills. Do not lie, double-deal, stagnate or become self-centred at work. Do not be opinionated or a part of the rumour mill. Do not be ruled by money. Do not spend all your time in meetings. Ensure that sufficient quality time is spent with your partner, family and close friends, watch your health and weight, and get enough exercise.

Now we come to one of the most critical periods in anyone's career, the mid-forties through to early fifties age group. This is the time when all your past mistakes can catch up with you, and there is little time to rectify them. If you can survive this period, you will sail through to retirement, but sometimes the period of the late forties through to early fifties is when, in terms of a person's career, the roof seems to be falling in.

What do people in this age group have to worry about? There is an increased chance of sudden death, for example a heart attack, cancer and so forth, whether this is themself or their partner. There is also the fear of finding yourself out on the street owing to a merger, acquisition, restructuring or divestment. The 50-year-old employee finds this much more devastating then the 20-, 30- or 40-year-old, because of their perception (often inaccurate) of the reduced chances of their being re-employed. Unemployment hits this age group especially hard, since individuals are used to a certain comfortable standard of living and cannot believe that the job is not there any more.

Their job search skills are rusty and even if they find a position, they often find it difficult to adjust and start all over again. Fifty-year olds who have allowed themselves to stagnate in their jobs, who have poor performance records or problems in the areas of chemistry and fit, will obviously feel the pressure of the axe more than those who are more successful performers. But sometimes in today's economic turbulence, the good must leave along with the bad. Fortunately, most organisations are willing to help the displaced employee find another job through the provision of outplacement services.

But key people in their mid-forties through to early fifties can survive this period with a little 'contingency planning', a lot of alertness to what is happening around them, a commitment to keeping up-to-date and competent work performance and fit.

As the wave of 'baby boomers' enters the 'big 5-0' years, it is horrifying to note that the Australian Bureau of Statistics has reported that nearly half of them are reported as being considered too old by prospective employers. In the case of those in their mid-fifties, nearly two-thirds have been reported as being considered too old. The trend appears to be deteriorating. In 1994 one-fifth of those in their mid-forties to early fifties were unemployed, compared to less than 10% in 1970.

At the executive level the situation is potentially even more serious—unemployed at '50+' may mean that the corporate career is over. If employed, how long is it likely to last? With chief executive job tenure now three-and-a-half years and dropping, the impact on those next in line is profound, with three to five years the likely maximum tenure in any senior executive position.

CASE STUDY

The costs associated with releasing mature executives can be substantial. Take the case of a $260 000 per year executive with 12 years' service. In the event of an imposed early retirement the separation payment was estimated at over $400 000. Why remove a knowledgeable asset who may be very content in considering lateral or even downward moves within the organisation, or indeed on a career which in its last corporate chapters, 'tapers'?

But for this to happen, executives like this have to be given the opportunity to review their future alternatives and to receive objective counsel from somebody with no perceived secret agenda or political axe to grind. This executive was 51 years of age when we met and he was fast developing an understanding that the early fifties age group is the most critical period in anyone's career.

In the case of this executive, his career consulting program enabled him to determine when he wanted and could afford to retire, the type of part-time consulting and contracting he would pursue during retirement and what he needed to do before retirement to get up to speed as a consultant/contractor.

Most importantly it helped him and his CEO determine what he would be doing in the company during his last three to five years with them, and how he would continue contributing as a valuable asset. For him this meant moving from a senior line executive role into more of an internal advisory and mentoring role, which was possible because of his unique know-how developed over many years. His salary plateaued and tapered over this period, but his company superannuation contributions were enhanced to offset this.

Some tips for the mid-forties through early fifties age group include further developing a sense of personal security by contingency planning. Develop and promote 'UMDs'—Unique Marketing Differentiators relating to your competencies and capabilities—in other words, your unique and marketable strengths that differentiate you against your competition. Your UMDs need to coincide with demands within and outside your existing organisation and they really represent your point of differentiation and competitive advantage compared with others. Remain aware of the political climate in your organisation and adapt to changing conditions. Keep abreast of developments in your field. Develop supportive social contacts and maintain a code of ethical behaviour, not blaming others for your mistakes and not taking all the credit for successes. Plan to continue working effectively until retirement, but be prepared with a plan of action, should the axe fall anyway. Finally, consider and plan 'second career' options of consulting, contracting, non-executive directorships for senior people and so forth, and in this regard be clear about, and further develop your UMDs!

In spite of the myths about older workers, there is no real evidence that productivity decreases with increasing age. Many people remain active and productive throughout their later years. Although individuals in the mid-fifties through sixties age group may be more prone to health problems, they usually take better care of themselves than do younger individuals.

People in this age group have an excellent record. If they have made it this far, they have usually proved their competence. The ability to adapt and change does not depend on age, as mature people are often quite flexible, while many younger people can be more set in their ways and in their expectations. Thus there is no adverse correlation between age and work performance, and often a positive consideration.

Issues of concern to individuals in this age group are time management, obsolescence, fatigue, and the speed of technological change. Many are bewildered by the developments in computing and telecommunications technology, and envy younger people who seem to cope better.

Some advice for people in their mid-fifties through sixties includes discussing your career and retirement intentions with your employer and asking for input or advice when needed. In fact, start planning retirement or 'second career' options if you have not already done so, and consider the alternatives for part-time work. Make decisions and be ready to say 'no'. Become involved in the community. Be honest, considerate and accessible, and keep a sense of humour. Above all, stay up-to-date, train your direct reports, delegate, and check your performance and fit continuously.

By linking the individual's career stage back to the lead-in discussions on the career environment, the career consultant is ensuring that career plans are laid having taken into account the real world, rather than the ivory tower approach of simply relying on self-assessment.

ALTERNATIVES TO PROMOTION

The third topic area I find particularly valuable in career consulting is alternatives to seeking and attaining straight promotion. Individuals should not automatically assume that moving up the organisation to higher level positions is the 'be-all-and-end-all' of career planning. They also need to consider 'central', 'sideways' or even 'downwards' options.

A move *centrally* means expanding the professional boundaries of your existing job, thereby increasing your value to the organisation and becoming perceived as a greater 'centre of excellence'. This central expansion is often accompanied by additional influence and even power. Individuals should not underestimate the potential for central expansion!

A *sideways* move, offering new responsibilities, may be just what an individual needs to meet their goals. It may not be possible to move upwards at that juncture and this may have to be a longer-term, rather then shorter-term objective. Upward promotion is always a tough proposition in today's smaller, flatter organisations.

A sideways move usually means a transfer to another area to take up a position at the same level as the present one. This may be a viable option for the individual if they want to remain with their existing organisation but feel they are better suited to another functional or geographical area, or department, or just cannot get along with the people with whom they currently work.

A *downwards* move involves giving up some responsibility. This may seem to be a step backwards, but for some people it is really what they need to meet their career objective. An example is technical people who have been promoted to senior management positions and find they can no longer practise what they do best. Not everyone is cut out for management, and such people may actually serve their needs and career objective best by moving downwards.

CONTINUING AND CONCLUDING THE TYPICAL CAREER CONSULTING PROCESS

The outcome of my career planning process includes a summary of the individual's career objectives and likely strategies, performance standards and feedback mechanism, and a personal development program—all devised by the individual with the consultant's help through discussion.

Third party interviews come next, using very much the same question areas as described in Chapter 6—'Core coaching processes', plus more specific areas as a result of the outcome of career planning. Interviews create the opportunity for verification and amplification of findings and conclusions, and represent above all, a robust reality-check. There is nothing worse than a career consultant attending a progress review meeting only to find that all the work undertaken with the individual on career planning has resulted in a career directional focus that is totally unrealistic in the eyes of the line manager and HR executive.

In fact, the various stages suggested in this typical career consulting process invariably render sound and pertinent outcomes which are accepted positively by the management and HR department. The key then is for the individual's plan to be put into action, rather than to be left as an afterthought.

Indeed, this is the role of the career consultant into the future, namely to work with the individual to ensure that traction occurs. Many years ago as a career consultant I used to conclude my work after the progress reporting stage which addressed the individual's career plan, only often to learn subsequently that there had been no implementation and the person had become demotivated or had moved on as a result. These days I find that three to six months of ongoing contact with the individual, line manager and HR executive is an essential prerequisite to the individual attaining some solid career development traction. Only then would I consider recommending the closure meeting.

Again, please do not assume that career consulting needs to be undertaken by anyone else other than the line manager. In my description I have assumed it is conducted by a third party, such as myself, but in the ideal scenario it should be undertaken by the person to whom you report, or an internal HR consultant can also enact the role of career consultant.

COMBINING EXECUTIVE COACHING WITH CAREER CONSULTING

As noted earlier, and is a recurring theme in this book, up until recently physical assets such as land, labour, buildings, plant, equipment and raw materials were tightly held by companies and relatively easy to manage. The industrial age executive simply 'controlled the what' by managing the factors of production via conventional top-down or scientific management.

The information revolution and the knowledge era have seen a greater emphasis on *intellectual* assets—people, patents, processes, skills and know-how, technologies, customers, suppliers and experience. Such assets are not so tightly held, and thus are far harder to manage. The information age executive needs to 'create the how' by facilitating people and processes via enlightened leadership and with a strong customer orientation.

Companies and their executives are transitioning between these two paradigms, creating complexity in terms of what is expected and how to develop as a manager and leader.

Competence as an executive of course requires ability in a broad range of management and leadership practices. With an increasing emphasis on leadership however, individual behaviour—the medium through which personality interfaces with your environment—has now become the focus for individualised and sustainable executive development.

And the fuel to fire competence is motivation, often underemphasised by companies, or believed sufficiently attended to by extrinsic rewards such as performance based pay, bonuses or options. But motivation is maximised through intrinsic rewards in the form of how satisfied you feel about your job, the organisation, whole-life balance and your future, something we refer to as 'career alignment' when in addition, individual goals and plans directly coincide with those of the organisation.

Results are often maximised by combining executive coaching and career consulting at the individual executive level. Coaching is aimed at performance development career consulting, at motivation and alignment. Invariably this leads to the retention of talent and their ongoing career success to the benefit of all parties.

The process to adopt is tailored to the needs, but typically entails needs-analysis, fact finding (incorporating existing management and HR processes), multi-level survey, career assessment, third party interviews and ongoing coaching and career consulting. Regular feedback is provided to the line manager and HR by the executive, ensuring full alignment with organisational needs and creating the opportunity for the line manager personally to assume a greater ongoing coaching role, as appropriate.

KEYNOTE

➤ As vital and effective as executive coaching, career consulting attends to the missing link of ensuring individual and organisational goal alignment, wherever possible.

➤ This maximises self-motivation which is the fuel to fire superior performance and effectiveness: 'why would I leave if I can achieve my career goals here?'

➤ Career consulting also adds value to succession planning, and helps people become more career resilient.

➤ It also helps individuals understand that 'up' is not the only way forward, growth in the current role and horizontal progression being just as opportunistic and even more attainable.

➤ However, to arrive at such conclusions, individuals need to do some soul-searching and be challenged. Career consulting offers each opportunity.

Chapter 9

A Typical Team Coaching

Process

❝ Most teams aren't great teams. At best they are a collection of stars, rather than a star team **❞**

Introduction

Example
A previously decentralised operating division of a substantial group decided to centralise operations and form a new executive team comprised of former business unit general managers and some new functional experts. With a major rationalisation program to be planned and implemented, it was essential that this team synchronised as quickly as possible. This was successfully attained through team coaching.

Change won't go away, it will only accelerate! And change creates new teams needing to get up to speed quickly in order to yield benefits from the synergies and leverage they should create. To enable this to happen, team members need to understand each other's behavioural styles and how their differences can be harmonised to create a star team, rather than just a team of stars.

In this, psychologists and behavioural scientists the world over agree that winning executive teams need to be balanced in terms of their composition. In other words, those teams generally perform best whose members between them represent all the main behavioural styles. But leading a team of clones can be a lot easier!

Leading a team of very different behavioural styles can sometimes see them 'clash' against each other like medieval knights jousting at a tournament, particularly when the team is working under pressure! This can become destructive rather than synergistic. Rather, teams need proactive input from each member and leader, contributed on the basis of mutual support, trust and cooperation.

Another important team consideration is that just as an organisation experiences different phases in its life cycle—start up, early and secondary growth, adolescence/ turbulence and maturity—so teams can experience similar phases. The last two are often a particular concern wherein the team needs to regenerate, if not reinvent itself. Adolescence/turbulence often coincides with interpersonal friction among team members. Maturity often coincides with 'meetings for the sake of meetings' and not a lot of creative output.

Through working with hundreds of executives and senior people in Australia over nine years and by drawing on third party research, I have been able to develop new approaches which bridge conventional wisdom with practical experience. This entails helping people better understand team processes (mission, planning, goal setting, roles and meeting conduct), as well as their own and each other's behavioural styles and how they can be harnessed to generate outstanding team outcomes. A typical team coaching sequence is summarised below, although each assignment is tailored to fit precise needs and sought outcomes.

After individual interviews with each team member and an introductory team meeting, each member completes a survey of self and other team members, to determine perceived behavioural styles and team processes. This is followed by individual and pair feedback discussion sessions with the coach. The program then moves back to the full team level with a half-day workshop. Thereafter, one-on-one coaching with the team leader is undertaken to help maximise and sustain ongoing team performance.

Results can be impressive and are designed not to fade as the coach moves on. Rather, the whole approach lays fresh foundations on which teams invariably develop their full potential.

A TYPICAL TEAM COACHING APPROACH IN MORE DETAIL

Again, in describing a typical team coaching approach I will refer to some of the core coaching processes in Chapter 6, although team coaching is somewhat different to individual programs because of its group orientation.

Introducing coaching to the line manager (in this case potentially the team leader) needs, of course, to emphasise the needs and benefits associated with further developing teamwork, and the considerations addressed in the introduction to this chapter can be used well for this purpose. Similarly this is so when introducing the coach to the coachees (team members).

In terms of needs analysis, this is initially undertaken with the team leader and subsequently with each team member. The classic core approach described in Chapter 6—'Core coaching processes' again serves well for this purpose.

The team coaching sequence typically then takes a different step, namely the conduct of a half-day (three hours may suffice) team presentation and discussion. The objective of this session is to help all team members examine their own team and commit to moving forward with the team development coaching program. I usually kick off the meeting with some thought-provoking discussion as to whether the ideal executive exists. By examining the very broad range of ideal executive traits, team members begin to realise that the ideal executive probably does not exist, hence one of the reasons for a team leading an organisation.

Taking this further, I help the team better realise that diversity in the range of operating styles or traits of each team member makes for the strongest executive team through the synergy it can produce. However, such diversity can cause interpersonal friction and can be hard to lead and manage.

And so, to create real synergy from diverse operating styles, there needs to exist strong interpersonal relationships, conducive in-team behaviour and effective team processes.

I then usually describe the six operating styles in the Adeptus Process® model (as related in Chapter 7—'A typical executive coaching process') in the context of team composition, the need for diverse operating styles of its members and the need to develop strong interpersonal relationships. These are the operating styles we all 'carry around' and the way we come across one-on-one. In the group or team setting, however, group dynamics can cause a different set of behaviours, and I call this 'in-team behaviour'.

Regarding in-team behaviour, I describe how four behaviours are most evident in team members: overly internally competitive; the same as others; fence-sitting until consensus is attained, which they then follow; and, loyal, proactive and contributing support to each other team member.

In addressing team processes, I then review: the importance of team vision, as to where the team is headed and what it seeks to achieve; team members' roles and accountabilities; appropriate team procedures; the need for attention to the human factor; and, interpersonal relationships with neighbouring teams.

I then review some of the factors which often represent unsuccessful team make-up. This can include when members are just all very clever, potentially rendering the team disaster prone! Similarly, when there are too many idea generators and not enough attention to follow-through. Or when teams are too narrow in terms of the composition of their operating styles—perhaps only two or three of the six operating styles in the Adeptus Process® model being represented. Finally, I allude to numbers of team members suggesting that fewer than six or more than ten is rarely ideal.

I then talk about the types of teams I often encounter, namely the *new or young team* which often operates along the lines of a collection of more or less independent people, requiring the appointed leader to demonstrate direction and support. Then we have the *divergent team* which seems to pull in different directions compared with the convergent team which is more focused and united.

A *developing team* is one which is working quite well but where there is an opportunity for further development.

A *synchronised team* perhaps describes the ideal team of members who work closely together and manage to extract the 'elusive butterfly' of real synergy—better decisions being made and taken jointly than could have been the case individually. Clearly, combining star players within a star team, the synchronised team, is what many teams seek to achieve.

I then usually hand out a copy of the overheads I have used to support the presentation so far, and I ask team members to comment about how they feel about their own team in the contexts presented. I then give them feedback on the aggregate results of my needs analysis, prior to presenting details about my ongoing work program, which I will now describe in some detail.

TEAM SURVEYS

The next stage is in fact the completion by each team member of a team survey which focuses on operating styles, in-team behaviour and team processes.

The operating style component I use is the same referred to in Chapter 7 and sourced from the Adeptus Process®. However, there is a range of other survey instruments that can be used for this purpose. The surveys need to be short, however, as each team member undertakes the survey for self and separately for each other team member.

The in-team behaviour survey element, undertaken in the same way, is also drawn from Adeptus, and I will describe in detail what it covers, shortly.

For team processes, each team member only completes this survey element once, namely, how the team appears to be faring against the team process criteria noted earlier, as well as against the following criteria in addition (which relate to advanced team processes at the executive team level):

➤ The team resembles a *leadership team*, whose members are highly committed to, and mutually accountable for, their reason for being, approach and total business performance. The team is comprised of no more than ten people ideally, with complementary capabilities and a strong commitment to each other (somewhat rare!)

➤ The team resembles a functional group, people who operate more as functional heads, their leader assigning them priorities, establishing performance expectations, facilitating encouragement and motivation, consolidating functional results into total business results and holding each person accountable for their individual input (somewhat usual!)

➤ Team members operate flexibly somewhere between a functional group and a leadership team. They reserve leadership teamwork for major opportunities, threats or challenges. They focus on, and balance their leadership team and functional responsibilities, rather than trying to mesh them in together or operate as a single, all purpose ongoing team. In this, they learn not to trade off one for the other, nor compromise leadership team and functional performance.

➤ The team decides when to operate as a leadership team, selecting times and events judiciously, where real opportunities exist for collective leadership team input. They understand that addressing all business performance matters as a leadership team inevitably leads to frustration, even a sense of boredom. They recognise the need for different types of meetings, sometimes as a functional group with a full agenda and tight schedule to get through the business of the day; sometimes as a leadership team with a smaller agenda and looser schedule.

➤ When operating as a leadership team, the team pursues a common purpose, intent, performance goals and monitoring. They commit to a mutually agreed and acceptable approach to how they work, including shared values and team processes and procedures. They believe in, and practise mutual accountability. They embrace and synchronise the diverse capabilities and operating styles of members, maximising synergy.

Individual feedback

Following completion and receipt of the surveys, I then conduct individual feedback sessions with each team member, lasting about 90 minutes each. The objective of these sessions is to discuss and maximise interpersonal differences, relationships and in-team behaviour with a view to enhancing overall team performance.

To accomplish this you need to: explain the operating style process being used and show self-perception, versus perception by the aggregate of the others, from the survey. Emphasise differences between 'preferred' self and 'perceived' self (by others by using the following type of statements):

'Do not be alarmed by the differences in scores between the various respondents. Your scores represent your "preferred" view of yourself, whereas the scores of other respondents represent their "perceived" view of you. If there is a big deviation between these views, then you must decide whether or not you are going to try to close the gap through further development and modification of your behaviour.'

Then discuss what, if any, actions the individual might undertake to move 'perceived' towards 'preferred' or another style using the self-management of development technique (see Chapter 6—'Core coaching processes'). Help the individual complete this. Then go through the self and aggregate of others results regarding in-team behaviour and the definitional write-up which follows if you are using the Adeptus model. Discuss team processes self results versus aggregate of others from the survey.

Then discuss and agree on preferred team members (rank order, based on where the greatest opportunities lie for improving interpersonal relationships, by and with each team member) for a pair feedback session (in other words, involving two team members and the coach), and attain agreement that the individual is prepared to share results with the other party in the pair feedback session. Make sure the individual brings the survey and related materials to the pair feedback session, and finish off by discussing the agenda and how they should prepare for this meeting.

IN-TEAM BEHAVIOUR

Turning to my Adeptus model for in-team behaviour, the model is based on the fact that some members of the team can be very proactive in terms of their input to team direction, others can be less so. Some members of the team can also be very proactive in terms of their support of team members, others can be less so.

By studying the degree of proactiveness in each area, I have evolved what I believe to be the four most common in-team behaviour descriptions. They have the following labels: *clones*, *knights*, *rooks* and *henchmen*.

➤ *Clones* from the biological perspective are genetically identical to one antecedent, or from the botanical perspective are transplants from one original seedling. Clones in the work or team setting can result from the 'mirror-image' effect of hiring, where the comfort level of the hirer is increased if the hiree is of the same ilk. Clones in the team setting do not provide much proactive input to team direction, but they do tend to be very supportive of, and go along with other team members, particularly the team leader.

➤ *Knights* were originally men of noble birth and are often thought of as medieval warriors wandering the land in search of chivalrous adventures. But knights also took part in pageants where they would joust by charging at each other with lances on horseback in an endeavour to dismount their combatant and win the tournament. A veritable 'I win—you lose' outcome! Knights in the team setting are very proactive in their input to team direction, but usually somewhat or even very unsupportive of team members, and in this are often seen as internally competitive.

➤ *Rooks*, often mistaken for crows, are very common in Europe where they live in large colonies or rookeries. They tend to do their own thing in the rookery— often seeming at odds with the other birds. Ultimately however, with reluctance and quite a lot of squawking, they will fly off with the others, rather than be left alone. Indeed, rooks really are 'fence-sitters' and only commit to a course of action if it seems to be the way all the other birds in the rookery are headed. Rooks in the team setting are neither proactive in their input to team direction, nor particularly supportive of other team members. They usually accept team consensus however, even if with some reluctance!

➤ *Henchmen* historically were squires or pages of honour, and could always be trusted and relied on. Henchmen were also full of cunning and native wit and would often come up with good ideas on behalf of their colleagues. Also, whatever the needs of an individual or team, henchmen would endeavour to support and provide for them, enhancing the overall effectiveness of the group. Thus, henchmen are proactive both in terms of their input to team direction and in their support of team members.

Teams need to be comprised of henchmen. In today's fiercely competitive environment, there can be no room for clones, knights and rooks! Again, if a team member identifies with this and wishes to behave more as a henchman, then the self-management of development technique can be used for this purpose, highly effectively.

PAIR FEEDBACK

The next stage is the pair feedback session. The objective of this 90-minute session is again to discuss and maximise interpersonal differences, relationships and in-team behaviour with a view to enhancing overall team performance. But this time the discussion involves two team members and the coach.

The following is the sequence of this session:

➤ Individual 'A' runs over their results of their individual feedback session with the help of the coach.

➤ Individual 'B' reveals their perception of the operating style of individual 'A' and in-team behaviour, as well as their own survey results on team processes.

➤ The comparison of the above is facilitated by the coach, who helps draw out implications.

➤ The steps noted above are reversed between individuals 'A' and 'B'.

➤ The coach then facilitates a discussion and agreement about what each individual plans to do to achieve the objective of the session, to record notes, to type up a draft memorandum of understanding and commitment, to have it approved by each individual, with their agreement that the team leader also receives a final copy.

➤ The coach then attains agreement from individuals 'A' and 'B' that they will be prepared to discuss their survey results and related information at the upcoming half-day group session.

The session concludes by discussing the agenda and how to prepare for the group session.

Group session

There then follows the half- (or one) day group session with the full team, the objective of which is, yet again, to discuss and maximise interpersonal differences, relationships and in-team behaviour with a view to enhancing overall team performance.

In brief, the sequence is as follows:

➤ The coach runs over (briefly) the progress made up to that time.
➤ The coach asks each individual to run through what they have learned about themselves in the process, namely: self-positioning of operating style ('preferred') versus others' positioning ('perceived') and what actions the individual may be taking to move 'perceived' to 'preferred' or another style.
➤ Similarly in-team behaviour and the action to become (even) more of a henchman.
➤ The coach then reveals team composition on a whiteboard version of the operating style model twice—firstly 'perceived' and then 'preferred', getting members to plot these positions themselves on the whiteboard model. The coach then facilitates a session on team composition and on how different operating styles might get on even better with each other.
➤ Similarly for in-team behaviour and how each behaviour type might become more like a henchman.
➤ Finally, team processes and what needs to be done to improve them is addressed through discussion, facilitated by the coach.

Throughout the session, note-taking is encouraged by the coach including how each member can help themselves and each other member: develop more appropriate operating styles; behave (even) more like a henchman; and, further develop better team processes.

Follow-through

In order to make sure there is follow-through, the team leader needs to have kept copies of the pair feedback session reports, the team composition model ('perceived' and 'preferred'), the in-team behaviour model ('perceived' and 'preferred'), and team processes survey results. Also, the main observations and comments, along with the team leader's own materials and notes from all sessions.

Ongoing follow-up by the coach with the team leader over the following three months is also advised, in order to ensure continuous and sustained improvement in teamwork.

Using the sports coaching analogy

Very much earlier in my career I had the good fortune to be a sports coach, of all places, at a Cadet College at Hasan Abdal in Pakistan!

I coached various sports which I had earlier, and in some cases subsequently, participated in as a player myself, namely rugby, shooting, boxing, swimming and field hockey.

I believe there are many aspects of sports coaching which lend themselves to the business team setting and which form a very useful checklist for follow-up coaching with team leaders, many of whom identify well with the sports coaching analogy.

Star teams

➤ Business and sports success is won through star teams, not just a team of stars. Yet moulding a team of very different individuals to become a world-class team requires as much focus on motivating and developing *the individual* as it does on the team.

   And individuals need to be treated like individuals, which requires a flexible tailored approach geared to bring the best out of each of them. How many chief executives, on the other hand, simply rely on team meetings to interact with their direct reports?

➤ *Individual motivation.* Whether it is the sports team or the business team, each individual responds to different stimuli in terms of their own self-motivation. For some it is a pat on the back. For others, it is the challenge of getting to the next level. Others are naturally competitive, and for them, benchmarking their own or team performance against others provides the stimulus to succeed. And the team leader needs to know the most appropriate stimuli to use with each individual, for each of them to attain and develop their best performance.

However, an overriding motivation in the team setting is camaraderie, team spirit and a mutually supportive and collegial atmosphere, 'We are in this together. Together we will win … or fail!'

➤ *Building confidence.* Any key person in any organisation can, at times fail, or certainly can find it lonely and tough to compete and perform at best, just like the professional sportsperson. Team leaders (just like sports coaches) have to concentrate on building the confidence of team members to attain new levels of performance.

To do this they have to create and develop a motivational environment, in which each team member sustains and enjoys incremental ongoing improvement, consistently. How many business team leaders you know are able to do this? And we are not talking here about team leaders needing to be loved, but they certainly need to be respected.

➤ *Respect.* Respect comes about if the team leader helps members put their own interests last and the interests of the whole team first, while at the same time recognises the achievements of individuals and directs credit to those deserving it.

Respect also comes about when individual or team failure is seen and treated as a learning experience rather than treated punitively. Failure plays an important role in team and individual development in fact, and this should be used positively (assuming failure is not overly recurrent!).

➤ *Moulding the job.* A job can be shaped to fit the individual. Clearly, sportspeople are far better at some sports than others. Similarly, individuals in the work environment will perform best when their roles as individuals and team members directly coincide with their interests, motivational capabilities, job requirements, values, motivational needs, operating style, leadership traits and in-team behaviour—all as addressed elsewhere throughout this book. 'A lengthy shopping list' might be your response 'Where do I start?'

Well, the team leader probably does not start anywhere, and an 80% rule often seems to apply. Eighty per cent of the responsibility for job moulding has to start with the individual, and intuitively if not planned, in 80% of individual cases there appears to be an 80% job fit. What the team leader does need to do, however, is to keep a watchful eye out for the 20% where job fit is less sure, and in the worst case a straight bad match. Under these circumstances opening up some career consulting dialogue (see Chapter 8—'A typical career consulting process') and putting the onus on the individual to think through job moulding options and potential, starts to lay some strong foundations for enhancing job fit.

➤ *Goal-setting and feedback*. Unless individual and team goals are mutually agreed, performance towards their attainment monitored, and supportive, motivational and, or corrective feedback provided, individual sportspeople or teams will never meet their full potential. Nor will business teams or individual members.

In this, as an executive coach, I often encounter huge gaps in establishing mutually held and understood expectations for results, and executives and managers often avoid providing real feedback. For the individual, such feedback needs to be spontaneous and ongoing, as well as planned and periodic through more formal performance evaluation or appraisal processes. For the team it can be self-generated feedback, initiated by the leader: 'How do you people feel we are tracking? What is going well? What is going not so well? What do we need to modify or change?' Responses by the team to such prompting—which again needs to be regular—can ensure team performance is enhanced and team development sustained.

➤ *Unique team players*. Unique individuals working cohesively as team members. Most successful sports team have sought, identified and worked with the uniqueness of each individual player, and galvanised them into a balanced and cohesive unit. And this requires each individual's willingness, indeed passion, to be a great team player as well as a great individual contributor.

Team leaders in business can again learn these lessons from the sports analogy, because as I have said earlier in this chapter, no single executive can have all the sought-after and ideal executive traits to run a company. But a team can, providing it is comprised of a range of unique characteristics in individuals who are team players.

➤ *Loss of key people*. Just as sports teams can lose key players—often to the competition—so business teams can encounter losses. This is a perfectly natural phenomenon in each case, and to be expected rather than worried about.

However, teams then need to realise that such a loss is a real opportunity to try out another player or team member. In this way, a potential negative can be turned into a positive, providing there is an adequate talent pool for succession. And the successor might not always be a perfect fit initially. Through coaching—whether in sports or in business—that successor invariably can be developed to become a more perfect fit and performer.

➤ *Continuous improvement*. When sports teams become comfortable with success, resting on their laurels, complacency sets in and their performance starts to deteriorate. When business teams become complacent, results can start to suffer or are certainly more at risk of doing so.

Teams, with the stewardship of their leaders, need continuously to seek new ways to improve their performance further. And in this the spirit of the 'malcontent'—never satisfied—but when applied positively, can generate great profits!

➤ *Team leadership*. Winning teams need effective leadership—and from behind, more than from the front—to create a sense of empowerment and shared leadership. And team leadership needs to ensure that appropriate plans and strategies are in place: where and how the team is headed, that the right environment is created wherein individuals and the team can thrive, along with positive reinforcement and leadership by example. In this, building on team and individual strengths and attending to the weaker areas, with commitment to continuous improvement, are the keys to ongoing individual and team success.

➤ *Continuous development*. To seek to attain continuous improvement in team and individual performance requires continuous training and development. Ask any athlete about the years of rigorous training they have to go through to attain their optimal performance and realise their full potential. If the world beating sports standards in Australia today applied to Australian business, then I probably would not be writing this book!

And do not forget 'the standards'. Athletes know the times they have to beat; executives and teams also need stretch standards or benchmarks, for them to attain their best, backed by continuous and rigorous training and development to help them get there.

CONCLUSION

Team coaching concludes, as far as the coach is concerned, with a closure meeting where the team leader addresses the following points:

➤ What were we seeking to achieve when we started the team coaching process?
➤ How successful were we?
➤ Main good points/outcomes?
➤ Areas we would have liked to have improved on even further?
➤ General level of satisfaction of our input?
➤ Enhancements next time around?

➤ Opportunities for referral to other teams within the organisation?

➤ Specifically to whom, and can the team leader make the introduction?

To conclude, I have again taken the orientation that the coach is someone other than the team leader. The individual facilitating team coaching can, in fact, be either. My preference is for the team leader to act as coach for their own team of direct reports, and this can be accomplished very successfully if, prior to taking on the role of team coach, the team leader has participated in a team coaching program within the more senior team of which he or she is a member.

KEYNOTE

➤ The most effective senior level teams comprise members with a diverse range of operating styles.

➤ Who operate in synchronism rather than compete internally.

➤ Where team processes facilitate team efficiency, effectiveness and interpersonal relationships.

➤ And whose members know when to operate as a functional group with a single leader.

➤ And as a true leadership team with mutual accountability.

Chapter 10

A Typical Assimilation Process for Newly Appointed Key People

66 Halve the time for new appointees to get up to speed, and the risks of early departure! **99**

Introduction

Doing more, with less, faster—in organisations where 'change is not going away, it's only going to accelerate'—is a given for established key people. Also it applies for those newly transferred or promoted internally, or hired externally.

Indeed, for recently appointed key people, honeymoon periods are getting shorter and expectations greater to deliver results, even though many companies still find it takes nine months for new executive appointees to get up to speed. And it is also estimated, based on my empirical research compared with the findings of others, that over 40% of executives are perceived not to achieve optimal performance within the first year in their new roles. Also, a significant proportion of such executives leave voluntarily or involuntarily within 20 months of their appointment—all at huge cost and lost opportunity for both the organisation and the individual executive. When do they start to experience problems? Usually after the honeymoon period, when reality really starts to set in and sometimes bite!

Why do they fail? In order of significance, we have established the following key factors which cause newly appointed executives to derail:

➤ not assimilating the new organisational culture;

➤ not developing strong interpersonal relationships at the team or individual level;

➤ not exhibiting appropriate leadership traits;

➤ insufficient understanding of expectations for results; non-attainment of key results on time;

➤ failing to assimilate organisational politics, power and influence.

Through specialised executive coaching over an initial 100-day timeframe, you are able virtually to guarantee greater haste up the learning curve. This vastly increases chances for the successful assimilation of newly appointed key people. Invariably this generates faster, more secure and more sustainable progress and results.

The first stage of the coach's involvement usually concentrates on helping the new appointees become very clear about the expectations of their manager and senior colleagues. This ensures their understanding of priorities, targets, timeframes and measures for delivery of results, along with other milestones, during their first year.

The second stage entails comprehensive and in-depth assessment of organisational culture—'the way they do things around here'. This includes the habits of the new population and key individuals. Many new appointees are there to be change-agents, and this can include changing culture, of course. In this case, a full understanding of where the organisation is coming from, culture-wise, as well as where it is headed (including pace of change) with the newly appointed person's leadership or help, forms the basis of coaching. The coach also helps the new appointee compare cultural idiosyncrasies with their own motivational needs and adopt appropriate coping mechanisms in the event of poor job fit.

The third stage concentrates on interpersonal relationships, with managers, key peers, direct reports, customers, suppliers and other major stakeholders. Operating styles are compared, and team behaviour is also addressed, to ensure that well-developed individual relationships are mirrored in all team settings.

The fourth stage concentrates on leadership behaviour. Just where is the organisation at in terms of its transition from *the industrial age*, where managers 'controlled the what' through top-down or scientific management to the *information age*, the era of knowledge, where leaders need to 'create the how' through enlightened leadership with a strong customer orientation? What does this mean in terms of expected management practices, leadership traits and change-agent competencies? Through coaching, the individual can quickly understand, and as far as possible pursue organisational expectations and preferences.

> **EXAMPLE**
>
> A recently appointed partner in a professional services firm needed to fast-track his assimilation into the partnership and to become a team leader rather than solely a technical expert. This was achieved quickly and sustainably through executive coaching and mentoring.

Finally, the coach addresses politics, power and influence, in a positive rather than exploitative sense. Understanding where the power resides, building allies, personal selling, networking and handling conflict all form the focus of coaching. This rounds off 100 days of fast-paced, yet secure and sustainable, transition into the new work environment. Follow-up coaching occurs during the next 100 days to ensure sustainability of results and progress.

> **EXAMPLE**
>
> On promotion to a senior executive role, through executive coaching and mentoring I helped an individual understand and prioritise key result areas—business performance, leadership and interpersonal relationship perspectives. Without such support during assimilation, it was deemed that the learning curve would have been longer, and progress slower, impacting adversely on business results.

The need for delivery of fast and sustainable results applies even more to the newly appointed sales executive. There is sufficient research and other evidence to suggest that an even higher proportion of sales executives are perceived not to achieve optimal performance within the first year of tenure of their roles, along with even higher and faster levels of turnover.

Their reasons for failure are very similar to other executives. They too can become derailed through:

➤ not assimilating the new organisational culture;
➤ not developing strong interpersonal relationships at the team or individual level;
➤ not understanding expectations for results neither/nor attaining key results on time;
➤ failing to assimilate organisational politics, power and influence.

However, another significant potential derailer, rather than not exhibiting appropriate leadership traits, is the sales executive not exhibiting appropriate professional consultative selling practices.

Thus, the fourth stage of assimilation coaching with sales executives helps them better adjust to the organisation's professional consultative selling practices. Where the organisation neither prescribes nor describes such desired practices, then the coach should be able to help them assess themselves. Appropriate development priorities can be pursued in the areas of: goal setting; psychology of selling; time management and prioritisation; lead generation; one-on-one communication; structured versus personalised approaches; use of visuals; closing; building loyalty; expanding influence; major account management; promotional techniques; and, writing effectiveness.

In place of the foregoing, or in addition, the coach should also be able to help them assess themselves and pursue appropriate development priorities in public speaking and group presentations. This could cover such areas as: first impressions; speaker styles; presentation development; presentation sequence; ending with impact; speech aids; visuals; convincing group communications and trouble-shooting; planning for success; and, meeting room layouts.

In all phases of assimilation coaching with sales executives, a heavy emphasis can be placed on role play and practice, which can be videotaped for critique and further development.

A TYPICAL ASSIMILATION PROCESS IN MORE DETAIL

As in virtually every coaching program, a typical assimilation process commences with some of the classic core coaching processes described in Chapter 6:

➤ *Introducing coaching to line managers*, the key benefit here being to target halving the time taken by a newly appointed key person to get up to speed and so lessen the risks associated with induction turnover.
➤ *Introducing the coach to the coachee*, and what an excellent hiring differentiator the availability of a coach can be to top talent considering joining your organisation!
➤ *Needs analysis*, which in this case may help prioritise the potential derailers in the context of case-specific hires, roles and organisation.
➤ *Career and role reviews.*
➤ *Review of previous feedback* and comparison to the new role and organisation.

➤ *SDOT analysis and development priorities.*
➤ *Self-management of development.*

Before going too far in the process however, in keeping with the vast majority of coaching programs, it is very important in assimilation to conduct a 'triangular' meeting between line manager, coachee, coach and HR executive (as appropriate), that is, assuming a third party coach is being used. However, again, we cannot emphasise enough the opportunity created by the line manager assuming the coaching role, and the powerful impact this can have on fast-tracking relationship development between line manager and direct report—the coachee.

Often an appropriate early step in assimilation is to develop a mutually understood and agreed expectation for activities and results against timeframes, between line manager and the newly appointed executive.

If there is a position description or job specification, then this can be used as a starting point in discussion with the line manager in order to understand expectations in-depth in terms of priorities, targets, timeframes, how results are measured and other activities and milestones. The focus is over the first year but broken down initially into quarters and then monthly.

In the absence of a job specification, then the checklist used in the role review in Chapter 6—'Core coaching processes' will work well for this purpose.

From this further analysis of results' expectations, you should be able to reassemble perceived result areas over the first year into the following sequence: result area; how measured; targets expected; dates; strategies; and, tactics (to attain result area).

This list of result areas should then be prioritised by applying 'Pareto', namely, selecting the 20% of result areas, strategies and tactics generating 80% impact during assimilation. This can be discussed between coach and coachee and submitted to the line manager for ratification. I usually recommend following 'results expectations' with 'assimilating the new organisational culture'.

ORGANISATIONAL CULTURE

Organisational culture forms the environment, or 'atmosphere' within which we have to live, survive and prosper. Understanding and adapting to the prevailing atmosphere—the culture of the organisation—is critical during assimilation. And if elements of the atmosphere are at variance with what we require, then we need to develop coping mechanisms. This is described in greater detail shortly in the form of a write-up on atmospheric needs.

The write-up is designed for use by the coachee in two ways. Firstly, as a checklist for learning more about 'how they do things around here' and in the event of intended culture change 'how they intend to do things around here'. Secondly, when any of the foregoing is at variance with the individual's motivational needs, appropriate coping mechanisms are adopted.

The following approach is therefore recommended:

➤ The coachee reads the write-up on atmospheric needs.
➤ The coachee discusses it with the coach.
➤ On advice from line manager and HR executive, the coachee meets with key influencers to address and learn to understand better, existing and intended cultural habits and idiosyncrasies 'the way we do things/intend to do things around here'. Also, when the individual has been hired as a cultural change-agent, pace as well as content needs to be determined, along with potential hurdles which need to be overcome, and props which need to be utilised.
➤ The coachee and coach then meet to discuss and summarise what has been learned, followed by a triangular meeting with line manager for ratification, where the emphasis is more on the cultural aspects than on the motivational needs (a more personal topic).

THE WRITE-UP

This is, in fact, quite a complex subject. In addition to the usual chemistry and fit assessments by individuals at the time of hiring, major organisational or 'atmospheric' needs of individuals—to maximise their self-motivation and personal effectiveness—include a range of characteristics of the organisation, its culture and its management style:

➤ *material needs*: remuneration, safety and security;
➤ *structural needs*: degree and type of structure, bureaucracy and systems;
➤ *behavioural needs*: management style and interpersonal relationships;
➤ *emotional needs*: trust, social needs, esteem needs and sense of achievement.

Newly appointed individuals need to assess their own atmospheric needs and ensure they are appropriately accommodated in the organisation, if at all possible. If not, self-motivation and, thereby performance, are unlikely to be at optimum unless appropriate coping mechanisms are deployed.

Atmospherics are a critical element of chemistry and fit, and yet are often ignored in management or selection and development, where an orientation of 'will the candidate fit in with us?' rather than 'are we right for the candidate?' usually applies.

In the context of assimilation, using atmospheric needs for purposes of assimilating organisational culture is an innovative and powerful approach as it represents a comprehensive checklist against which culture can be assessed. This assessment has a five element focus: what is the culture today? where is it headed and what is it intended it should look like in the future? at what pace should it develop? where is it at variance with my own atmospheric needs? and, what coping mechanisms should I adopt accordingly?

Material needs relate to the base-level needs as described by the well-known behavioural scientist Abraham Maslow. They include all the basic needs for living and working: remuneration for food, clothing, shelter, health and education; and, safety and security at work, and even 'comfort' at work, be this the office environment, cafeteria arrangements, style of car, or fringe benefits.

Clearly, if the material needs of an individual are not satisfied, this may create, on the one hand, self-motivation to progress within the organisation and via promotion to improve material returns to a more acceptable level. Or, as is often the case, cause dissatisfaction, poor morale and poor performance, potentially leading to a voluntary or involuntary separation.

Structural needs relate to the way the organisation is structured which can include degree of centralisation versus decentralisation and levels of autonomy accorded. Other factors include: degree of bureaucracy and red tape versus a more free-wheeling environment; complexity and intensity of management reporting and supporting systems; degree and type of computer-based information versus paper-based, and requirements for computer literacy; and, rigidity or otherwise of policies, rules and regulations.

Again, the organisation, in terms of structure, may either meet the motivational needs of the individual, or may be diametrically opposed to them, causing an adverse reactive and often stressful behaviour, and apparent 'poor fit'.

Behavioural needs start to get more complex and can become somewhat of a moving target because of the coming and going of senior people in corporate life to whom an individual reports. For example, an executive may be hired by a chief executive who displays ideal behavioural characteristics for the newly hired individual. However, chief executive job tenure now spans less than four years and so there is a strong chance that any executive is likely to report to a new boss—it is simply a matter of time! That new boss may display very different behavioural characteristics from the original hirer, and these characteristics may not meet the motivational needs of the individual.

However, behavioural needs are not only met (or not met) by the senior executive to whom you report, but also by the culture of the organisation, and so these needs and how they are satisfied are well worthwhile examining in detail. Behavioural needs, in fact, fall into two main categories: *management style* and *interpersonal relationships*.

Management style encompasses such aspects as planning, organising, monitoring, decision-making, motivating, delegating, adaptability, entrepreneurism, resilience and communication, which are summarised below in the context of assessing atmospherics:

➤ Planning: the degree to which and how executives plan, set objectives, develop strategies, monitor, control and review the performance of direct reports; how 'top-down' or 'bottom-up' the planning processes are within the organisation; and, how fixed or flexible plans are during implementation. Some individuals are motivated and perform well in a highly planned environment, whereas others operate better in a more spontaneous setting.

➤ Organising: in addition to the structural aspects of the organisation as addressed earlier, individual executives clearly have an impact on 'organising', for example, the degree of formality or informality in terms of team structure, reporting relationships, responsibility, accountability, authority, delegation; and, span of control. Some individuals prefer a well-organised environment, others prefer a more informal or 'loose' setting.

➤ Monitoring: the degree to which the monitoring of performance is preventative or maintenance; the number and specificity of major result areas and standards of performance; the form of monitoring, be it on-the-job supervision or hands-off, via reporting and information systems; and, how individual development and learning needs are identified and addressed. Some individuals perceive close and formalised monitoring as an unpalatable invasion of their autonomy, whereas others see this as the norm and need regular feedback about their performance.

➤ Decision-making: the degree to which decision-making is involving direct reports or imposed; problems and opportunities are fully defined or understood; a range of prospective solutions is developed and assessed; root causes as opposed to symptoms are addressed; and, how much creative thinking 'outside the square' is encouraged in the development of best possible decisions. Some individuals need an environment where decisions are made quickly, where there is neither ambiguity nor 'shades of grey'. Others prefer and operate better in a more reflective environment, where there is ample time for decision-making, particularly when complex issues are being addressed.

➤ Motivating: the degree to which a motivational environment is created through a climate encouraging personal development and advancement; democratic rather than autocratic leadership; trust and integrity; job interest and satisfaction; recognition of individual or group contributions; alignment of personal and corporate goals; and, an egalitarian as opposed to status-based culture. Some individuals need and can only survive in a motivational environment, others are more self-motivated.

➤ Delegating: the extent to which executives delegate in terms of being clear about what and to whom responsibilities are delegated; sufficient resources and authority being provided so that the delegation can be carried through effectively; delegation to maximise the skills and personal development of direct reports; and, delegation to free up internal bottlenecks and to allow senior executives to concentrate on higher level matters. Some individuals have an insatiable appetite for delegated responsibilities, whereas others prefer to work to their own agenda and perceive an environment where there is a lot of delegation, as one where being continuously on the receiving end of 'passing the buck', adversely impacts on personal freedom, initiative and autonomy.

➤ Adaptability: the degree to which individuals appreciate and offer variety and change; adapt to changing circumstances rather than resist them; and, take a flexible management and leadership style depending upon the competence of direct reports and the urgency of tasks. Some individuals thrive on change, others resist it to the hilt (and it can become the cause of their undoing!).

➤ Entrepreneurism: how far the organisation is prepared to experiment with new ways of doing things; innovate in terms of products, services, processes or systems; and, display a certain amount of daring in this (yet balanced by an appreciation and application of risk management). Some individuals need to work in a highly entrepreneurial environment, others fit best in slower-paced or more predictable settings, and perhaps in bureaucracies.

➤ Resilience: the degree of resilience in individuals in the form of handling and managing stress; capacity to persevere when the going gets tough; seeing change as a way of life rather than a hindrance; and, generally displaying that 'dogged streak' of perseverance at times of particular difficulty or uncertainty. Some individuals fit best in a 'tough' or resilient environment, others prefer a 'softer' work setting.

➤ Communication: the degree to which people engage in open, two-way communication; seek to understand the other party's point of view; minimise the physical and behavioural barriers which can so often detract from effective communication; and, are considered approachable by direct reports. Some individuals thrive on open two-way communication and indeed need this to be effective, others prefer a more traditional hierarchical setting, and are more used to communication which is primarily top-down.

Newly appointed key people need to be very clear about their needs regarding management style, be this the executive to whom you report, or from more of a management culture perspective across the organisation. If such needs are met, self-motivation and performance are invariably enhanced. If such needs are not met, this will likely cause difficulty and in the extreme case, a negative stress reaction. Yet, how many employers even are aware of, or consider chemistry and fit from this 'reverse' perspective?

Interpersonal relationships is the second main category relating to *behavioural needs*, and executives need to be clear about their preferred operating styles of the senior executives to whom they report, which may include one or a combination of those described in Chapter 7 under the heading 'Interpersonal relationships'.

We may have preferences regarding the operating styles of others and to whom we report, and yet we may not always be able to choose our line managers in organisational life! But even understanding that there are differences in operating styles, and that these differences in the team setting are actually needed in order to provide for balanced team composition, all helps. However, in selecting a new role within your existing organisation or a new job outside it, there may be some extremes in operating style you might be better to avoid. *You* have to decide!

As mentioned earlier, although the initial focus in assessing the degree to which your behavioural needs are met is the executive to whom you report, and this executive may change and be replaced by another, many of the elements of management style and interpersonal relationships also relate to the culture of the organisation, and so need to be assessed in this dual context: will my behavioural needs be met by the person to whom I report; will they be met by the culture of the organisation?

In considering the final category of needs, *emotional needs*, we revert again to the behaviour scientist Maslow and the higher levels of his hierarchy of needs, which include trust, social needs, esteem needs and sense of personal achievement.

Trust relates to the organisation being seen as fair and reasonable in its approach to dealing with staff, that senior management is trustworthy, results will be rewarded and that there will be no undeserved penalties or dismissals. Social needs encompass the theme of individuals feeling they 'belong' and are part of a group. Esteem needs are satisfied by executives being recognised as individuals, and for their contributions, capabilities and achievements. Sense of personal achievement is where the executive feels a sense of high level accomplishment in terms of attaining what has been strived for, which brings great personal satisfaction and self-confidence.

Most of us need an environment where our emotional needs can be met in one or more ways. Yet in today's era of organisational turbulence and uncertainty, even large, apparently well-managed organisations seem to have lost the plot with many in their senior level ranks.

Trust has walked out the door as a result of a hire-and-fire mentality. Social interaction has deteriorated as individuals in the group jockey for survival and the apparently fewer opportunities for promotion in today's flatter organisation structures.

Esteem needs may be only partly met as achievements go less recognised, the pressures of 'doing more with less faster' leaving little time for such pleasantries and a sense of achievement becoming an even more elusive butterfly.

Since some career management experts have estimated that more than 50% of unsuccessful executive career episodes are caused by the atmospherics of organisational life being at variance with the motivational needs of the individual, newly appointed individuals should keep this in mind. The following strategies may be useful: determine their main atmospheric needs from the various categories and items noted above; endeavour to position themselves in organisations, and under people where their atmospheric needs are best attended to; and, judiciously select new roles or new employers with the same considerations in the forefront of their minds.

When the atmospherics are seriously out of alignment with individual needs, prepare and implement a defensive strategy which may include: better understanding and accepting the situation; changing your own needs and expectations; communicating with others about your concerns with a view to changing the atmospherics in the organisation; 'attacking' it (but who is likely to win, the organisation or the individual?); or 'retreating'—moving on within the existing organisation or moving out.

Getting atmospherics right or coping better when they are at variance with your needs helps create a 'I win-you win' situation for both the individual and the organisation. Getting it wrong or not coping can cause grief and lead to casualties.

In using this write-up on atmospheric needs in assimilation, the coachee needs to work out, with the coach's help, what the individual actually needs, the relevant and current cultural idiosyncrasies of the organisation, any gaps and how to close them through appropriate coping mechanisms. The coachee also needs to address the intended future cultural style of the organisation again using the atmospheric needs write-up as a checklist, the desired pace of change, how the individual can facilitate progress, and any hurdles to be encountered or props to be deployed along the way.

INTERPERSONAL RELATIONS

In sequencing coaching input during assimilation, I find that 'fertile ground' has now been created to address further the key area of interpersonal relations.

For this, the operating style element of executive coaching in Chapter 7 and of team coaching in Chapter 9 works extremely effectively. As does the in-team behaviour element of teamwork, also in Chapter 9.

However, I only use these methodologies for and with the newly appointed individual, rather than sending out surveys to other respondents which could cause alarm: 'What's going on? Peter Stephenson has only just joined us and now wants us to participate in a survey? Come on!'

Regarding leadership traits and the need to be displaying desirable leadership traits, I also use the methodology described in Chapter 7 for the executive coaching process. This enables an individual to assess what the organisation expects and to compare this with their own leadership traits, allowing the individual to modify their behaviour as needed. The theme of motivational delegation also addressed in

Chapter 7—'A typical executive coaching process' can be used to good effect in the leadership context also.

In helping the coachee understand where and how to modify their behaviour, the core coaching process of self-management of development invariably works effectively (Chapter 6—'Core coaching processes').

And finally, at this stage of the assimilation process, do not forget another core coaching process, namely that of progress reporting.

POLITICS, POWER AND INFLUENCE

Politics, power and influence represent another key topic in assimilation. Every organisation has its networks and I am not talking here about the formal lines of power and authority, but the ones which operate 'behind the scenes'. The sooner a newly appointed individual becomes aware of these networks, the sooner they can begin to use them for the further development of their image and for their own career success.

This does not mean fighting or clawing at other people's expense; such an attitude will backfire on you eventually. What it does mean is that you do not stick your head in the sand as to how the organisation really operates and who the real decision-makers are. The new hires need to take the time to look around and ask themselves the following questions:

➤ Whose advice is sought and followed?
➤ Whose criticism counts?
➤ Whose ideas carry weight?
➤ Whose opinion causes others to change theirs?
➤ At whom do people address their remarks when they make a recommendation?
➤ Who confides in whom?
➤ Who backs whose suggestions?

Endeavouring to answer these questions is not just an exercise in people-watching, but a necessary requirement for an individual's ongoing success, career protection and advancement. Once the coachee has identified the power plays and networks, they will be in a better position to use them to their own advantage and enhance their own influence. To do this effectively, they will also need feedback on how they are seen in terms of their work performance and their relationships with others. This feedback can come from the executive to whom they report, their peers and even their subordinates.

The new hire needs to be aware of how people respond to them in terms of tone of voice, their desire to know your opinion, and unspoken signals. Newly appointed individuals should not neglect to ask for feedback directly on how they are doing and where they may need improvement. In this way they can set up channels for communication and feedback which will prevent potential problems and keep them informed, rather than isolated.

However, the biggest potential obstacle in the context of 'power'—and also the most significant opportunity—is to work out where the power *really* resides in the organisation.

CASE STUDY

Take the case of the newly appointed CEO of a major division of a large group. He was appointed to follow through on some recommendations that he had made earlier while acting as a management consultant and advising on divisional strategy and operations improvement. This newly appointed divisional CEO had been told by his boss—the CEO of the overall group—to watch out for one of his direct reports, an older-style general manager who managed, in a highly autocratic fashion, one of the companies in the division.

It went further than this. The division needed rationalising and part of that rationalisation might include the early retirement of the 'difficult' general manager, who had apparently been a thorn in the side of the group CEO for years. However, the group CEO had obviously lacked sufficient intestinal fortitude to do anything about it.

The new divisional CEO went about his task and found, indeed, that rationalisation and the phasing out of the general manager in question made sense. Pressure was applied in the context of the need for change and improved bottomline performance.

Just a few short months into the job, the divisional CEO was called into a meeting with the group chairman, who had flown in from the overseas group head office. The meeting was a fight from start to finish. The chairman challenged the divisional CEO from the outset and it became clear that he was in real trouble, although the reason for this was unclear to him at the time.

The group CEO watched the confrontation like a salamander, watery-eyed and licking his lips, but making no comment and certainly not leaping to the defence of his new divisional CEO, who up to that point had made an excellent start in his new role.

Shortly after this disastrous meeting the divisional CEO received the bullet—several actually, over a period of a couple of weeks, until the coup de grâce finally came. He never knew at that time what hit him, alas.

Now for the bitter truth! The group CEO did not, after all, hold the power. The power—and in this case the forces of darkness—actually resided with the general manager. It turned out that he had a strong personal relationship with the group chairman because they had worked together closely, earlier in their careers.

The exiting divisional CEO learned a lot about power, politics and influence from this episode, although it took him quite a long time to recover from the experience! I should know—he was me!

PERSONAL SELLING

I have been involved, directly or indirectly, in executive and management development for some 25 years, and over that time I have advised countless numbers of executives and other people on how to become successful in organisational and business life, through winning at power, politics and influence. One of the key success ingredients in this area is perhaps best described by the phrase 'It's not *what* you know, but *who* you know!'

Indeed, it is clear that personal selling—selling your views, ideas and yourself to others, networking to expand your contact base of allies, and effectively negotiating with others within and outside your immediate work environment—is a critical success factor in this. The newly appointed individual needs to remember this, with the help of their coach at the outset, and into the future in their new role and career with the organisation.

I have found that people can accomplish this by developing an understanding of professional consultative selling techniques, adapting them to their own unique circumstances and honing such skills to an advanced level. In a word, what the individual is trying to achieve here is greater 'influence' and this can only be accomplished through effective personal selling and the development of informal 'alliances'.

CASE STUDY

Here are two examples of personal selling. The first was human resources director of a major food group. He used to spend core office hours circulating and meeting with senior executives and others in the company, to the extent that they took him into their confidence and depended on him for advice. They saw him as their 'ally'. He became the one person in the company with his finger on the pulse of the organisation's climate and employee morale. He also developed a strong external network of allies by working with the local chapter of the Human Resources Institute and serving on its national committee. In addition to excelling at personal selling, he was a strong delegator and relied heavily on the functional expertise of his team. He eventually became CEO and was an outstanding success in this role also.

The second example relates to another human resources director, this time of a major resources group. She attained this role because she was acknowledged as an authority on most, if not all, of the key human resources functions. Indeed, she spent much of her time in keeping up-to-date through reading (even during office hours) and attending, participating in and sometimes leading human resources seminars. Unfortunately she did not last in this role because executives and line managers within her own company found her to be inaccessible and 'above them'—too theoretical and concerned with perfection rather than Pareto (in this context, Pareto means focusing on the top 20% of work requirements which generate the 80% beneficial impact.) Clearly, personal selling was not her forte and it may never have occurred to her that, in effect, this oversight cost her her job.

The first step in making a success of personal selling is to acquire the attitude of an entrepreneur—the executive or manager seeking greater influence has the responsibility to run their business of personal selling efficiently and profitably.

Goal-setting is the starting point of achievement—we have to know where we are headed and what we hope to achieve, before we can take the steps necessary to get us there and effectively monitor our progress so that we stay on course. Goal-setting in personal selling involves the following principles: the setting of realistic, specific achievement goals; and, monitoring your goals regularly.

In order to be effective, goals must be realistic. They should be attainable, but set a little higher than would be required for easy achievement. You should have to work hard to achieve them. Setting them way out of reach, however, will only result in discouragement and eventually work against you.

The coachee's goals should also be specific, so that they can easily tell whether or not they are achieving them. To set a goal of 'improving personal selling performance' or 'making more contacts' is so general as to be meaningless. Some examples of specific personal selling goals might be:

➤ Liaise with each member of the board of directors, monthly.
➤ Touch base with each senior executive in the organisation or division at least once a week.

➤ Make four presentations a year to external groups.

➤ Develop four new external contacts and two supporters or allies per quarter.

➤ Telephone two former external contacts and one ally per week for an update.

The coachee needs to make sure their goals remain realistic in the light of current developments and changing circumstances. They should not be tempted, however, to revise their goals downward at the slightest excuse. Their goals should stand, regardless of their current performance, unless there have been major positive or negative factors beyond their control. Continuous monitoring will keep them on track and help keep their personal goals and objectives in sight and attainable.

COMMUNICATION

The coach would be wise to discuss with the coachee the fact that selling yourself, finding allies and negotiating your way to success comprise basically a communication process. Selling yourself successfully depends on your communication skills. These skills can be learned and improved upon, so as to upgrade the quality of communication and all subsequent contacts with your target audience.

What do I mean by communication? According to the common definition: 'Communication is a process by which meanings are exchanged between individuals, through a common set of symbols.' The symbols take the form of speech, written messages, facial expressions, gestures and actions. Effective communication requires both a transmitter and a receiver. Simply 'saying something' to a contact does not guarantee that communication has taken place.

In moving from you (the transmitter) to your contact (the receiver), or vice versa, there may be interference, or 'noise', which prevents the message from being properly understood. Some examples of 'noise' are:

➤ Ambiguous words and phrases such as, 'We'll meet as soon as possible'. Be more specific, such as 'We'll try to meet next Friday'.

➤ Speaking too quickly, or mumbling words.

➤ Failing to clarify. You may know what you are talking about, but your contact may not understand you.

➤ Failing to use terms which are easily understood, and trying to impress with 'jargon'.

➤ Not taking into account the mood, attitude and corresponding attention span of the receiver, your contact, in delivering your information.

➤ Not taking into account the operating style of the other party and not adapting to their style, their 'wavelength'.

Effective communication implies the correct usage of language and grammar, as well as tone of voice and volume. But it also implies the effective use and reading of body language (such as posture, facial expressions and gestures). Finally, effective communication implies 'active listening', since communication is a two-way process. Here are some rules for active listening:

➤ Be committed to *concentrating* on what your contact is saying, rather than on formulating what you will say next.
➤ Take an active *interest* in what he is saying and express your interest through your responses, facial expressions and body language.
➤ Be willing to hear your contact out fully. *Never interrupt* or try to take the words out of their mouths, as the complete story may throw more light on the situation.
➤ Try to prevent *distraction*, by shutting out background noise and movement as much as possible. Focus on the contact's face and voice.
➤ As you listen, rather than interjecting your own thoughts, *summarise* what the contact is saying, and pick out the key points.
➤ *Practise* your active listening skills at every opportunity. As with most skills, practice makes perfect!

MEETINGS

Meetings are really the meat and message of developing alliances. These are where—as with the professional salesperson—all your careful preparation, experience and training should come together eventually to convince the other party to treat you as if you were an ally. The main advantage of the face-to-face meeting is that it can be tailored to the other party. It provides you with instant feedback on their response, so that immediate adjustments can be made if necessary.

Since the communication process is two-way, you are not only giving information, but receiving it. In fact, most of those effective at personal selling act more as receivers rather than transmitters in the meeting by 'tuning in' to the other party and by practising active listening skills. Without a certain amount of empathy (where you sense reactions and respond to them), it will be difficult to establish a relationship of trust, so essential to building a close alliance.

There are six steps to conducting an effective meeting: gaining attention; arousing interest; building desire; winning conviction; getting action; and, writing notes of appreciation.

GAINING ATTENTION

Your opening statements should be such that you gain the other party's attention immediately. This does not mean that you should do somersaults or make wild, impossible claims! What it *does* mean is that you should have prepared an opening statement which introduces you and then launches into a discussion about the benefit of the topics you wish to discuss which will grab the other party's attention right away, since you know this to be a very high priority for that particular individual.

AROUSING INTEREST

Once you have gained the other party's attention, you should maintain it by arousing interest in what you are saying. This can be done by introducing a little touch of drama into your discussion. You don't let everything out of the bag at once—try to encourage the individual to become involved by holding back some aspects of the topic you wish to discuss, which you know will be of interest and thus encourage questions.

Unless you can get the other party to talk, you won't get very far. Encourage a two-way dialogue, where both you and the individual ask and answer questions. This will maintain their interest throughout the presentation and discourage distraction or 'tuning out'. If at any time you sense the individual's attention is wandering, you can bring them back by asking an open question which needs some thought to answer, rather than just a 'yes' or 'no' response.

BUILDING DESIRE

Psychologically, before the other party can make a positive decision to accommodate what you seek, they must actually want to do this. Once they reach this stage, they have a definite desire to follow through.

You can build them up to this desire by making frequent reference to how accommodating what you seek will benefit them, how their interests or needs will be satisfied, their problems solved and so forth. This should be explained in language they can understand—jargon and overly technical terms will turn them off, rather than build desire.

WINNING CONVICTION

This is where someone, or something other than you and the content of the discussion, convinces the prospect to accommodate what you seek. This can be a personal endorsement from another satisfied ally, a visit to your area, or a practical demonstration which gets the other party more involved in what you seek. In other words, at this stage you must provide the individual with proof that what you have been saying is true.

Getting action

The final step of the meeting should focus on getting the prospect to act, by signalling agreement to accommodate what you seek. There are several effective ways of doing this, often referred to as 'closing', which will be addressed later.

Writing notes of appreciation

'Thank-you' is one of the most important phrases in personal selling. By sending an email which says 'Thank-you', you will be leaving your mark or impression on the potential client. Such notes should be sent:

➤ After first and all subsequent meetings with prospects and allies.
➤ After the prospect or ally has helped you in some way.
➤ To referrers.

Other occasions include when you have had a positive telephone conversation with a contact, prospect or ally, or after an encounter with anybody who can potentially refer other prospects to you.

Pressure and stress management

These are a few of the personal selling and ally building topics the coach can usefully discuss with the coachee to their great benefit in their assimilation. Indeed, having talked over with the newly appointed individual all the major topics relating to assimilation, the coachee should be making secure and great haste up the learning curve by now. However, new working environments can still cause a lot of pressure, and 'in reserve' the coach may need some guidelines on how to survive such pressure, as noted below.

For example, the inevitable periodic conflict experienced in jobs—whether physical, emotional, interpersonal or professional in origin—causes stress. In terms of your ability to succeed and progress, a new hire may have to deal with it some day, somehow.

When you encounter a stressful situation on the job, which is not going to go away, you have basically seven courses of action open to you, as briefly alluded to earlier:

➤ *Attack it.* Dig in your heels and hold your ground, until something works out.

➤ *Ignore it.* Pretend the conflict does not exist, and keep up outward appearances.

➤ *Develop resilience through imagery.* The way I do this is to imagine I am wearing a suit of medieval armour. When the slings and arrows come my way, I do not let them through my defences. 'Ping!'—they bounce off! You really can develop resilience through imagery—try it!

➤ *Change it.* Change the situation by persuading others to change or get your role or responsibilities revised.

➤ *Change your behaviour.* Speak up more or listen more, learn to say 'no' or 'yes' to demands, or work at a different pace.

➤ *Change your attitude.* View the problem positively as a challenge or an opportunity to remain alert.

➤ *Retreat.* Remove yourself from the conflict by transferring or resigning.

Of these seven possible reactions, the first two should be avoided as they are non-productive, don't get rid of the stress and will continue to eat away at you. Each of the other five reactions will be appropriate in different situations.

There will be times, however, when you should change your own behaviour, and other times when the only sensible thing to do to preserve your career and your sanity is to quit. Before leaving, however, examine the other alternative responses, to see whether or not the conflict can be effectively handled in a less dramatic way.

We all experience stress to greater or lesser degrees, and there is a tendency to regard stress as a negative force since it seems to be the cause of so many problems, both personal and professional. If not handled properly, stress can stunt career growth and development, but it can also be a very positive force in our lives, spurring us on to greater achievements.

The problem arises when the stress becomes excessive, or our ability to deal with it is limited. People differ in their opinion of what might be a stressful situation, as what produces stress in one person may not affect another at all. Stress is a very subjective thing, depending on the individual's capacity to 'roll with the punches', the workload taken on, the tendency to worry about things in general, or how much is expected of you.

Some people are able to cope with a great amount of stress and use it in a positive way as a motivator to achievement at a very high level. However, prolonged exposure to stress in the work situation, coupled with an inability to deal with it, produces the occupational condition commonly known as 'burnout'.

Burnout has been described as an exhaustion and cynicism, which often develops after repeated exposure of people, in an intense, involved, stress-producing way, for a prolonged period of time.

How can you recognise whether you, your coachee, a partner, a friend or colleague is suffering from burnout? Symptoms will vary depending on the person's individual response to stress and on the extent or degree of burnout being experienced. Common symptoms include:

➤ Irritability with others at home or at work.
➤ Often feeling tired and lacking in energy.
➤ Feeling a lack of purpose or direction in your life, or a longing to escape.
➤ A loss of, or low, confidence.
➤ Indifference to your work.
➤ Easily becoming impatient with family and friends.
➤ Increased usage of alcohol or drugs.

These symptoms brought on by work stress illustrate a sense of 'uncaring'. Advanced burnout victims literally stop caring about the work they do or the lives they live. They stop caring about themselves and everyone around them.

In its most advanced stages burnout causes individuals to stop even going through the motions of work—they stop working altogether. This is when, if nothing has been done to solve the problem up to this point, employers are forced to take action—all too often by firing the victim. Fortunately, most burnout cases do not get to this point. The victim seeks help in time, or is forced into seeking help by a worried partner or concerned employer. Obviously, the earlier the symptoms are recognised and dealt with, the better for all concerned.

Here is a useful exercise to use with a coachee apparently suffering from excessive stress. What are your idiosyncrasies? Do they suggest you are prone to stress or avoiding it? Read over the following statements:

➤ I believe 'If you miss the plane, there will be another one soon—no need to worry about it'.
➤ It doesn't worry me being late for a meeting.
➤ I like talking about matters other than the successes I have enjoyed.
➤ I really relax with a game of tennis, handball, by swimming or by participating in other sports.
➤ I really enjoy taking a holiday and just doing nothing.

➤ I couldn't care less if I lose in a game, even if I am really good at it.

➤ I enjoy working steadily without making any fuss about it.

➤ I never seem to feel hostile or angry with the world.

➤ I lead my life so that I am hardly ever rushed.

➤ I never feel impatient.

Now read over the following group of statements:

➤ My schedule is usually crowded and I find it hard to refuse people.

➤ I enjoy being ahead of others, especially others who are competitive.

➤ When I am doing something else, such as playing squash or cards, some of the best solutions to problems at work come to me.

➤ I usually feel guilty if I do not make good use of my time and it is hard for me to relax and do nothing.

➤ I like to talk about things that are important to me; small talk bores me.

➤ Rather than wade through a whole book, I prefer reading book summaries.

➤ What really irritates me is a slow driver ahead.

➤ I am a fast eater.

➤ When I'm talking, I tend to accent key words.

➤ I always walk and move rapidly.

The coach then continues as follows.

Which group of statements sounds more like you? If the first group, then you tend to have stress-avoiding idiosyncrasies; if the second group, stress-prone idiosyncrasies. It has been determined that stress-prone idiosyncrasies are much more likely to cause heart disease, regardless of diet, weight, and even smoking patterns. Stress-avoiding idiosyncrasies enable people to handle stress better, and are more conducive to good health.

Since burnout is the result of prolonged exposure to stress, it follows that burnout can be prevented or controlled by learning how to handle stress more effectively. Even those who have not reached the burnout stage will benefit from an effective stress management program, of which there are five basic elements:

➤ *The supportive element:* being able to talk about it with a partner or close friend and developing a support structure.

➤ *The physical element:* taking exercise regularly, reviewing diet, ensuring periods of relaxation, having a health check-up annually.

➤ *The behavioural element*: resolving conflicts, reviewing your behaviour, reordering your values.

➤ *The spiritual element*: prayer or meditation, confronting ageing of self or family members, and in some cases illness or even death. Develop a philosophy of life—'What's it all about? Why am I here? What's my reason for being?'

➤ *The organisational element*: identifying causes of stress, using group problem-solving, improving work and home environment, managing time more effectively, allowing time for leisure pursuits.

In concluding with stress management, I have covered all the major topics relevant to assimilation, which the coach needs to have covered with the coachee during the first 100 days or so of the individual's appointment.

PROGRESS REPORTING AND CLOSURE

Returning to the core coaching processes (Chapter 6) the coach, line manager and coachee (HR executive too, as relevant) may meet for a closure meeting if all has progressed well, or for a progress reporting meeting if it is felt that ongoing but tapering coaching input is needed over the next, say, 100 days.

Either way, inevitably the benefits of assimilation coaching are likely to have been experienced, namely, securer, faster progress up the learning curve and in the generation of sought results, at the same time lessening the risks of costly and largely unnecessary induction turnover.

KEYNOTE

➤ Executive coaching can help new appointees assimilate with their new organisational culture.

➤ Coaching can help them quickly develop strong interpersonal relationships with key stakeholders.

➤ It helps them understand and adapt to expected leadership traits.

➤ It helps assimilate organisational politics, power and influence.

➤ Coaching can deliver mutually agreed expectations for activities and results.

➤ Why let a new appointee just 'sink or swim?'

Chapter 11

A TYPICAL EXECUTIVE MENTORING PROCESS

66 It's lonely and exposed at the top, and you can't let your guard down, ever! 99

INTRODUCTION

During the recession in the early 1990s and since then, restructuring of organisations largely centred around 'downsizing' to effect cost savings. However, this has tended to hide what also has been happening to organisations:

➤ *Globalisation*—as companies have expanded their international horizons, their competitors have become more evident in their own home markets.

➤ *Information age*—not only have computers and telecommunications enabled organisations to 'de-layer', but they have also shortened the various phases of the organisational life cycle, and opened up new 'reveal all' communication channels with customers and suppliers. The information age, with its increasing emphasis on intellectual assets, is becoming far more complex than the industrial age when managers simply managed top-down and controlled the 'factors of production'.

➤ *Leadership*—greater competition and increased customer and shareholder expectations have driven executives to become highly responsive and adaptable to the external environment. This, coupled with the changing nature and expectations of the workforce, demands competent change management and visionary leadership.

The impact of all this on organisational life is 'revolution' rather than 'evolution', the rate and pace of change accelerating to the extent that we now have the 'variable' (rather than the 'fixed') organisation. The variable organisation anticipates change, and flexes and adapts to the needs for change.

'You have to be very conscious of the fact that change is going to accelerate,' says John T. Ralph, former Chief Executive Officer, CRA Limited, when interviewed about the book *Leadership, Australia's Top CEOs Finding out what Makes them the Best*, by James C. Sarros and Oleh Butchatsky. 'You may think that we've had a lot of change in the last ten years, but there is going to be more in the next ten ...' (*The Bulletproof Executive*, HarperCollins, 1997).

It is no small wonder then that CEOs and senior executives can sometimes find it lonely and exposed at the top. And so this is where an objective, independent, confidential and very experienced mentor makes all the difference, whether providing input on a specific issue, or acting as a more general sounding board. Mentoring enables executives to tap confidentially into the highest level of intellectual capital available in such areas as: leadership, management of change, interpersonal relationships, team development, career and whole-life balance.

Whatever the orientation of the need, top executive mentors can be accessed confidentially on a regular or *ad hoc* basis. Often the mentor's input is provided over a three- to six-month timeframe, or longer, 'unseen' to other members of the organisation.

A Typical Executive Mentoring Process In More Detail

The key point to remember is that executive mentoring is an 'open agenda' form of program, reserved for senior executives who may not wish to be overly involved in a specific 'process'. However, if there is to be an organisational benefit from the program, the mentor clearly needs to focus their input either towards competence (executive coaching) or motivational alignment with the organisation (career consulting) or both. Elements of team coaching also may be usefully incorporated, according to needs.

However, as with any of the coaching programs described in this book, the mentor needs to diagnose before they can help the executive self-prescribe development opportunities. The mentor should not automatically assume, however, that any particular sequence, or the one alluded to in this chapter, is the only sequence.

For example, it may be that the core coaching needs analysis sequence (Chapter 6 —'Core coaching processes') of its own accord leads to sufficient diagnosis. If not, then there are other suggested steps which are most helpful in avoiding simply a 'talk-fest', and in making the program a high impact and beneficial experience for both the executive and the organisation.

A final point is that if the executive is averse to process, the mentor should not hand out guidelines and so forth for the executive to complete. They can be used instead as discussion prompters at the meetings—and the mentor can also make notes on them and remind and reinforce the executive at subsequent meetings.

And so in considering a typical process, and bearing in mind the caveats about sequence and handouts, many of the core coaching processes in Chapter 6 can still be usefully deployed, particularly: introducing coaching to line managers; introducing the coach (mentor) to the coachee (senior executive); needs analysis (as noted above); career review; role review; review of previous feedback; SDOT analysis and development priorities; self-management of development; psychological assessment; coaching meetings and counselling.

NEEDS ANALYSIS

In needs analysis, because of the more open agenda style which mentoring embodies, I will describe the types of questions you might use in meeting the line manager of the person to receive mentoring. If this person is the CEO, the initial needs analysis may be with their HR director.

Firstly, in addressing background, status and things which are going well in the organisation and for the individual to receive mentoring, the following questions serve as good 'openers':

➤ How is the company performing? *& what is the impact*
➤ How is the business unit/division/department of the individual potentially to receive mentoring performing?
➤ How is this individual finding things in their role?
➤ What is going well in their role?
➤ What are their strengths?

In turning to matters which may lend themselves to improvement, the following questions provide opportunities for focus:

➤ Does the executive in question, confronted by so much change and complexity in organisational life, find it lonely and exposed at the top, and difficult to keep up to date on all fronts?

➤ Do they need or would they benefit from periodic or *ad hoc* input in such areas as broad-based strategic or operational advice, specific functional expertise (people, finance, IT, acquisitions or marketing), or particular industry know-how?

➤ Are they concerned about the more conventional forms of receiving this input, from consultants or non-executive directors, the former usually requiring significant and very obvious consulting assignments and fees, and the latter potentially signalling to the board that they are weak in the area needing input?

In moving to the downside if required improvements are not attained, the following sequence of questions can be a powerful way to help the other party understand the degree of need for mentoring input:

➤ What might be the potential downside if these concerns are not overcome?
➤ The company/business unit/function being led by someone who is not up-to-date on all fronts?
➤ Inadequate understanding and attention by the executive to the following key areas: strategy or operations; functional management; industry sector know-how?
➤ If there is reluctance by the executive to avail themselves of expertise in these critical areas, then are not the best interests and performance of the business unlikely to be maximised?

By now, if the questioning process is having the desired effect, the other party is probably looking somewhat concerned, if not uncomfortable! The role of the questioner is now to turn such concerns into optimism through the next set of questions:

➤ Could the advantages of resolving your concerns include:
➤ Up-to-date effective leadership of the company/business unit/function?
➤ Leading-edge understanding and attention to strategy or operations; functional management; industry sector know-how?

➤ Maximising the best interests and performance of the business?

➤ The executive feeling less lonely and exposed at the top?

➤ And performing better, making better decisions, feeling better and being perceived to be operating at optimum?

The time should now be ripe, through more questioning, to have the needs and sought outcomes of mentoring tabled explicitly. The following questions help establish whether your needs could therefore be:

➤ For an approach which enables the executive in question to keep up-to-date on all fronts particularly in the areas of strategy, operations, functional management and industry know-how?

➤ For the best interests and performance of the business to be maximised?

➤ For the executive to feel supported and safer at the top?

➤ To significantly improve their performance, decision-making, the way they feel and the way they are perceived to be operating?

The final element of this classic needs analysis sequence is for the mentor to describe how mentoring can really add value in helping the individual to receive mentoring, attain the stated needs and sought outcomes. The core coaching processes of introducing the coach (mentor) to the line managers and introducing the coach (mentor) to the coachee (individual to receive the mentoring) (see Chapter 6), can be used as a reference point for how mentoring can add such value.

The needs analysis with the individual to receive the mentoring can be along very similar lines, as follows.

Regarding background, status and things which are going well:

➤ Tell me about your role/yourself?

➤ How is the company performing?

➤ How is your business unit/division/department performing?

➤ How are you finding things in your role?

➤ What is going well?

➤ What do you believe are your strengths?

Regarding matters potentially lending themselves to improvement:

➤ Confronted by so much change and complexity in organisational life, do you find it lonely and exposed at the top, and difficult to keep up-to-date on all fronts?

➤ Do you need or would you benefit from periodic or *ad hoc* input in such areas as broad-based strategic or operational advice; specific functional expertise (people, finance, IT, acquisitions or marketing); or, particular industry know-how?

➤ Are you concerned about the more conventional forms of receiving this input, from consultants or non-executive directors, the former usually requiring significant and very obvious consulting assignments and fees, and the latter potentially signalling to the board that you are weak in the area needing input?

Regarding the *downside* of required improvements not being attained:

➤ What might be the potential downside if these concerns are not overcome?

➤ The company/business unit/function being led by someone who is not up-to-date on all fronts?

➤ Inadequate understanding and attention to the following key areas: strategy or operations; functional management; and, industry sector know-how?

➤ If there is reluctance to avail yourself of expertise in these critical areas, then are not the best interests and performance of the business unlikely to be maximised?

Regarding the *upside* of the required improvements being attained, could the advantages of resolving your concerns include:

➤ Perceiving yourself to be an up-to-date more effective leader of the business?

➤ Your leading-edge understanding and attention to strategy or operations; functional management; industry sector know-how?

➤ Maximising the best interests and performance of the business?

➤ Feeling less lonely and exposed at the top?

➤ Performing better, making better decisions, feeling better and being perceived to be operating at optimum?

Regarding tabling the precise needs for mentoring, could your needs therefore be:

➤ For an approach which enables you to keep up-to-date on all fronts particularly in the areas of strategy, operations, functional management and industry know-how?

➤ For the best interests and performance of the company to be maximised?

➤ For you to feel more supported and safer at the top?

➤ To significantly improve your performance, decision-making, the way you feel and the way you are perceived to be operating?

And then the sequence is concluded by the mentor again describing how mentoring can really add value in meeting the explicit needs which have been tabled.

Clearly, from the above examples of typical needs analysis sequences, a range of mentoring topics can come forward and be addressed.

Selection of the mentor is of course critical. While most senior people who regularly engage in executive coaching, career consulting and mentoring can undoubtedly add value in most mentoring assignments, the needs analysis may uncover requirements for a mentor. Perhaps an additional mentor is required with specific strategic or operational expertise in such areas as people, finance, IT, acquisitions, marketing, and so forth, or for particular industry know-how. Given the vagaries of organisational life, restructuring and downsizing, fortunately the available talent pool of such expertise has been growing!

GETTING STUCK

As the mentoring program unfolds, because of its more open agenda style, the mentor may find the process 'runs out of steam' prematurely. Having said that, I rarely find this to be the case personally when mentoring, as issues and opportunities for input always seem to be abound!

But I have heard it be said that mentoring programs can get 'stuck'. When this happens, a useful trigger to generate new areas potentially benefiting from mentoring input, is to use what I term an 'effectiveness beyond leadership' checklist. I developed this checklist following my first five years in this field, based on my experience of working with some 300 senior people.

The first part of the checklist which can be used in discussion with the individual receiving mentoring, addresses *job performance* and business results, and suggests that truly successful executives:

➤ Understand, give sufficient time and priority attention to, and apply the management practices of: planning, organising, monitoring, decision-making, motivating and delegating.
➤ Know what their single most important business objective is, the primary drivers of attaining that objective, and spend their time prioritising these essential areas, rather than on less essential matters.
➤ Keep themselves fully informed about 'futures', the fast-developing external environment which impacts on their business—the economy, the market place,

the competition, their customers, technology and the business sector in which they operate; rather than taking too much of an internal perspective on organisational or administrative matters.

➤ Attract, select, retain and develop staff of the highest calibre available and have few problems in achieving all this.

The second part of the checklist addresses *personal performance* and self-motivation and suggests that for successful executives:

➤ Their main occupational interests are represented in their job, be they technical, computational, practical, medical, scientific, social, persuasive, literary, clerical, musical, outdoors or artistic.

➤ Their main capabilities—and those ones they enjoy using—are represented in their job, be they memory, verbal comprehension, numeracy, spatial ability, perception, fluency, reasoning ability, creativity, social ability, or clerical speed and accuracy.

➤ Their main values are represented in their job and work environment, be they security, integrity, social, community or environmental responsibility, personal or financial success, prestige or variety.

➤ They have developed a sense of ownership, confidence and control over their own career destiny and they know where they are headed, rather than relying on their organisation for career direction and development.

The third part of the checklist addresses leadership of change and suggests that successful executives:

➤ Exhibit the competencies of adaptability, entrepreneurism, resilience and open two-way communication with managers and staff; rather than being inflexible, status quo-oriented, stressed or overly transmittal in communicating (insufficient listening).

➤ Understand and manage the various phases associated with organisational restructuring: planning, launch, break-up, recovery and re-fire and joint gain; resulting in continuing good morale and productivity and performance improvement objectives being attained on time.

➤ At times of organisational change, emphasise the human factor, avoid 'slash-and-burn', 'hire-and-fire' and dismissals, and nurture talent (rather than talent fleeing the organisation).

➤ 'Deliver' presentations and speeches well, rather than solely concentrating on their content.

The fourth and final part of the checklist addresses personal chemistry and fit and suggests that for successful executives:

➤ Their motivational needs—material needs (remuneration, safety and security); structural needs (degree and type of structure, bureaucracy and systems); behavioural needs (management style and interpersonal relationships); and, emotional needs (trust, social needs, esteem needs and sense of achievement)— are met by the organisation for which they work.

➤ They understand and apply what their organisation expects of them in terms of leadership traits, that is the required emphasis towards people or output, creativity or control.

➤ Their operating style enhances their team effectiveness, adding value to team-work, and, they act in a fully supportive manner towards other team members, while still contributing proactively (rather than simply going with the flow).

➤ They understand and respond to organisational politics, power and influence by selling themselves, networking and negotiating their way to success.

VALIDITY

If the executive challenges the validity of these success factors—which is perfectly acceptable and can generate healthy discussion—the mentor may wish to refer to my book, *The Bulletproof Executive*, which describes these success factor areas in greater detail. Not only were they drawn from 300 or so case studies, as mentioned earlier, but my findings were also checked out with an 85-member independent executive panel before going to print, and so my empirical research does seem to have, at the very least, some good face validity. *The Bulletproof Executive* can also be used as a mentoring resource for purposes of following through on any of the themes addressed in the above checklist.

As for the rest of content or process regarding mentoring, I find the concepts, principles and practices which I have alluded to throughout this text provide a wealth of appropriate and powerful resource.

But beware! If you are personally considering offering mentoring at the senior level, until you are well versed in the various applications of, and processes for executive coaching and career consulting as addressed in this book, you could find yourself on dangerous ground! The bottomline is that executive mentoring, particularly at the senior level, is only for highly experienced, highly trained and well-supported senior mentors.

KEYNOTE

➤ There is no need to feel lonely and exposed at the top, if you have a confidential experienced mentor.

➤ An objective and independent mentor can make all the difference as to how a senior executive feels and is perceived to be operating.

➤ Mentoring can be geared to a specific issue or offered as a general sounding board.

➤ Mentoring can tap into the highest level of intellectual capital available.

Chapter 12

A Typical Major Change
Leadership Coaching Process

66 Change won't go away, it will only accelerate! 99

Introduction

The statistics are alarming. To recap, two-thirds of restructures (including mergers) do not yield sought-after bottomline improvements on time. Less than 20% produce satisfactory outcomes. One-third yield unsatisfactory levels of performance improvement or the time taken to achieve it. Seventy per cent of organisations downsizing find no immediate increase in productivity and more than 50% fail to improve profitability the year after.

The common causes of these woeful statistics are usually cited as morale and productivity. I take a different stance. Based on my nine years of Australian empirical research, I see the cause invariably as poor change leadership by the organisation's executives. Not that all executives don't know how to lead at times of change. More, that they themselves need to adjust to change quickly, if they are to be effective and timely change leaders of others. Five factors prevail:

➤ *The first factor*—As noted earlier, some companies find it takes key people in new roles or reporting relationships after a restructure or merger, nine months to become 'profitable', that is, to perform at an acceptable level.

Some perceive over 40% of them not to be performing at their personal optimum within the first year, a significant proportion of whom leave within 20 months. Clearly, if it takes this long for individuals to get up to speed, the multiplier effect on their teams and staff can be punitive.

➤ *The second factor*—Restructures create new teams. Any newly constituted executive team also needs to get up to speed quickly to generate the much needed synergy and leverage they can produce. But what often happens is a sense of caution, guardedness and even mistrust on the part of new team members. In the worst case, self-interest and powerplays can predominate, and business imperatives assume lesser priority. Again, the multiplier effect hampers, if not freezes, the progress of others dependent on team outcomes.

➤ *The third factor*—The bell-shaped curve is alive and well when it comes to an executive population's competence range in terms of change leadership. Some are natural change-agents, some are more cautious or feel more effective with dealing with the known, rather than progressing into the less well known and the inevitable ambiguity caused by organisational change. Change leadership competencies include adaptability, entrepreneurism (innovation balanced by risk management), resilience, management of restructures and above all, open two-way communication. The success of any change program correlates to the strength of these competencies in the leaders of change.

➤ *The fourth factor*—Restructures leave some key people in roles and reporting relationships wherein their comfort levels, motivation, capability and performance deteriorate. Several feel they have lost out, or their future promotional prospects are shot. This can cause negative reactions on the part of affected individuals, which can degenerate into serious interpersonal or performance issues. Until any such misalignment is fully addressed, working out the causes and implementing appropriate solutions, then the multiplier effect will again take hold, and progress by affected people and their co-dependents, will stall.

➤ *The fifth factor*—At times of major change executives and managers often find they are spending their time working with the problem areas which include lower performing staff. Higher performing employees, the talent—who often adapt to change more quickly—are thus left to fend for themselves. This can be the ideal time to poach them, the external forces, including search consultants, raising the doubts about their staying at times of 'instability' and the benefits of their moving to greener pastures. Just at the time the organisation needs them most!

I have carefully researched and developed important applications of executive coaching which add great value in attending to the factors highlighted above.

Through a new executive assimilation program (Chapter 10—'A typical assimilation process for newly appointed key people') you are able to help key people with new roles or reporting relationships significantly reducing the time it takes for them to get up to speed after restructuring, and lessen the risks of early turnover.

A team coaching program (Chapter 9—A typical team coaching process') for newly constituted executive teams fast-tracks the development of team processes and, in particular, interpersonal relationships—the base ingredients for effective teamwork.

Through a variation of the straight executive coaching program in Chapter 7 —'A typical executive coaching process' and as described in this chapter, you are able to help executives develop advanced change leadership competencies.

A career consulting program (Chapter 8—'A typical career consulting process') is a powerful way to address 'square-pegs-in-round-holes', invariably generating win-win outcomes through a sense of mutual re-alignment.

And finally, through executive coaching and/or career consulting (Chapters 7 and 8)—seen as intrinsic rewards and a statement that the organisation really cares—talented key people are less vulnerable to the poachers.

The starting point of potential involvement is an informal review with the CEO or group leader and the HR director, followed by developing a tailored solution according to group and individual needs. Once the work is under way and executives and managers themselves feel they are adjusting well to the new modus operandi, they increasingly devote their time and attention to the priorities of the day—the change leadership of their people.

A TYPICAL EXECUTIVE COACHING PROCESS DESIGNED FOR MAJOR CHANGE LEADERSHIP IN MORE DETAIL

The overall blueprint for such coaching is addressed in Chapter 7—'A typical executive coaching process'. However, the following emphasis needs to be built into all elements of the coaching process.

CHANGE LEADERSHIP COMPETENCIES

Besides knowing how to manage restructures, required competencies for the leadership of change include adaptability, certain elements of entrepreneurism, resilience, and above all open, two-way communication. Which executives and managers whom you know display adaptability, entrepreneurism, resilience and skills in open, two-way communication? How do their leadership of change competencies compare? What can they learn, and how should they adapt their behaviour to become outstanding leaders of change?

Being an outstanding leader of change is inspiring others to embrace, cope with and, indeed, excel in times of change. This requires not only being a leader of change yourself, but developing a culture and a set of business processes within the organisation which stimulate change and experimentation, and celebrate risk-taking.

Yes, leadership of change is not about charismatic leadership. Rather, leadership of change embodies the capabilities described, and ensures the necessary organisational environment exists to seek out, embrace, and exert maximum leverage from the impact of the changing external environment, for the organisation, its objectives and its people. The following anecdotes describe executives whom I believe display particular capabilities in these required competency areas.

CASE STUDY

Adaptability. One of the most adaptable executives I know is a senior executive in the information technology sector. When confronted by challenges at work, he is able to take a flexible approach to solutions, rather than assuming 'business as usual'. Indeed, he seeks variety and change at work, rather than routine, and when experiencing new situations, is curious and inquisitive.

Although upholding corporate policy, he can be seen by colleagues as sometimes being non-conformist, adapting to changing circumstances rather than resisting them, comfortable with the unexpected and interested in the unconventional. His management and leadership style changes according to the competence of the particular direct report and the urgency of the particular task, and is seen by direct reports as flexible rather than rigid in day-to-day operations.

In problem-solving he thinks 'outside the square' and actively seeks input from others when confronted by changes at work.

CASE STUDY

Entrepreneurism. *I would describe a marketing manager of a food service company as an excellent example of an 'entrepreneurial' executive. She is good at experimenting with new ways of doing things and is successful at innovation, be this in the form of new products, services, processes or systems. Indeed, she displays a certain 'daring' and tries out brand-new concepts at work, not only taking the initiative, but also accepting accountability for the results from the initiative—good or bad.*

Displaying an independent style and acting autonomously, she is as good at development as she is at straight maintenance of ongoing operations. This includes taking risks when the rewards are high, but also understanding the possible benefits and adverse consequences of taking risks. Indeed, she is good at managing risks, and at applying preventative monitoring appropriately.

CASE STUDY

Resilience. *An executive displaying this characteristic runs a medium-sized transport company. He can handle and manage stress: he avoids the negative impacts of stress at work, leaves 'troubles' at work rather than taking them home, and sleeps well and 'enjoys weekends' rather than worrying about work. Resilience also implies a capacity to persevere when the going gets rough. Indeed, he is considered to be extremely tough and forges ahead at times of adversity, getting the desired results even when confronted by difficult work situations.*

He confronts change as a way of life rather than as a hindrance, and accepts change positively. Even though the challenge may be extreme when given a job to do, he completes it and is seen as a good ally by colleagues when the going gets rough and when everyone is up against it. Resilient executives like him have to have a 'dogged streak' of perseverance, particularly at times of change or uncertainty.

CASE STUDY

Open, two-way communication. *An executive who is an excellent communicator manages a major public hospital. One of the secrets of her success is that she communicates well with direct reports, peers and superiors, keeping them informed as and when necessary. This includes her understanding of the other party's point of view before responding, and listening twice as much as talking in interpersonal communication.*

The 'physical' barriers to effective communication are understood and minimised by her—noise, outside interference, incoming telephone calls and other interruptions—as are the 'behavioural' barriers—the expectations of other parties which may be different to her own and influencing what they choose to hear. Her written communications are usually planned and well thought-out, rather than 'dashed off' too spontaneously. Similarly, her presentations to groups are well planned, with a clear objective of what is to be achieved with each particular audience.

At times of organisational change, she communicates the changes to all affected parties, both in person and in writing regularly. She has found that communicating changes once or twice is not enough at times of restructuring. She believes that the better organisations encourage employees to ask difficult and even embarrassing questions. In her view, the human resources function should champion such mechanisms.

Finally, she is seen as approachable by direct reports, encouraging questions and concerns and seeking to hear quickly about bad, as well as good, news.

In addressing these change leadership competencies, clearly the coach needs to be able to facilitate some diagnosis as to the coachee's effectiveness in these areas (which the Adeptus Process® multi-level survey includes very effectively), followed by appropriate coaching.

MANAGEMENT OF RESTRUCTURES

Similarly, when it comes to the management of restructures (also addressed by Adeptus), diagnosis and guidelines for self-prescription by the coachee are needed. The guidelines I use, this time in the form of case studies, are as follows.

CASE STUDY

First, the case of the food factory relocating some of its production lines to a new factory in another state. Unfortunately, I was involved in this exercise as a consultant too late to have any impact on the outcome.

Two years earlier, the accounting and administration departments had moved from the site to head office, an exercise which was far harder and took far longer to implement than senior management had believed possible. The casual observer might have thought that management had learned some lessons from this, but they obviously had not, for the relocation of the production lines turned out to be an even more unsatisfactory experience, for all parties.

The problems started when employees perceived that managers appeared to 'go missing'. For some reason, weekly and daily routines started to change as managers attended extra meetings, some of them off-site. During breaks and in the canteen, employees from production, warehousing and distribution compared notes. Yes, senior managers across the company seemed to be involved in some sort of planning exercise. Could it be another restructure, or worse, a closure?

The signals were certainly there that something 'big' was going on. The factory started to miss a beat or two as these signals converted to speculation. With unsettled minds on the shop floor, productivity dipped. Managers seemed not to notice. Meanwhile, a group of supervisors were heard to be talking in the canteen about the earlier centralisation of accounting and administration, and how it had never really worked out. 'Another bad decision by management!'

By the day of the announcement of the relocation of the production lines, speculation was so intense that, when employees were assembled to hear the news, there was an air of inevitability and bad omens. The upcoming changes were announced and employees learned that the decommissioning and relocation of the three production lines would be phased in over the next 12 months, and production moved to a newer factory in Queensland. The critical point made by management was the need for continuing productivity, quality and output, as consumer demand for the product lines affected was increasing. The news was received with anger and scepticism. Not only were people going to lose their jobs, but also the plan for a running handover to the new factory clearly 'wouldn't work'.

Indeed this prophecy by the sceptics became a reality, as productivity dropped and quality problems soared during the transitionary period. It was clear that building the required stock levels by the time of the handover to the new factory was going to be an insurmountable challenge.

Eventually, what the company had to do was to invest in completely brand new production lines in Queensland, rather than phase in the relocation of the more modern process and packaging equipment from the existing factory. This was at enormous extra cost, and the whole exercise took more than two years to complete.

A BETTER EXAMPLE

However, restructuring can work well provided it is meticulously conceived and even more carefully implemented.

CASE STUDY

The anatomy of a more successful restructuring can be demonstrated by the insurance company which decided to contract out its information technology department and 'call-centre' (inbound and outbound telemarketing and customer service). Rather than rush this exercise, even though cost savings and other benefits appeared significant, the company decided to take a well-planned approach in order to minimise disruption, employee resistance, and the potentially adverse impact on customer service if things went wrong during the changeover.

Six months before initiating the contract-out option, management stepped up its proactiveness in the context of staff communication. Briefings were conducted on the 'changing face of the insurance sector' and information was shared about responses by competitors to these changes. Communication was two-way at these briefings, and feedback, questions and ideas were encouraged. Managers increasingly were encouraged to become more available to staff and a more open, positive and communicative environment developed. In this way 'development opportunities' for the company were more regularly addressed and discussed, as was the need to 'move forward in response to external change'.

By the time the 'contract-out' plans were announced, the organisational environment was so fertile to receive such news, that even those directly affected seemed to accept the decision as being right for the company. What helped was the painstaking efforts by senior management to describe how this change tied in with the vision of where the company was headed, and the values or principles which drove how the exercise would be implemented, including extremely fair separation arrangements for those who would have to leave the organisation (some of them joining the two external contractors).

From initiation onwards, the exercise was a success. All staff seemed clear about their changing goals and roles, and a 'can-do' atmosphere prevailed. As progress was made, staff not only cooperated but also took the initiative and necessary modifications were made on the run in order to facilitate the changes. In this, managers seemed to be leading more from behind, staff often seeking and implementing their own solutions.

As the new information technology and call-centre arrangements settled into place, everyone felt themselves to be winners. Morale and productivity were at new heights, bottomline results flourished, and the size of annual salary increases recognised the efforts made by all and was funded by the cost savings.

Although successful restructuring can be accomplished as demonstrated, time and again, thunderbolt 'slash-and-burn' staff cuts have not resulted in the desired cost reduction and other goals. The reasons often relate to the trauma caused by such draconian measures and the negative impacts on remaining staff in terms of reduced morale and productivity.

World best practice standards

More enlightened organisations seek to attain any necessary reduction in staff in two ways. First, they do so by improving their forward planning and relying on natural attrition, internal redeployment to other more buoyant areas of the organisation, early retirement, leave of absence, study leave, secondments to other organisations, part-time work, pay cuts, job sharing and selective voluntary redundancy (retaining and rewarding talent, however).

Secondly, if they do need to move faster than this as a result of unexpected externally driven forces, for example, happenings in the market place or economy, then they do to world best practice standards.

Case study

Take the case of the finance company which decided it needed to centralise operations, reduce the number of staff and develop more of a customer focus. At the time I was called in, the company had not been performing well in terms of financial results and other benchmarks. It appeared to be overstaffed, and head office seemed to be unable to control the highly decentralised organisational structure and state-based operating business units. A recent customer survey suggested that the company was overly product-driven, and was remiss in understanding and attending to the real needs of customers.

A new managing director had recently been appointed from a consumer product manufacturing and marketing background. In his previous position he had turned a substantial food product group from a loss to a healthy bottomline.

He had achieved this by: successful new product development based on extensive consumer market research, supported by innovative 'above and below-the-line' promotional campaigns; centralising operations and closing down marginal plants; substantial staff reductions, undertaken according to world best practice standards; and, development of morale and productivity through his own inspirational leadership and the progressive implementation of a range of rebuilding initiatives.

Although the board of directors knew there was some risk in hiring a new managing director from a non-financial services background, they felt reasonably secure knowing that the company's senior executive team was comprised of excellent people with strong finance company track records. What they felt they needed was a strong new leader with a customer and employee orientation who could breathe new life into the organisation and turn around its performance through the development and implementation of innovative business strategies.

I recognised these qualities in the new managing director when I first met him, and since then I have admired the way he approached what turned out to be an enormous task, the outcomes of which exceeded even the board's expectations. I was called in early enough to get involved in some initial business strategy development sessions conducted off-site, led and facilitated by the managing director himself. In this way, each member of the senior executive team personally bought into the need for change, as well as the need for specific business development and profit improvement goals and supporting strategies.

My input concentrated on the human factor and the need for meticulous planning of the restructurings, and the team agreed that anything less than world best practice standards would be inadequate and unacceptable. The restructuring and downsizing was going to be significant, with some 350 people needing to leave over a 12-month period, from top to bottom in the organisation and throughout Australia.

The first phase of the restructuring process mirrored the earlier insurance company example: an ethos of open management was initiated by managers 'walking about' more, frequently articulating core statements about the state of the financial services industry and the need for change, along with the active solicitation of feedback to management from all employees. Concurrent to this, the organisation went into planning turbo-drive to ensure that all aspects of the change program were thought through and linked against timeframes, actions and responsibilities in a comprehensive master plan. A project planning software system was used to facilitate this.

An initial element of the schedule was my further coaching of the line managers in successful change management practices, and in how to communicate with their staff about their job losses, be they on a voluntary or involuntary basis. Included in this coaching was how to recognise and handle the emotional responses of departing staff at the time of announcing the restructure and job losses, how to risk-manage the exercise from humanistic and legal perspectives, logistics on the day of terminations, and how to communicate with and manage the 'stayers'.

The next phase looked into the dismissal avoidance strategies: natural attrition, early retirement, part-time work, job sharing and selective voluntary redundancy—all being fully considered and deployed, where practicable. In fact, the voluntary redundancy option was offered to all employees for their consideration, but with no guarantee it would be granted in each case. Loyalty bonuses were promised to key staff where their requests for voluntary redundancy were declined, the bonuses payable after restructuring and when the company attained its business growth and profit improvement goals.

As the restructure was launched, there was a dual emphasis on vision and values for the stayers, and attendance on-site by my team of outplacement consultants for individual and group meetings with departing staff. These meetings focused on the staff themselves, allowing them to express how they felt about their changing employment status. Also, a brief introduction was provided to the outplacement programs to be provided.

In selecting an outplacement provider offering world best practice standards, the managing director and his team attained exceptional results: 76% of departing staff found new jobs within 16 weeks. Because such staff were treated well during their career transitions, they reported this back to remaining staff and customers alike, which as predicted, further enhanced employee and customer perceptions of the company, morale, productivity and business results.

As the break-up of the old organisational structure was happening back at base with the financial services company, the firm continued to adopt world best practice standards by prioritising the key elements of successful leadership of change. Goals and roles were clearly identified and linked from the organisation to each individual. In moving to the recovery of the organisation, all managers—topped up with additional coaching—increasingly allowed their teams and direct reports to decide on and implement improvements 'on the run'. In fact, managers were by now truly leading from behind, rather than micro-managing from the front.

Additionally, at the break-up and recovery stage, my consultant colleagues and myself were called in to advise on, and provide progressively, a range of rebuilding interventions including counselling, coping and managing, team coaching and career consulting.

Time and again, organisations seem to underestimate the impact of restructures on remaining staff, which is why such rebuilding initiatives are invariably needed, in order to:

➤ Facilitate the timely attainment of performance improvement goals after restructuring.
➤ Enable managers to cope with change better and manage others more successfully at times of organisational change and uncertainty.
➤ Offset the risks of remaining staff feeling betrayed or becoming angry, anxious, depressed or resentful about staff departures and necessary internal changes.
➤ Similarly offset the risks associated with such emotional responses, including reduced productivity and risk-taking, role ambiguity, increased absenteeism and bailouts of talented executives, managers and staff (often the first to go when the organisation is in strife).

Thus the objectives of special rebuilding initiatives are based around rebuilding morale, productivity, performance and commitment. In this, counselling often represents the first step, as was the case with the financial services company. At the break-up stage I advised the managing director that he would need to have counsellors available, both to advise line managers on how to attend to any anxiety, trauma or grief experienced by remaining staff, and to be available themselves for direct intervention where needed.

Coping and managing skills development was provided by my colleagues and myself in two forms. First, a skills development workshop was provided to all line managers which focused on:

➤ How to cope with changes personally.
➤ How to manage others at times of change and uncertainty.
➤ How to recognise and handle the predictable elements inherent in organisational restructuring.
➤ How to minimise the intensity and timeframe of reduced productivity during transitions.
➤ How to develop leadership of change competencies.

The outcome was a much more confident and positive management group, who in fact became a much better equipped and more effective group of change leaders. Back to back with this, we provided half-day 'coping with change' workshops for all employees addressing very similar topics, yet from the employee's perspective.

The double impact of both managers developing their leadership of change skills and employees strengthening their coping skills has a highly potent effect. In fact, the managing director once remarked that he felt these particular interventions enabled the organisation to accelerate through the break-up stage to recovery, far faster than he had seen in any other organisational environment at the time of restructuring, in his more than 20-year executive career.

As new teams were brought together, we were able to assist through the provision of team coaching and group discussion sessions. The objectives and outcomes of these initiatives were the rapid development of interpersonal relationships between new team members, and the enhancement of team composition and processes.

Finally, as the organisation nudged towards the re-firing stage, and as the 'I win-you win' theme of improved motivation, productivity, organisational performance and individual reward was increasingly becoming an attainable reality, we addressed career focus by providing career consulting at mid-to-senior levels in the organisation. Outcomes *sought and invariably attained were a greater sense of control by executives and staff over their own destinies, the better development of ideas and strategies as to how to progress their careers within the restructured, flatter organisation, and the greater alignment between personal and organisational goals.*

The company re-fired and attained 'I win-you win' within its desired timeframes. End of story. No wonder the company quickly achieved sought-after employer status!

All companies can do what this company did, and derive the same benefits. Out with slash-and-burn! In with restructuring world best practice standards!

MAJOR CHANGE GUIDELINE

The final guideline I use in coaching individuals charged with the responsibility for leading and implementing major change, which involves restructure and downsizing, is as follows.

CRITICAL SUCCESS CONSIDERATIONS

Before describing an effective sequence, I will outline what I perceive to be the top seven critical success factors which need to be at the forefront of the minds of those responsible for leading and implementing major change:

➤ *Firstly*, internal changes (over which leaders have some control) are often caused by external changes, for example, market forces (over which no one has any real control). The information revolution means that change will not stop, it will only accelerate, causing one wave of change to be followed by another—even before the first wave has passed. Certainty is gone, ambiguity prevails, and leaders and their people need to understand this and adapt accordingly.

➤ *Secondly*, change is uncomfortable and rarely implemented without problems, even when well planned. This is one of the reasons why people resist change—it is hard. This resistance consumes energy, saps morale and impacts on performance and productivity—a 40% to 50% productivity drop can be experienced, and expected, as major change is implemented (yes, 40% to 50%, and over how many weeks and months?!).

➤ *Thirdly*, transitioning through major change, as a leader is like a teacher taking their class on an outing to the park, and leading them across busy roads. So join hands, make haste, focus on the priorities, route and the end game, dodge the obstacles, communicate frequently and lead proactively. And seek and celebrate early wins.

➤ *Fourthly,* major change means individuals lose things from the past. This creates confusion, uncertainty and suspicion, and causes individuals to look out for and look after 'Number 1'—themselves. That is why some of the talent will jump ship, although more lacklustre mortals are less able to do this. And where do the leaders spend their time in periods of major change? With the lacklustre mortals who need the help. Meanwhile, the talent, left largely unattended to, become wooed by the headhunters and enticed to greener pastures.

➤ *Fifth,* resistance to major change is passive as well as active. The resistance is caused through worry. Worry about: 'What's going to happen to me and to the organisation; what will we lose from the past and what's in store in the future?'

➤ *Sixth,* don't underestimate the need to communicate with staff at times of major change. If you can describe where the organisation is headed, then they need to have this communicated up to ten times for them to internalise it. If you can't describe where the organisation is headed, the continuous communication has to be the order of the day, and remember that listening rather than telling, is the important part of such communication.

➤ *Seventh,* at times of major change, don't let things get out of hand: an internal organisational focus rather than focusing on the customer and competitors; time being spent on silly things which really don't count or have little effect; time being spent on things largely outside your control; an assumption by those responsible for the planning and initiation of the major change, at the time of its launch, that everyone understands and identifies with the end game as they do, and that everyone else just needs to get on with it; an assumption by everyone else that it is management's role to implement major change, whereas everyone actually is responsible and accountable for making major change work.

EFFECTIVE SEQUENCE FOR PLANNING AND IMPLEMENTING MAJOR CHANGE

Having set the scene regarding the critical success factors, I will now describe an effective sequence for planning and implementing major change:

➤ *Planning of restructure.* Planning can be either a good news or bad news story. Even the most confidential planning process imposes change into executive routines, and staff notice this. Those extra meetings, those off-site 'seminars' all generate signals and speculation that something is going on, 'probably another restructure'. The best planning environment is one where, through a climate of 'open management', staff all realise and accept that organisations have to respond to the changing external environment, and see this as representing opportunities.

Open management requires prioritising the *proactive leadership* of the restructuring process, *an open environment*, and the *encouragement of feedback* from direct reports.

Proactive leadership includes:

➤ A preparedness to discuss the needs for, and drivers of change in organisational life today.
➤ 'Management by walking about'—rather than being office-bound.
➤ Frequent use of core statements emphasising the party line and the need for continuous adaptability in the face of ever-increasing external pressures.

An *open environment* requires that teams are encouraged to learn and to convert criticism to remedy—making necessary improvements rather than complaining about the need for improvements. Team meetings may also benefit from the chairmanship being rotated, and participation in team meetings by others from elsewhere in the organisation experiencing change.

Encouragement of feedback requires further developing the means for upward communication—feedback from the team and individuals about any issues or concerns. These matters need to be discussed and shared, and should be acted upon.

However, over the past few years when I have shared restructuring models of this nature with executives, I sometimes receive the initial response of: 'If we suddenly start emphasising open management at the planning stage of a restructure, we are at risk of causing the worst case scenario—employees will read the signals that another restructure is being planned.'

My response is usually two-fold. First, you should graduate the open management approach and initiate it in the context of improving the organisation's management practices, rather than implying—or allowing it to be inferred—that a restructure is imminent. If one is imminent, the signals will be seen anyway and open management will improve the chances of success. Secondly, employees expect and prefer open management, and perform better as a result of it, and so executives should be practising it anyway. It's never too late or too soon to move further down the path of open management!

➤ *Launch of restructure.* The launch of a restructure will either be received with scepticism by staff, who feel they have seen it all before and believe it will not work, or will be accepted positively and seen as making sense. In order to ensure the latter, vision and principles need to be emphasised at this stage and the vision as to where the organisation is headed should be presented with impact. The principles—the guidelines on what is important to the organisation and how it should operate—need to be shared and to gain group commitment.

The vision needs to emphasise benefits for all parties, and to be presented in a way which really means something to the listener. For example, rather than long-winded statements about continuous improvement, a short and sharp headline statement such as 'we will be the best in our industry' is more effective. This may seem trite to senior management, but their intended audience, staff and customers, can understand and accept such headline statements.

Vision also needs to define how the organisation will look in terms of structure, as well as the impact the restructuring will have on teams and on each individual. In fact, all the key elements of vision need to be emphasising the where, when, why and how: 'We will be the best in our industry within two years. Our customers deserve and expect this, and we will attain market leadership by providing uncompromising customer service and delivering best value for money. For this to happen we need to decentralise and work in independent business units based on each of our major product lines. You will be working in smaller work groups.'

Principles need to cascade down to individual teams, so the way each team should behave and operate should be discussed and agreed by team members. Behaviour is addressed at the individual level in terms of what is expected and what is unacceptable. The agreed principles and behaviours need to be referred to regularly, and represent the 'glue' between team members—'the way we behave and operate around here.'

➤ *Break-up of the old structure.* At the break-up stage and in the worst case scenario, resistance can often be fierce and a dogged determination not to accept the changes can prevail. However, a 'can-do' atmosphere needs to be created by executives clearly detailing goals and roles. Goals should be specific and clearly understood, and new roles should be defined, sold to, and accepted by each affected individual.

To be meaningful, organisational vision and goals should be clearly linked to individual goals. Achievement or otherwise of individual goals needs to be monitored and any adverse variances quickly and positively addressed.

Roles are invariably altered at times of organisational change, usually with an emphasis of 'doing more with less, faster'. Therefore it is a good opportunity to make jobs and work content more streamlined and thus more efficient. Efficiency improvements should be tested and modified as necessary on the run, to maximise effectiveness and productivity. No matter how well planned the restructure or the definition of new roles, modifications will always be necessary and are to be expected.

➤ *Recovery of the organisation.* As noted, it is estimated that two-thirds of restructures fail to achieve their goals within the desired timeframes. For recovery to happen more rapidly, teams need to start to feel empowered in their new roles in the different structure and to be able to make decisions and act promptly. Self-improvement through education should continue to be encouraged. In this, the manager needs to delegate more, enact the role of resource rather than controller, monitor progress and manage by exception.

Self-improvement also means that staff are encouraged to seek their own solutions, so that the work environment becomes more participative and less autocratic, and so that managers concentrate on leading from behind rather than 'micro-managing' from the front.

➤ *The organisation re-fires.* For the organisation to re-fire, all parties need to 'win' at this stage, in the context of high levels of motivation, productivity and rewards. Motivation and productivity are optimised through a sense of achievement and commitment. For this to occur, staff need to own, believe in and be inspired by the changes which have been implemented.

> *Two-way rewards.* The organisation derives bottomline benefits, and so should individuals in order to create a truly 'I win-you win' situation. Individual rewards can be intrinsic in the way individual jobs have developed—inherently more interesting and satisfying—and extrinsic, via improved remuneration. Indeed, 'shared gain' needs to be the ethos as the organisation re-fires and benefits from improved productivity and bottomline performance compared to pre-restructuring.

And so in summary, the 'bottomline' at times of major change is putting people first, constantly communicating with them, helping them see the advantages of the way forward and helping and encouraging them to handle the hurdles in getting there. This will generate the sought results!

KEYNOTE

> Most major organisational change does not produce sought-after results on time or to the extent desired.

> Executives and their teams are the cause of this—look no further!

> By displaying appropriate change leadership competencies, and by attending to five critical success factors, major change can work.

> Organisational restructuring can also work, providing best practice is understood and pursued in order to maximise the positives and to minimise the negatives in the entirely predictable restructuring cycle.

Chapter 13

A Typical Individual

Turnaround Process

> **"** If a machine, computer or system breaks down, you fix it, you don't throw it out. What happens when an executive or someone else isn't delivering? **"**

Introduction

The costs of hiring and helping executives and other key people develop can run into many hundreds of thousands of dollars. As can the costs of letting the person go—often said all-too-easily—in this era of continuing change and ever-increasing expectations for results and appropriate leadership behaviour.

Yet based on my empirical research, as well as studies conducted by several leading international outplacement companies, executives are rarely fired because of straight performance issues. Perceived operating style, levels of motivation and 'fit' often form part of the rationale, as does 'out with the old and in with the new' attitudes when leadership or ownership changes hands.

Most executives moving on in their careers, as a result of someone else's decision, invariably target and attain new roles wherein they are perceived to add great value and which they find satisfying. Their replacements in their former organisations take six to twelve months to get up to speed and are by no means guaranteed to be more successful than if their predecessor's potential had been maximised. And meantime, the 'churn and burn' causes great concern on the part of an organisation's executive cadre and staff, diluting trust and loyalty, and adversely impacting on external image as both employer and supplier.

And so, in response to client needs, I have developed a better way of resolving these 'performance' issues, which represents another powerful application of executive coaching. A typical sequence follows.

The organisation determines that, for whatever reason, an individual is entering the 'derailment zone'. If their performance, leadership behaviour, attitude, fit or other aspects of the way they operate do not show marked improvement relatively quickly and sustainably, then they are likely not to make it.

The coach provides input to the line manager in terms of identifying possible causes, needs, sought outcomes, business economic case and an appropriate form of turnaround program. Also, on how the line manager communicates all this with the individual in question. The emphasis here is best kept positive and towards upside potential through necessary improvement over an appropriate timeframe (usually three months). Over this period the coach helps facilitate the sought-after changes in the way the individual operates. In the event, as intended, that necessary performance improvement is met, then coaching continues for a further three to six months or longer, to ensure sustainability of improvement.

If perceived incremental improvement does not match expectations (progress reviews are held monthly) then the individual needs to understand from the outset that alternative roles within (subject to availability), or outside the organisation will need to be pursued, with the ongoing career transition support of the coach.

If the individual needs to leave the organisation, then appropriate separation arrangements can be made which include a level of financial support to cover the transition period. This may be more cost-effective to the organisation than in the case of a straight dismissal which backfires. The individual wins in this too, as chances are, by keeping better informed as to how they are perceived to be progressing, or in this case *not* progressing, they will resign rather than be dismissed, leaving their track record more intact. Even a 'mutually agreed separation' is better in this context.

In the worst case scenario when the individual has to be dismissed as a result of the turnaround program and the 'warnings' (even if only implied rather than expressed) at the outset and at the end of each month's progress review, the termination can be immediate and may be less risky and costly.

The organisation wins further in this. 'Fair play' has taken place and been seen to have taken place, with a beneficial impact on the morale of others within the company, and on the organisation's external image, as perceived by potential employees or customers.

To ensure such turnaround programs are appropriately planned, initiated, conducted and risk-managed, we also advocate some specialised legal counsel from a leading IR practice.

And so there is another way, a far better way of resolving individual performance issues. The sooner a possible derailment is foreseen, and the sooner the coach is called in, potentially the better for one and all.

A TYPICAL INDIVIDUAL TURNAROUND PROCESS IN MORE DETAIL

A typical approach to the turnaround process is very similar to executive coaching (see Chapter 7) but usually with greater sense of urgency, shorter initial timeframes, and more regular progress review meetings.

Turnaround or performance improvement programs can usefully be applied, following an unsatisfactory performance appraisal or, at other times, when an individual's performance is perceived as being below satisfactory or deteriorating.

Such programs are often given a timeframe, anything from three to six months, and indeed, have a start and end date with specific objectives, action plans and review dates which more often than not are monthly.

In addition to ongoing reviews, regular discussion is needed regarding all key incidents—good and bad—between the individual and their manager. The human resources function can also usefully be involved, with an HR executive present at pre-, interim- and post-reviews. The goals, of course, are to improve personal performance and to prevent the situation deteriorating into a dismissal, which is invariably avoided when such processes are given the attention and priority they deserve.

If, however, they do not result in improved performance to the extent required, then the process can be extended, or the individual may be transferred to another job position, demoted (and what has happened to the demotion option? It is rarely seen these days) or dismissed. The key is that all concerned in the process understand and agree on the goals and the alternatives at the very outset of the program.

Additional key elements of such programs include:

➤ Regular feedback regarding progress and regular coaching sessions—continual emphasis is needed.
➤ Specific written objectives which spell out the results to be achieved, the extent of the desired achievements and the timeframe.
➤ The results being sought, not just effort.
➤ Mutual acceptance of objectives, attained by their joint establishment and agreement.
➤ A mutual understanding of what non-achievement may result in, for example, demotion or relocation (internal or external).
➤ Fewer objectives rather than too many—'less is more'—and too many objectives may be received negatively by the incumbent, reducing their tolerance for the whole exercise or negative feedback.
➤ Opportunities for the individual to have progress recognised, and to receive help with any required corrective action.
➤ Written records regarding progress.
➤ A supportive approach throughout.
➤ When progress is not being realised, the restatement of possible outcomes and benefits of making progress, and possibly the establishment of new interim objectives.

What are some of the reasons for needing turnaround or performance improvement programs?

JOB PERFORMANCE

First, even the most basic management principles and practices can be missing at the executive or manager level, and you do not have to go to business school to learn them. Short courses abound, but there has to be at least some basic motivation and organisational support to bring new knowledge back to the workplace and convert it into applied skills.

People management can also be a deficiency. There has to be quality time devoted to the process of staff management, which in itself can be a challenge, given the shortage of time in today's climate of 'doing more with less, faster'.

In this, many executives and managers fail to attract and develop staff of the highest calibre available, as a result of:

➤ Selection and development practices which do not ensure 'career alignment'—the alignment of the goals of the individual with the goals of the organisation.
➤ A 'slash-and-burn' approach to downsizing and staff reductions.
➤ A 'hire-and-fire' mentality towards staff.

Clearly, executives and managers need to ensure the organisation has a favourable public image and is a sought-after employer in order to attract talent—the starting point of exceptional job performance for individuals *and* their line managers. Compounding all this, over the past few years, spans of control for executives and managers—the number of staff directly reporting to them—have increased and widened substantially, as a result of decentralisation and the 'de-layering' of organisations. This means, in effect, that there is a danger of the manager being spread too thin and spending a disproportionate amount of time on non-essential matters.

This coupled with a failure to prioritise the primary 'drivers' of the business— either financial, physical or human (usually a combination of the three)— can result in the executive or manager operating across too broad a front, rather than being focused on the main result areas. They often fail to succeed as a result.

Additionally, with all the organisational change and restructuring which has been occurring and which will continue to accelerate as we move into the 2000s, executives and managers can often become too inward looking and fail to realise what is developing in their external environment. This can either be at the customer or competitor level.

The fast developing environment within which the organisation operates presents opportunities and threats. Resources and priority attention need to be dedicated to the assessment of these external 'futures' and the development of appropriate business strategies.

However, less than 20% of executive and manager problems potentially leading to dismissals, if uncorrected, are triggered by straight job performance inadequacies in the areas I have described. More than 80% of the problems result from one or more of a range of criteria, as noted below.

Personal performance

One potentially derailing problem area is when the executive, manager or key person is perceived not to be performing at their personal best. Sure, the business results may be there, but the individual seems not to be giving of their all and is perceived as 'going through the motions' at work. Self-motivation seems to be the problem. Left unattended, the situation can deteriorate into a separation, be this voluntary or involuntary.

On closer examination, the reasons for this often relate to the fact that the individual's main occupational interests are not represented in the job. We all have different interests, for example for some it may be helping people, for others it may be being persuasive, for others, problem-solving. As noted in Chapter 8—'A typical career consulting process', if your interests—what you ideally like to do—are not to be found in your job, then job satisfaction can be adversely affected, as well as self-motivation and personal performance.

The same can be said of your capabilities, what you excel at. If the capabilities you were born with, or which you have developed over the years, and in particular, those capabilities you enjoy using ('motivational capabilities') are not represented in the job, then the situation can again deteriorate in terms of job satisfaction and self-motivation. Capabilities include numeracy, fluency, reasoning ability and several other categories.

The same is the case with your values—what you believe in. Values are the beliefs we uphold at work, home and in the way we live. Integrity, security, financial success and a range of other values can exist in differing mosaics in us all. If our values are not upheld in our work, dissatisfaction often results. These values become less negotiable as the years unfold and so are particularly significant at the executive and managerial level.

Additionally, most people these days perceive their employers with mistrust. 'The days of the career-for-life employer are over' and 'Cradle to grave is a thing of the past' are now commonly held beliefs.

Yet, ironically, executives and managers usually spend more time planning their holidays or home extensions than their careers. Few have replaced mistrust and a sense of vulnerability with a sense of personal confidence and control, through career direction and 'ownership'. The missing ingredients so often are the tools for personal career planning and necessary self-development, which together can make senior people impervious to the vagaries of organisational life and continuously employable (no matter who your future employer may be!) Developing a sense of control over your own career destiny in this way, significantly improves self-motivation and personal performance with your current employer.

CHANGE MANAGEMENT

Next, change is here to stay. Technology has accelerated the various phases of the organisational life cycle—start-up, early growth, subsequent growth, the adolescent/turbulent years, maturity and decline. Change in organisations has advanced faster than anyone's expectations and will continue to do so. This, coupled with the return to the core competencies of the organisation—process re-engineering, mergers, acquisitions and divestments, and never-ending changes in the external market place—has meant that change is a major part of ongoing organisational life.

Executives have to be able to embrace change personally rather than resist it, and to lead others at times of change, uncertainty and turbulence. Indeed, executives and managers have to be 'leaders of change'. Yet, how many executives and managers are born with these characteristics, and how many have had help from their organisations in developing the required competencies? What are these leadership of change competencies? Where do you start?

As addressed in Chapter 11—'A typical executive mentoring process', certainly adaptability will help, as will more of an entrepreneurial approach. A dogged streak of perseverance when the going gets rough will also be needed, as organisations continue to flex and adapt to the fast developing external environment. Additionally, understanding the various phases of restructures and how to manage them requires competencies very much in vogue for as far into the future as anyone can see.

Leaders of change always need to prioritise the human factor, avoiding staff dismissals, whenever possible, and continuously seeking to select, align and retain talent. An organisation, its executives and managers are only as effective as their people.

Finally, leaders of change require skills in proactive, open, two-way communication. This includes group as well as individual communication. At times of change in particular, executives and managers need to be able to generate presentation impact in the way they communicate with groups. However, most presenters concentrate too much on the 'content' of their speeches and too little on 'delivery'—the real driver of impact. In fact, delivery accounts for more then 90% of the group presentation success formula.

EXAMPLE

A very bright executive was in the habit of talking too quickly and apparently not listening to others. This, coupled with a dominant streak, put people off. Executive coaching has since enhanced the individual's ability to engage with others and attain their greater support and contribution.

PERSONAL CHEMISTRY AND FIT

In looking at that other potential derailer, personal chemistry and fit in addition to whether the executive or manager 'fits' in the conventional sense, the organisation's culture and management style or 'atmospherics' need to meet the expectations and needs of the individual in order to maximise personal effectiveness. For example, the bureaucrat trying to develop a career in an entrepreneurial environment, or the entrepreneur in the government bureaucracy. They don't fit.

It goes further than this in fact. As noted in Chapter 10—'A typical assimilation process for newly appointed key people', atmospherics also include material benefits, interpersonal relationships and the need to achieve. If individual motivational needs in these areas are not met, it can cause a negative and even stressful reaction on the part of the individual, which is then perceived by others to be a chemistry or fit problem.

And as discussed in Chapter 7—'A typical executive coaching process', organisations often expect quite specific types of traits in their executives and managers. They often seeking 'modern' leadership traits to help propel them into the future, and at the same time discarding, via dismissals, the 'old' style of leadership traits.

Modern leadership traits include a visionary approach, open-mindedness, a customer service orientation, and an emphasis on developing people. Old style traits often are more autocratic, bureaucratic, unaccepting of diversity in people, and emphasising supply and production.

Executives and managers also need to be perceived as making a significant contribution to the team, by exhibiting and adding value through different personal operating styles, perspectives and viewpoints to their colleagues.

Yet so often we see the case of the 'halo' effect at times of hiring—the CEO recruits an executive of similar operating style, causing in the worst case scenario, a cloning of the executive team. Initially, the new recruit may well 'fit' in the team, but as the months go by the individual's team contributions may not be seen to add significant value—too much 'me too'.

Teamwork can cause problems too, both for the team, and the individual. As explained in Chapter 9—'A typical team coaching process', time and again researchers reveal that the best performing senior executive teams are balanced in terms of the operating style of the members. A combination of styles is required, some, perhaps, great analysts, others more creative in their approach, others more results orientated, and yet others focusing on the human perspective. But even *with* balanced team composition, some team members seem preoccupied with jousting with each other—a potentially destructive rather than synergistic activity—whereas others just sit on the fence!

Finally, executives and managers may fail to understand or respond appropriately to organisational politics, power and influence. As noted in Chapter 10, they often fail to realise that those in real power may not be those in the senior ranks. In this way they may also fail to sell themselves, develop a supportive network of allies and negotiate their way to success.

Like it or not, politics, power and influence are alive and well in even the most results orientated environment, and executives and managers need to learn how to play this game constructively, and win!

And so having overviewed the primary causes creating the need for turnaround or performance improvement programs, I will now go into greater detail about some of them, which so far I have not addressed in detail in other chapters: primary business drivers, basic management practices and external futures.

PRIMARY BUSINESS DRIVERS

As noted earlier, one of the biggest problems in business today is the breadth of responsibility held by most executives and managers, exacerbated by the removal of middle management positions. Whereas in the past, management science suggested that seven direct subordinates (each representing a discrete management function) was about an ideal span of control, it is not uncommon today to see senior executives with a dozen or more direct reports.

Even if an executive or manager has a smaller team than this, compare today's breadth of additional responsibility to ten years ago in terms of such time-consumers as equal employment, age discrimination, unfair dismissal, protection of the environment, enterprise bargaining, occupational health and safety, quality accreditation and so forth. The list is seemingly endless. Senior people often feel spread too thin. Time and effort is dispersed across too broad a front. Primary business drivers are insufficiently attended to, as secondary business drivers and time-consuming matters predominate.

Clearly, executives and managers need to withstand being sucked into this vortex, determine what the principal business objective is and devote maximum time, effort and resource to the primary business drivers which will best deliver this objective. Developing this further, what is your single most important business objective right now or in your last executive or managerial position? You are only allowed one objective, the most important one! What are the two main drivers of your principal business objective? In other words, the two activities and result areas which will have the greatest impact on attaining your principal business objective? Which secondary drivers drive your two main drivers? Which supporting drivers drive your secondary business drivers? Which of all these drivers, if prioritised, can be most improved and will have the greatest impact on your principal business objective?

This approach, which I refer to as the hierarchy of business drivers, leads to a better understanding of the *primary* business drivers, usually found at the secondary, or other supporting levels, which can have the greatest impact on overall business results.

CASE STUDY

By way of an example of primary business drivers, let us examine the case of an autonomous division of a large manufacturing and distribution company. We helped the general manager develop his hierarchy of business drivers as follows.

The principal business objective in this case was return on total assets expressed as a percentage, as supported by the two main businesses drivers of net pre-tax profit and assets employed in the business. These two main drivers were supported by the secondary drivers of sales, operating expenses, fixed assets and current assets, which in turn were supported by a range of supporting drivers—a fairly classic hierarchy of business drivers for a company, in fact.

Given the need to attain the principal business objective of maximising return on total assets, and by developing a complete hierarchy of drivers, the general manager with our help then determined which drivers were 'primary'. In other words, he determined which drivers he was able to improve most and which had the greatest impact on improving his principal business objective, and the ones he therefore needed to prioritise.

In addition to the hierarchy of drivers approach, enabling executives like the general manager to determine their primary business drivers, and which ones to prioritise at any given time, the hierarchy can also be superimposed on the organisation structure of the business, with relevant direct reports and their teams being held accountable for results in primary business driver areas.

The general manager in this case did this with great success. He found that the superimposition of the hierarchy of drivers on his organisation structure had a strongly unifying effect on his team—they all pulled together in the pursuit of maximising return on total assets, which they nearly doubled in three years!

CASE STUDY

Another example of primary business drivers is the case of the general manager sales and marketing, let us say, of a 'tobacco products manufacturing and marketing company'. He had inherited a new CEO who had initiated a broad range of process improvement programs, to the extent in fact, that wheels were spinning and results suffering.

In trying to help the general manager prioritise, I decided to use the primary business drivers approach which went something like this.

We agreed that his principal business objective was to substantially increase profitable sales growth (I would rather not quantify this objective in this book, the quantified target being commercially confidential). The two main business drivers were increasing sales revenue and increasing margin.

These two main drivers were supported by the secondary drivers of selling more to existing grocery and route customers and increasing the number of new vending and route customers (for increasing sales revenue); selling more to the more profitable route customers and decreasing costs in the case of less profitable grocery customers (for increasing margin).

The next level of drivers was improved category management and competing more on the basis of quality of service (for selling more to existing grocery and route customers); exploiting underdeveloped channels and increased distribution in existing channels (for increasing the number of new vending and route customers); identifying and prioritising the more profitable customers as well as tailored growth plans for them (for selling more to the more profitable route customers); and, better identification of cost drivers and a tailored plan to maximise returns (for decreasing costs in the case of less profitable grocery customers).

Having mapped out the hierarchy of drivers in this way, further analysis indicated just three major strategies to be prioritised. These previously were just three of the broad range of process improvement programs initiated by the new CEO, causing spinning wheels and slipping results. And these three were clearly seen to have a major and sustained impact on helping the general manager sales and marketing and his 1000 strong permanent and part-time team, better achieve their principal business objective of substantially increasing profitable sales growth. They were:

➤ *Maximising profitable sales revenue growth through existing grocery and route customers by selling more to them and increasing market share through advanced category management techniques and the acquisition of permanent secondary space.*

➤ *Increasing margin by better understanding the cost structures and tailoring specific plans for high volume and low profit grocery customers, in other words, developing profit and loss statements for each major grocery customer and implementing margin improvement plans.*

➤ *Increasing revenue by identifying new customers in existing vending and route channels and implementing appropriate service plans.*

By concentrating on these three major strategies—having put together a convincing case based on primary business drivers to the new CEO—results improved dramatically and the principal business objective was achieved.

BASIC MANAGEMENT PRACTICES

Turning to basic management practices, the areas which can often represent one or more priorities for purposes of turnaround or performance improvement include planning, organising, monitoring, decision-making and communicating. These are in addition to other management practices addressed elsewhere in this book, for example, delegating and motivating in Chapter 7—'A typical executive coaching process'.

Below, I provide checklists which can be used both for diagnosis and self-prescription (by the coachee with the help of the coach), as well as for ongoing coaching focus.

PLANNING

➤ Is good at planning and objective setting, and establishing the strategies to accomplish these objectives.

➤ Anticipates problems in progressing from planning to implementation, and reviews progress.

➤ Updates plans according to progress and external conditions, making necessary changes to plans.

➤ Ensures objectives are quantified and stretching, yet attainable, and address what, when, where and how.

➤ Ensures staff are involved in the planning process and understand what is expected.

➤ Is proactive rather then reactive to external changes which impact on the organisation.

➤ Sees planning as continuous rather than one-off (i.e. not just an annual event).

➤ Displays a capacity to conceptualise, be creative, think outside the square and take an external perspective.

➤ Ensures planning receives top management commitment, priority attention, necessary time and resources.

➤ Ensures planning focuses on effectiveness (outcomes and achievements) and efficiency (inputs and processes).

ORGANISING

➤ In terms of organisation, ensures that all relevant parties understand the structure and reporting relationships.

➤ Ensures people are organised in the most effective, efficient and flexible ways to attain desired objectives.

➤ Ensures coordination is enhanced by everyone knowing who is responsible for what and accountable to whom.

➤ Ensures jobs are well defined but 'broad-banded' and flexible enough to adapt to changing operating conditions.

➤ Ensures span of control—number of job positions reporting to him/her—is neither too broad nor too narrow.

➤ Ensures people are clear about with whom they need to liaise and to whom they report.

➤ Ensures opportunities for delegation are maximised, but 'abdication' is avoided.

➤ Ensures organisational arrangements maximise morale.

➤ Ensures teams comprise people with different operating styles, rather than 'clones' of the team leader.

➤ Ensures teams are empowered and encouraged as far as possible to be self-directing.

MONITORING

➤ In monitoring progress, ensures that goals and objectives are attained according to plan.

➤ Ensures monitoring is orientated towards preventing problems, rather than having to resolve them.

➤ Ensures preventative monitoring helps employees know what is expected with regard to: quality, quantity, time, cost.

➤ Ensures employees know their job parameters, scope of responsibility, authority and accountability.

➤ Ensures maintenance monitoring focuses on key result areas, signalling if progress according to plan is adverse.

➤ Ensures key result areas for staff are specific: orders, units, errors, complaints, dollar volumes and costs.

➤ Ensures monitoring takes the form of on-the-job supervision and management by exception.

➤ Ensures mutually agreed personal performance standards define the outcome of tasks satisfactorily performed.

➤ Ensures appraisal processes regularly check performance against standards and development needs.

➤ Ensures development needs are quickly and effectively addressed via counselling, coaching or training.

DECISION-MAKING

➤ Ensures decision-making is sound, selecting a course of action from a range of alternatives.

➤ Ensures decision-making starts via fully defining and understanding the problem or opportunity.

➤ Ensures all facts are analysed, evaluated and interpreted in the context of the problem or opportunity.

➤ Ensures a range of solutions or options is developed, and alternative potential decisions addressed.

➤ Ensures alternatives are compared and ranked, the overall ranking determining the decision.

➤ In defining the problem, ensures root causes as opposed to symptoms are addressed.

➤ In collecting the facts, ensures they are true and valid facts, rather than guesses, opinions or lies.

➤ In examining all possible solutions, ensures creative, 'outside the square' thinking is encouraged.

➤ Ensures problems and opportunities are shared, and that all parties to contribute to decision-making.

➤ Ensures a 'bottom-up' as well as a 'top-down' approach in decision-making is undertaken.

COMMUNICATING

➤ Communicates well with direct reports, keeping them involved, whenever necessary.

➤ Communicates well with peers, keeping them informed, whenever necessary.

➤ Communicates well with his/her more senior colleagues, keeping them informed as necessary.

➤ Listens twice as much as talks and understands the other party's point of view before responding.

➤ Understands and minimises the physical barriers to effective communication, such as noise and outside interruptions.

➤ Understands that expectations of others are often different to your own and impact on what is heard.

➤ Communicates precisely and concisely in writing, planning written communications.

➤ Plans formal oral presentations and is clear about what is to be achieved with the audience.

➤ At times of change, communicates with all affected parties, both in person and in writing, repeatedly and regularly.

➤ Is seen as approachable, encouraging questions, and wanting to hear about bad, as well as good news.

EXTERNAL FUTURES

Moving to external futures, the emerging changes external to but impacting on organisations, the same reasons which prevent executives and managers from determining and concentrating on primary business drivers—too much to do, too much an internal focus on time-consuming activities, being spread too thinly—prohibit many of the same individuals from remaining alert to the developing external environment. And this too can be a potential de-railer. Although turnaround in this area may take some time to transfer into results, where there is perceived to be a potentially derailing deficiency through an individual being too internally focused, at least being *seen* to becoming more externally focused may alleviate the threat of derailing, assuming results follow.

In these rapidly changing times, we can no longer assume that past trends will repeat themselves in some predictable cycle. It is highly likely that the future will bear little or no resemblance to the past. In order to assess futures, we must look forward, not backwards, to try to get an idea of where the future opportunities will be in the context of several external areas: technological, economic, political, social, customers and competition.

TECHNOLOGY

There seems to be no disputing the fact that the rapid growth of technology is having, and will continue to have, a dramatic impact on executive management. What new kinds of businesses will new technologies create? Where will future business opportunities lie? Which sectors will experience growth in the years ahead? Which sectors will experience decline?

The impact of technological change must be viewed in relation to your own organisation and executive and managerial aspirations. For example, the continuously increasing trend towards automation in offices and factories has shifted the focus from manual to mental skills. Specialised knowledge, skills and decision-making abilities are in demand more than ever, and those organisations and individuals possessing and developing them will hold the power, as others come to depend on their expertise.

How can you make sure that you will be ready to respond to the technological and indeed other changes when they arrive? You can do this by keeping a close watch on the environment for 'signals'. It commences with innovation, when someone or a company develops some form of breakthrough or discovery. Next is the media stage when it is written up in publications, papers or other forms of print and media (for example, radio and TV announcements). This is the time to be alert and monitor such indicators of future developments. Next is the material stage when prototypes, models, or pilot batches take the innovation concept to a more material form, often a test launch or limited initial release. Again, careful monitoring is needed. The next stage is that the material form becomes refined, modified or made more effective, and indeed is produced and made available on a wider scale. The final stage is widespread usage, in other words, market acceptance, and by now it is history!

By monitoring at the media stage, and then at the material stage, an individual may well be able to predict future trends and influences to their own and their company's advantage.

Thus the impact of innovation can be determined years before it actually affects your business or yourself in any major way. All it takes is to be aware of developments around you, stay up-to-date with your reading, talk to people who are involved with technology and other forms of innovation, and know what the predictions are and how they may affect your business plans or you. Constant monitoring is essential in order to plan effectively to take advantage of future business and personal opportunities.

ECONOMIC VARIABLES

Economic variables in the environment can certainly affect business as well as personal performance, as some of us are painfully aware today. For example, a prolonged recession causes many people, who might otherwise upgrade their buying patterns and behaviour, to stay put. It is precisely in times like these that previous contingency planning pays off, because it provides options not available to those who neglected to plan ahead. Knowing how to prepare for economic conditions will lessen the chances of your organisation or yourself being 'left out in the cold' when hard times hit, or when the economy swings upward again.

In looking at the economic environment, we are basically looking at those factors which influence the demand for your products or services, their supply from other sources, and the competition for marketing them in the economy. Too many executives and managers ignore the impact of economic cycles when business planning. In good times the tendency is to reap the benefits of demand with little concern for the future. Then, when the hard times hit and the demand falls off, there is a struggle to develop new products and services, which should have been developed earlier in anticipation of a downturn in the cycle. This all takes its toll in time, money and frustration. Economic cycles and a variation in demand are a fact of life.

POLITICAL VARIABLES

In developing business plans, it is also becoming more and more necessary to take into account political and legal implications. As we are all aware, the various levels of government are affecting our lives to an ever-increasing degree. For example, tax legislation has a great influence on personal lifestyles and business performance. It can also affect business decisions such as whether or not to develop and launch new products.

SOCIAL VARIABLES

Environmental shifts in social attitudes, behaviour and values, should also be taken into account in business planning. Understanding social trends puts the executive or manager in a better position to take advantage of potential business opportunities.

For example, we see an increasing number of dual-career marriages, where the career plans of one partner must take into account the career aspirations of the other. We also see a switching of 'breadwinner'/'housekeeper' roles with more men tending families, while women provide the family income. Such social trends can affect your business and personal performance, but should be seen as opportunities rather than threats, with careful business planning and full consideration of external futures.

CUSTOMERS

The four external areas already mentioned also affect the lifeblood of any commercial organisation—customers—and their requirements from your organisation. Being aware of the impact and how it converts into customer demand is perhaps the single most important area relating to external futures. Continuous customer monitoring and evaluation is needed, rather than an assumption that they will continue to purchase your products or services in the same or increasing volume as in the past and through the same methods of distribution.

COMPETITION

Competition is also affected by all these external factors, in terms of competitor responses to the changing market place, and their reactions to your organisation as a competitor. Unless you are carefully tracking your competitors, it is only a matter of time before you get caught out. Yet it is surprising how poor competitive intelligence can be, or how quickly it can become outdated. Continuous tracking is required both formally (perhaps via external specialists, who may be better placed to do this) and informally through the eyes and ears of customers, suppliers and staff.

These are but some of the areas representing opportunities for turnaround and performance improvement, or threats relating to potential derailment if they are left unattended to. The former can prevail and the latter be avoided, by incorporating them into an executive coaching program, as appropriate, and with the help of the coach and line manager. The best coach is, of course, the line manager!

Clearly, to address where major problems lie in turnaround or performance improvement programs needs careful and comprehensive diagnosis. This can be undertaken through needs analysis and other feedback. One example is use of the Adeptus Process® which in fact surveys or assesses every single subject area described in this chapter.

KEYNOTE

➤ Executives and other people can be turned around, just like businesses can be turned around.

➤ They need to know expectations for activities, behaviour and results along with clearly articulated shorter term objectives and timeframes.

➤ They need encouragement and a support structure along with regular feedback as to how they are progressing.

➤ And in all of this, the coach's role is vital to make sure that it happens, and it usually does!

Chapter 14

A TYPICAL CAREER TRANSITION

PROCESS

❝ You can be sure about one thing in your career. There will come a time when you have to move on! **❞**

INTRODUCTION

Over the past 15 or so years economic rationalisation in Australia has caused tens of thousands of executives to change jobs or occupations. Organisational life has become far more complex, unpredictable and competitive. This means that any executive or indeed any individual in career transition—whether moving to another role within the organisation or externally—needs to focus on the future and carefully define personal directions based on a clear understanding of self-image in the changing career environment. They would also be wise to look back and learn from the lessons of their past for purposes of risk managing their future career directions and success. They also need to take great care during the assimilation period in their new role, in the context of getting up to speed quickly and sustainably.

Career transition support needs to gear coaching and career consulting solely towards what each individual requires, rather than make bland assumptions. This places the full value of input to where it is needed most, compared with the bundled, costly approach which outplacement consultants seek to provide in largely undifferentiated and outmoded fashion. Options for input at the executive level include:

➤ *Agreed reasons for career change and references*—in order to facilitate a successful transition, both for the organisation and the executive, the development of mutually acceptable, supportive, credible 'agreed reasons' and 'references'.

➤ *Career planning and strategy development*—to help the executive evaluate career options. For a range of processes some may use my proprietary Australian Adeptus Process® methodology developed from my self-assessment instruments.

➤ *Lessons of the past*—an optional in-depth review of previous performance evaluations, psychological tests and related diagnostic data. This could be bolstered where possible, by third party interviews to assess strengths and development needs as a vital input to self-image and career targeting, followed by appropriate development coaching.

EXAMPLE

I had been consulting with the particular organisation and senior executive on internal career moves, and the time had now come for the individual to move on in her career externally. The executive chose to continue working with me since career transition is yet another application for career consulting and coaching. The latter in this case enabling the executive to learn from some of the lessons of her past—not to repeat them when selecting, attaining and excelling in her next career step.

➤ *Career attainment*—covers all aspects of career strategy implementation. A particular emphasis is placed on self-presentation, self-marketing channels, interview skills and negotiating.

➤ *Direct marketing*—offers a self-marketing opportunity often poorly attended to in terms of targeting and materials (typically letter and résumé). While I always advocate networking as a priority, followed by executive search, and management recruiters, the coach needs to be able to utilise direct marketing expertise to help design and implement a campaign. Direct marketing is particularly relevant to 'baby-boomers' who are often precluded from shortlists by executive search firms because of their age.

➤ *Portfolio careers*—assessment of relevance and fit, and comprehensive support and advice in pursuing the options of contracting, consulting, non-executive directorships and not-for-profit.

➤ *Own business*—I used to consult, and lecture in small business management in North America and produced and ran courses in evaluating and starting a business, cash flow and financial management, small business marketing, and HR management. Having owned and operated five small businesses myself, I am able to make my experience and expertise available to those considering their 'own business' option, in addition to my proprietary new business feasibility and planning processes. If a coach does not have experience running his own business, at the very least the individual in career transition will need to network with other business proprietors and seek their counsel.

EXAMPLE

After a long and successful career with a major group, a director of one of the subsidiaries decided he would move on in his career and seek to start his own small business. During the notice period I was able to sharpen his focus through career consulting and help him determine preferred options, facilitated by use of my proprietary new small business evaluation and planning processes.

➤ *Assimilation into the new work environment*—the coach should help the individual understand and adapt to the new job, boss, stakeholders and organisational culture, in order to achieve and secure early success. Coaching input and support should be sustained beyond the 'honeymoon' period, after which reality sets in, and sometimes bites!

➤ *Office facilities*—with the advent of the home office, and today's greater acceptance of the near inevitability of job change, experience shows that executives in career transition often do not need such facilities, or at most, only use them on a very occasional basis. Also, for many executives there is a stigma associated with attending and using outplacement facilities, where no matter how hard the service provider tries to segment the audience—

that is, keep and treat executives separately—they are bound to 'bump into' people they would rather not meet at an outplacement facility. And so office facilities can often represent an unnecessary and costly expense.

➤ *Other services*—from time to time executives and others in career transition may need financial planning and advice, psychological support, a health check-up, industry and business research, and international referrals (in the case of an international job search). Coaches need to refer individual executives with such requirements to appropriate service providers.

A TYPICAL CAREER TRANSITION PROCESS IN MORE DETAIL

Career transition processes initially are very similar to career consulting (see Chapter 8) and also contain many of the core coaching processes described in Chapter 6.

This chapter will therefore address the main differences, starting with how the coach can assist in planning, line manager coaching and attendance at the time the individual is notified of their career change. The following points address this:

➤ Who notifies the individual of the career change? Preferably the line manager in the presence of an HR executive.

➤ Who has advised the person on legalities of career change, how notification will be made and on separation package? Always advise the individual to involve the company lawyer or refer to an external IR specialist lawyer. Emphasise the complexities from the legal perspective and do not advise— coaches are not lawyers!

➤ When will the change be notified? Preferable early in the week and late in the day, as professional support (the coach and others) is available. Never on Friday!

➤ Where will the change be notified? Preferably in neutral meeting room, away from peering eyes, with coach available close by so that he or she can be brought into the room as the line manager and HR executive leave.

➤ Coach's role at post-notification meeting? I suggest the following sequence: handshake; introduce self; 'How are you so-and-so?'; 'Were you expecting this or was it a complete surprise?'; allow the individual to vent and don't feel you have to talk; try to draft 'agreed reasons for career change' list or at least get the individual to consider it; in the event of any resistance to coach input, use the *needs analysis* core coaching process (see Chapter 6); schedule next meeting and invite partner to join meeting; advise the individual not to make contact with any business people until after next meeting you and until 'agreed reasons for career change' list is agreed with line manager and HR executive.

➤ Next steps? Need to be agreed with line manager and HR executive previously, but ideally entail individual going home and collecting belongings later. Avoid 'frog-marching' off premises at all costs. Offer taxi in lieu of car in event of trauma. Goodbyes should come later. Suggest the individual leaves relatively quickly to 'get on with rest of life'.

INITIAL GUIDELINES

Either at the first or subsequent meeting between coach and individual, some guidelines will need to be given and understood on transitioning through today's employment market and on managing their career. They may sound something like this:

'So you are now moving on in your career. You know you must look upon the career transition process as a job in itself, and treat it as such. Anything less than full commitment will not get you very far.

Fortunately, there are many great jobs available. Finding them, however, demands hard work and perseverance, along with careful research and planning.'

Give them some practical tips to help confront today's job market:

➤ Exit your current job position smoothly. Many people do not realise how an abrupt or acrimonious departure can damage their chances when seeking another position.

➤ Develop a good personal profile or résumé—no more than four pages long. This is your door-opener and should present you in your best light, while omitting things which could limit you, such as salary requirements and job objectives which are too narrow.

➤ Maximise the use of your personal and professional contacts. Enlist the help of family, friends, business acquaintances, former customers and other contacts, and give them a résumé they can potentially pass on, or which will prompt them to refer you to a prospective employer.

➤ Manage your time efficiently and effectively. Treat the job search as a serious job and aim to make at least five direct contacts a day, in person or by telephone, preferably to people with decision-making authority in organisations.

➤ The process may take far longer than you think it will initially. Landing an executive or management job these days can take anywhere from one month to a year, and the average timeframe is between three and six months, so you need to be tenacious and stay on track.

➤ Make twice as many applications as you think you need to. In making job applications, try to use the direct or indirect referral approach as much as possible, rather than mailing out hundreds of application letters 'cold'—this simply does not work and is a waste of time and money.

➤ Expect some initial negative reactions. 'No vacancy' may be the formal responses to your initial enquiries, but openings still become available through the need for new skills, organisational change, retirement and resignations, so endeavour to arrange meetings anyway, and match and promote your capabilities to the current or future needs of the organisation you are targeting.

➤ Are you unrealistic in your demands? The executive and management market is highly competitive, so be prepared if necessary to lower your sights accordingly with respect to job targets, salary requirements, job location and other criteria. But *do not* lower your sights too soon, as you never know what might be waiting for you, just around the corner!

➤ Don't throw in the towel! Maintain your momentum throughout your job search—it will help if you regard the process as a regular job—taking frequent, short breaks rather than doing nothing for weeks on end and thereby losing touch with possible opportunities out there.

➤ Remain in touch with prospective referrers and employers. An executive or management job opening can come up at any time, so make sure you stay on the 'active list', by telephoning back once in a while and getting an update on the organisation's status and outlook.

Once these important criteria have been explained, regarding transitioning through today's employment market, the full career assessment process used in career consulting should ideally be deployed, through homework and follow-up counselling and coaching. The outcome should be some clearly defined career directional options.

The next steps, clearly, are implementation and attainment. A considerable range of topics need to be addressed, through coaching, over several weekly meetings at least. The total story-line for such meetings typically goes something like this:

'We will now address the vital elements of how to track down that next ideal job opportunity. Playing and winning the career game requires preparation, rehearsal and perseverance, and our next meetings will arm you with the top, proven techniques which will enhance your self-confidence and your effectiveness on this challenging journey.'

The very first step in any career change should be to make a point of changing your present job position with goodwill in the case of all parties, as far as possible. If you must begin your search while still employed in a particular job, carry on in your role as normally as you can and do not make any lack of interest too obvious. However great the temptation, don't vent your pent-up frustration as you move on.

In fact, leaving gracefully really makes sense, as it will leave a lasting, positive impression. Make no mistake, this last impression of you will be remembered if your future line manager calls your last line manager to check you out, as will likely be the case. Try to stay on good terms with everyone, and increase your chances of leaving with your reputation intact and with a good reference later on when it is needed.

THE RÉSUMÉ

Your résumé is the foundation of your job search, and will save you time and effort later if you do a superior job compiling it well the first time around. Dragging out an old résumé and adding a few lines is not good enough.

Also beware of professional résumé writers. They will never know you as well as you know yourself and you will have to make running adjustments to the document as your campaign progresses anyway. For example, you may recall something in your background which you neglected to include but which is extremely relevant to your next prospective job position or employer. Also, professional résumé writers have their own particular style and no matter how good that style is, it is not your style and this becomes apparent at the interview. Those people who are used to reading résumés can recognise the characteristics of many professional résumé writers.

What might this say about you? It might indicate that you lack ability or confidence in written communication. So take the time to develop the résumé yourself—it will be well worth the effort, and the process of compilation will prepare you for discussing your background coherently over the telephone, or at interviews. The money you might spend on professional résumé services would be better spent elsewhere.

Before you sit down to develop your résumé, remember that its sole purpose is to obtain an interview by presenting some of your credentials in a way which gains the reader's attention, interest and curiosity—enough curiosity to invite you to a face-to-face meeting. No one hires on the basis of a written résumé alone—you will be hired on the basis of the face-to-face interview, and so gear your résumé towards attracting enough interest to 'get your foot in the door'.

Although the final product should be no longer than four pages, résumé preparation is a very lengthy and detailed process. It will take you several hours to complete but will ensure that all the important information required for your job search is recorded, organised and instantly available as required. Having this information on hand will not only increase your self-confidence but it will also save you a lot of time later on.

There are basically two types of résumés, a career-oriented version and a capability-oriented version. Examples of each abound in the many books available on the subject (including my book *The Bulletproof Executive*).

The career-oriented résumé is particularly useful for line management or operational jobs, or where your most recent experience, say over the last five to ten years, is highly relevant to the job position you are considering.

The capability-oriented résumé is more relevant for technical, specialist, functional, advisory or consulting type jobs, or where your earlier—rather than more recent—experience is more relevant to the job position you are considering. This type of résumé is also useful if you have had a long career with just one employer, or where taking the career-oriented approach may emphasise a particular skill-set other than the one you are trying to portray.

For example, 25 years in banking and using the career-oriented version may well cast you as a 'banker', whereas by using the capability-oriented version you can cast yourself as a 'general manager', 'operations manager' or whatever your skill-set and career objective dictates. I refer to this as 'repackaging' and it is most useful where career moves entail changes in business sector or job function and when you need to promote yourself in this new idiom, rather then historically.

Always commence the résumé development process by completing a career-oriented version first, even if you actually need a capability-oriented version. By completing them in this order, you will develop a better capability-oriented résumé, since the achievement statements, more easily derived by assessing your chronological career experience, can then be transferred verbatim across to the capability-oriented version of your profile.

Achievements are the most important statements in your résumé, covering letter and, indeed, even at interviews. Using well-developed achievement statements is akin to selling the 'benefits' of a proposition, rather than the 'features'—one of the rules of professional selling which transfers directly across to personal selling—features in your own case being statements about your responsibilities and duties. Salespeople are always told to sell the benefits; executives and managers in career transition need to sell their achievements.

Never send out a résumé to a prospective chairperson, CEO or other senior executive without a covering letter. Personalise your approach by addressing your letter to the key person within the organisation who has the power to hire you, and gear both letter and profile to the organisation's needs, as far as possible. First, assess your skills and talents and where you want to go in your career, and then understand what organisations look for in job candidates and how you can differentiate yourself from the crowd.

Avoid writing to personnel or human resources directors if possible—you will merely be one of the crowd—and your chances of getting an interview may be very slim. Aim for the top decision-making person. Don't be afraid to approach these top people by telephone first, and try to arrange a brief meeting to drop off your profile in person. You have nothing to lose, and they may be impressed with your proactiveness enough to want to see you. If they do not, then ask if you can mail them your profile and letter.

Make the most of your covering letter. It can be a very effective tool for marketing yourself, as it is more personal than the résumé, and if developed correctly, can make the person reading it really interested in meeting you—this is what you are aiming for!

An alternative approach is not to send your résumé at all, but to send a three-page letter entirely geared to your perception of the needs of the other party, and how you believe you can meet these needs, again by noting some of your relevant past achievements. This is a highly potent form of direct target marketing, and its needs-orientation makes it particularly effective. However, before sending out 'cold' letters and profiles, try to get introductions to your target audience by using your contacts. (Seek your contact's permission to do this first.)

FINDING JOBS

Most people find jobs either through personal, family or business contacts. For this you need to get introductions to others and so develop your 'contact network' and use it effectively.

Surprisingly, advertised jobs comprise only 20% or less of all jobs available at a particular time. This means that at least 80% of available positions are not advertised. Whether internal or external, I call this the 'invisible job market', and this is where you should be directing most of your efforts. There is 'more out there than meets the eye', and you will greatly increase your chances of success by tapping into this fertile area.

The fact is most employers fill job openings with people they know through personal contact, or with people who are recommended to them by someone they know. This makes sense to many employers. It reduces their risk of hiring someone who turns out to be completely unsuitable, and it also saves them the time and cost involved in putting the position out to an executive search firm or management recruiter. For many employers this is also a sensible strategy in order to help track down the very best candidate available.

You can increase your exposure to this invisible job market by using your contact network effectively, and by approaching key people within your target organisations through introductions and word of mouth referral. By staying in touch with your contact network on a regular basis, you are using the law of averages to increase the probability of being in the right place at the right time— being available just when an organisation needs someone with your capabilities.

Many openings are found and secured this way—by direct and continued contact with prospective employers—regardless of whether or not any positions are initially available. Direct most of your efforts to this 'invisible job market' and learn to play the career game!

Winning the career game requires a game plan. I have already mentioned where most of your efforts should be directed. Staying in control of the game requires that you sit down and plan your time and effort for maximum efficiency and effectiveness. You need also to check up on yourself from time to time to make sure you are staying on course, and not getting bogged down in unproductive activities.

Make yourself a game plan or course of action, and stick to it. There are several alternative courses of action open to you in your job search campaign, if leaving your current organisation. Your best move is to cover all these bases, but apportion your efforts according to the probability of success with each alternative.

For example, try apportioning two-thirds of your effort to personal or business referral contacts, in other words your developing contact network. Try assigning the other one-third of your effort to direct approaches to employer organisations (only if you cannot be introduced or referred to them); job advertisements; and, executive search firms and management recruiters.

You can adjust these proportions of effort percentages once you find out how each alternative works for you specifically. Allocate your time and financial resources accordingly. Set up a daily plan of action with a goal of so many contacts a day or so many letters written and update your card file or database continuously. This is the only way to keep track of where you are in the game as you will be covering quite a large volume of contacts, and a missed follow-up call, or letter not sent in time could cost you a job.

If you are a senior manager or executive, it is important to get on the database of several executive search firms, which rarely advertise. Management recruiters usually reveal themselves when they advertise for specific positions. Try to get some introductions to the key players in search firms through your network contacts, with a view to meeting them and discussing your career objectives. Make sure they have your résumé on file and your full details on their database.

THE INTERVIEW

So you have learned to play the game, made a game plan, and made all the right moves. Sooner or later you are going to score a goal, this being the *interview*. In fact to win the game, in other words to land the ideal job or career position, you will probably need to score several goals—interviews—and prove your superiority over your competition.

So how can you sail confidently through what many consider to be the most nerve-racking stage of job-hunting? Nothing is insurmountable, if taken in a logical sequence, and this applies to job interviews as much as anything else. The trick is to be well-informed, and well-prepared.

Up to this point, all of your efforts have been aimed towards getting interviews. In the highly competitive senior level job market you will need to be creative and persistent without being obnoxious. Some interviews will come more easily than others, but keep trying and land as many as you can which relate to your target areas.

The two main forms of interviews are 'screening' and 'in-depth'. The screening interview is usually conducted by an executive search consultant, management recruiter or HR director, who tries to find out your strengths and weaknesses, and how you compare with other candidates. If you pass this stage, or if there is no screening stage, you will undergo an in-depth interview by the line manager, for whom you will work if hired.

The interviewer will try to see how you fit the specific requirements of the job, the extent and nature of your expertise and how well you get along with people. From your point of view, the objective of the interview is to convince the interviewer that you can offer whatever is needed. In short, you must sell yourself. Therefore, you must present yourself in the best possible light, ensure you have a neat, businesslike appearance and a confident, responsive manner.

A good interviewer will evaluate you on a broad potential range of criteria which will certainly include:

➤ *Capabilities*: qualifications, experience, skills, aptitudes and competencies.
➤ *Motivation*: achievements in the past and the degree to which and how the individual has been self-motivated to achieve these results.
➤ *Personality*: ability to fit in with superiors and peers, and to get results through subordinates and other people.
➤ *Chronology*: early family life and schooling, university achievements (academic and other), track record in career, progress in terms of promotions, perceptions of strengths and weaknesses, non-work interests and how time is spent, career aspirations and particularly reasons for leaving jobs.

Handling the interview successfully requires that you are well-informed about the organisation and the position, and well-prepared for the questions you will likely be asked. It also requires that you project a professional, confident and relaxed image. As well as answering questions, you will be expected to ask some of your own and so prepare them accordingly. Now for the three golden rules on how to win at interviews.

Firstly, the interviewee needs to answer all questions and provide all commentary from the interviewer's perspective, in other words, responses should be geared 100% towards the needs of the employing organisation. Indeed, the candidate really has to enact the role of the professional consultative salesperson, and in this be very clear about the other party's needs, and respond entirely to these needs. Many interviewees fail to realise this, and answer questions and make their responses 'according to the story of their own lives' rather than 'according to the story of the other party's life—*their* needs'.

To establish what those needs are, the candidate should undertake extensive research about the organisation and at the interview, and use pre- and post-check questions and responses. For example, in response to the statement 'Tell me about your strengths', the candidate should pre-check by saying 'I'm told I have quite a broad range of strengths. In which business or functional areas are you particularly interested?' Another example question: 'Tell me about your career/about yourself' could be pre-checked with 'I've had a long, varied and successful career. Which parts interest you most?'. Or, 'I'm not sure where to start—what particularly would you like to know about my career?'

Post-checking phrases, after responding to questions, include: 'Was that what you were seeking?', 'Does that answer your question adequately?', 'Have I demonstrated that adequately?'

Using pre- and post-checking techniques makes sure that you are responding to the needs of the other party, that you have adequately overcome any possible hidden doubts or objections, and that you are engaging in discussion rather than simply answering questions. Remember, good interviews are a two-way exchange of information.

Secondly, always proliferate your answers and responses with examples of your achievements, including results attained and your actions taken to attain them. This type of response provides verification and coincides with behaviourally oriented selection procedures which seek to gain a clear understanding of the candidate's past behaviour in critical areas relevant to the new job. The thinking behind this is that past behaviour is a predictor of future behaviour. You are, therefore, advised to spend a great deal of time on developing your achievement statements and memorising them.

Finally, focus on the start and end of the interview. 'The sale is lost or won in the first 30 seconds' is the salesperson's first rule, and you have to try and win the interview from the outset! Think through all the possible questions you might be asked first, and rehearse your responses. The particularly difficult ones are 'Tell me about yourself?' or 'Why do you think you are the right person for this job?' or 'What do you think we are looking for?' Plan for these and rehearse!

Similarly, plan and rehearse your closing statements. 'The order is not placed until you have closed' is the final rule for the salesperson, and this is just the same for the interview candidate. Closing statements generally need to summarise your interest in the job and why you believe you are well-qualified to win it—restating your key relevant achievements in brief, for closing impact.

After every interview write a follow-up letter to the person who interviewed you, thanking the person for the interview and restating your interest in the position. Also, remind the reader how your background, experience and achievements fit the position requirements and needs of the employing organisation.

The waiting period between the final interview and a possible job offer can be nerve-racking. Protect your best interests, in preparation for possible negotiations later, by keeping the following tips in mind:

➤ By all means do some follow-up if you have heard nothing after ten days, but no earlier than this, nor too frequently, as you may weaken your position if you appear too anxious.

➤ Keep the details of any other ongoing negotiations to yourself—do not mention other companies or prospective job positions or salary levels.

➤ No matter how close you feel you are to a good job offer, keep going full steam ahead with your other leads and lines of inquiry.

➤ Don't commit yourself too quickly to an offer, without thinking it over and weighing it against other possibilities.

➤ Do make sure that whatever job opportunity you select, really fits *you*.

➤ Revisit your career objective—does the job opportunity fit this objective really well? If not, what are the trade-offs, and what are the opportunity costs?

All the foregoing can form the focus of an appropriately oriented executive coaching program (see Chapter 7), also utilising many of the core coaching processes from Chapter 6.

Closure

As the process unfolds and the individual successfully attains a new position, closure meetings may be conducted, as follows:

➤ *With the individual*:

How satisfied are you with your new role?

How satisfied are you with your career transition program?

Most helpful program elements?

Improvements?

To what extent can we feed this back to your former employer organisation?

➤ *With the former line manager and or HR executive*:

How satisfied are you with my input?

Most effective program elements?

Least effective program elements?

Improvements?

Provide feedback from the closure meeting with the individual (as above) but preserve confidentiality.

The final consideration, of course, is who should provide career transition consulting? Conventionally, it has and is provided by external consultants. However, there is certainly potential for internal people, such as HR consultants, to provide this type of valuable input to individuals leaving their organisations, and particularly while working their notice periods. Providing this internally can be very cost-effective, and the career transition consulting capability can represent an important development opportunity for those engaged in its provision.

Keynote

➤ Facilitating someone's career transition helps them leave as an ally, not as a foe.

➤ Remaining colleagues see them as treated fairly as does the customer base.

➤ The days of outplacement are nigh.

➤ Career transition support needs to be geared to what each individual requires, placing the value of the input to where it is needed most.

➤ This is preferable to the bundled, costly approach which outplacement consultants seek to provide in largely undifferentiated and outmoded fashion.

Chapter 15

A TYPICAL COACHING PROCESS FOR PROFESSIONAL CONSULTATIVE SELLING

66 Attracting, developing and retaining clients is the discerning competitive characteristic for successful professional or business-to-business service firms **99**

INTRODUCTION

Over the past three decades I have either started, owned or operated professional or business-to-business service firms in a broad range of fields: career guidance; small business consulting; economic development consulting; technology transfer consulting; training; information technology; home-based health services; executive contracting; outplacement; and, of course, executive coaching, career consulting and mentoring! In most of these fields I have also personally enacted the role of service provider, often as a management consultant or executive coach.

A key given in the success or otherwise of such firms is the intrinsic value of the service provided to the customer or 'client' (the term I will use henceforth), the integrity of the service delivery processes, and the capabilities and experience of the service providers themselves.

However, the key success factor for such firms is the attraction, development and retention of clients. In my experience this is the discerning competitive characteristic which drives success, mediocrity or failure in professional or business-to-business service firms. Frankly, I believe this is the one area where such firms fail to maximise their full potential!

The reasons? Basically one reason, and that is a preoccupation with service delivery and in many professional service firms, 'chargeable hours'. Whereas a preoccupation with professional consultative selling and appropriate business development and marketing support is what really counts, and is what drives 'chargeable hours' and the ultimate success and longevity of the business.

But to make this happen requires those engaged in the revenue generation effort—often technically or functionally gifted professionals—to develop new attitudes, behaviours and habits, namely those of the professional consultative sales person.

And for this to happen, sales training courses are only the starting point in the journey to proficiency, let alone excellence. Building and applying new skills as if they are habits requires sustained effort and input over quite a considerable timeframe. This includes pre-brief, role play, test, debrief and continuous improvement under the watchful eye of a senior coach, who has sufficient time, talent and technique to make the difference.

EXAMPLE

For a team of senior management consultants in a major 'blue chip' professional services firm, I designed, developed and delivered tailored small group and individual coaching sessions in professional consultative selling. The impact was huge in the successful further development of their practice, my input and its effect having 'exceeded expectations'.

A TYPICAL COACHING PROCESS IN MORE DETAIL

In describing a typical process I will again include reference to the core coaching processes in Chapter 6.

In introducing coaching to the line manager the economic benefits orientated business case can be developed quite easily, as improved performance in professional consultative selling flows directly across to increased sales revenue. Also, the sports coaching analogy can be used powerfully in describing sales coaching.

At the time of needs analysis, quite apart from identifying the specific development needs of the individual to receive coaching, you should also develop a clear understanding of the degree and content of any sales training the individual has received to date. In this I find a broad range of scenarios. In many cases little, if no formal, training has been provided. In other cases 'We were put on a course two to three years ago … I might be able to find you a copy of the training manual we all received … I'm not sure where mine is, however!' In other cases, training has been provided regularly and the whole firm uses a particular selling method.

And of course, in the true idiom of The Stephenson Partnership coaching, the coach needs to work out with the organisation and particularly the coachee, which, if any, already existing training and sales processes need to be used for purposes of both diagnosing the coachee's strengths and development needs, and guiding them to improved selling performance.

When introducing the coach to the coachee for the first time, there is rarely, if any, concern by the latter. Rather, they see sales coaching as an opportunity to improve both business and personal performance, potentially transferring into improved earnings for each!

Similarly, the further needs analysis discussion with the coachee is invariably an open, positive meeting, with the focus almost more on the professional consultative sales function and process, rather than on digging too deeply into the self-image of the coachee. However, even in sales coaching, 'peeling back the layers of the onion' to help the coachee better understand himself/herself and what drives attitude and behaviour, in other words the emotional intelligence stock-take, lays a strong foundation on which to build modified sales behaviour and habit.

Career review, role review, review of previous feedback, SDOT analysis and development priorities, and self-management of development are all core coaching processes usefully to be deployed.

However, instead of embarking on 360° survey, I tend to rely more heavily on third party interviews, including interviews with customers or clients which also represents a great public relations opportunity: 'We want to make sure you are receiving the best possible service.'

In terms of psychological assessment, there are in fact a range of assessment tools which can be used very effectively in the selling environment, and which provide good additional diagnostic feedback. Rather than go into detail about these here, suffice it to say that any experienced organisational or business psychologist should be able to access appropriate tools, according to each specific circumstance and need.

In the event the client organisation or coachee does not have access to sales coaching guidelines, methods and so forth, then these could possibly be sourced externally. The following is an extract from my own guidelines, and is used section by section as both homework by the coachee and for follow-up discussion, pre-brief, role play, and debrief (after testing) at coaching meetings. If you recognise some of the content, don't be surprised, as it bears similarity to the personal selling guidelines in Chapter 10—'A typical assimilation process for newly appointed key people'.

And herein lies a learning point. The more often coaches uses core-type processes, the more proficient they become as coaches. Just imagine the opposite, where the coach has to scramble for some form of guideline not previously used, nor is likely to use again. This leads to huge inefficiencies, and questionable effectiveness, to the disadvantage of both the coachee and the sponsor of the program. Core processes render efficiency, effectiveness and results!

EXTRACTS FROM MY PROFESSIONAL CONSULTATIVE SELLING GUIDELINES

The first step in making a success of professional selling is to acquire the attitude of an entrepreneur—the executive seeking sales success has the responsibility to run their 'business' of selling efficiently and profitably.

Goal-setting is the starting point of achievement—we have to know where we are headed and what we hope to achieve, before we can take the steps necessary to get us there and effectively monitor our progress so that we stay on course. Goal-setting in selling involves the following principles: *the setting of realistic, specific achievement goals*; and *monitoring your goals regularly*.

In order to be effective, goals must be realistic. They should be attainable, but set a little higher than would be required for easy achievement—you should have to work hard to achieve them. Setting them way out of reach, however, will only result in discouragement and eventually work against you.

Your goals should also be specific, so that you can easily tell whether or not you are achieving them. To set a goal of 'improving selling performance' or 'making more contacts' is so general as to be meaningless. Some examples of specific selling goals might be:

➤ Liaise with each client, monthly.
➤ Touch base with each senior executive in each key account at least once a month.
➤ Make four presentations a month to new contacts.
➤ Develop four new external contacts per month.
➤ Phone two former external contacts per week for an update.

Make sure your goals remain realistic in the light of current developments and changing circumstances. Don't be tempted, however, to revise your goals downward at the slightest excuse. Your goals should stand, regardless of your current performance, unless there have been major positive or negative factors beyond your control. Continuous monitoring will keep you on track and help keep your personal goals and objectives in sight and attainable.

THE FOUNDATIONS OF SUCCESSFUL SELLING

The increasing need for expertise and knowledge relating to market and industry developments is making unprecedented demands on today's professional sales executive. The human mind can only absorb so much. Rather than try to take in everything, the trick is to try to pick out what is essential and to concentrate on absorbing as much of that information as possible, while ignoring the rest, or relying on your direct reports.

Now the focus of selling yourself is the person with whom you wish to develop an 'alliance' (a client-supplier relationship) leading to sustainable sales development. All the knowledge in the world will not be of much use, if that knowledge cannot be related somehow to genuine interests, needs and wants of other people.

The psychology of selling yourself attempts to understand the behaviour of other people, and for this the guidelines on operating style in Chapter 7—'A typical executive coaching process' and Chapter 16—'A typical coaching process for professional presentations and public speaking' can be used with good effect.

EXAMPLE

A relatively new partner in a professional services firm was so intent on chargeable hours and technical excellence, he completely lost the plot with interpersonal relationships both within and outside the firm. Executive coaching helped him re-appraise priorities and he now puts people first.

The psychology of selling yourself also requires that you understand what motivates other people potentially to develop an alliance with you. This knowledge of behaviour and motivation will be useful to you in tailoring your selling approaches to individual contacts. Flexibility is the key—the 'canned approach' is out. Remember initially to focus on the interests and needs of your contact, not on your underlying reason for wishing to develop an alliance.

In selling yourself at the executive and managerial levels you are not always dealing with independent contacts. You are often dealing instead with 'organisational' contacts, who may be in some way involved, directly or indirectly, in helping you gain greater influence. These contacts may include executives in other businesses, manufacturers, wholesalers, retailers, agricultural and resource companies, government agencies, associations and so forth.

In attempting to focus on organisational characteristics, you should realise that there are some major differences between independent and organisational contacts. For example, organisational contacts:

➤ Normally associate with others, particularly those outside their employer's organisation, for fewer *personal* reasons than do independent contacts.
➤ Are sometimes restricted by well-defined company policies and practices, as well as the inevitable time pressures.
➤ Typically distribute liaison with external contacts among several other people.

Thus, in trying to understand behaviour and motivation, you must consider not only the individual with whom you wish to develop an alliance, but also the organisational characteristics which will impact on this alliance. For example:

➤ What are the policies of the organisation?

➤ Apart from the contact I am targeting, how many other people are likely to be involved in developing this alliance?

➤ Who is the main influencer?

➤ Is it one individual or a group?

➤ If it is a group, who are the vital people, who tend to sway group opinion?

➤ What kind of individual operating style (or styles) am I likely to encounter, and to which I must adapt and respond, in order to get desired results?

Being able to answer such questions, as they relate to each of your organisational contacts, obviously takes some preparation.

Now, if you want to be effective in developing alliances and generating greater influence with organisational contacts, you need to understand the process—the 'how' of a decision, whether or not to develop an alliance with you, will throw some light on the 'way'. Remember that all decisions take time and generally speaking, they will follow the following steps.

NEED RECOGNITION

The identification or recognition of a need sets the decision process in motion of whether or not to develop an alliance with you (remember, this is a client-supplier relationship, clients are in fact allies). Once begun, the process continues until the alliance is cemented or rejected. But in order to get the process started, the individual or individuals with whom you are liaising must be motivated to form such an alliance.

Thus, the first task in selling yourself is ideally to identify and appeal to an unsatisfied interest, need or want on the part of your target contact, as this will serve as the motivating force. Before an unsatisfied need can motivate behaviour, however, it must be recognised and acknowledged by the contact—some people have needs of which they are unaware, until this is pointed out to them.

There are two ways in which contacts become aware of their needs, by receiving new information and by re-evaluating their current situation. You can be instrumental in either case. Contacts generally need to be reminded or told about your experience and capabilities and how they can satisfy their particular interests or needs. They also have to be appraised of the need itself, because sometimes the need is latent and it is up to you to convert the latent need into an obvious need, and into a 'want' which you can satisfy!

SEARCH FOR INFORMATION

Once the need has been recognised and acknowledged, the contact will then require a certain amount of information. All contacts, whether independent or organisational, have two major sources of information: internal and external. Internal sources of information are those facts which are already known to the contact, whether through reading, discussions with others or actual experience. Organisational contacts may have extensive databases, files and records at their disposal, catalogues, trade journals, company brochures, correspondence records and so on, to help with information gathering.

Even with all of these internal sources, however, most contacts look to external sources, perhaps to you to supplement their information needs. This is why one of the most important characteristics in selling yourself is credibility. Less than honest claims and approaches are easily exposed and you need to be a knowledgeable, believable source of information for your contacts.

SELECTION AMONG ALTERNATIVES

Once the contact feels that enough information has been gathered, there must be a selection. This selection may be between similar external contacts, or between associating or not associating with a specific contact—perhaps you!

You need to realise that in this stage of the decision-making process the outcome will depend upon two things: which factors the contact will consider in making the decision to develop an alliance; and, the relative weight or importance attached to each factor. Identifying these factors, and their relative importance to the contact, is not as difficult as it sounds. A little preliminary investigation, coupled with some careful questioning, should bring these out. This is an area in which selling yourself usually improves dramatically with experience.

ONGOING ALLIANCE

You can and should seek to have some influence over the strength or longevity of the ongoing alliance, by following through to ensure that your contact is satisfied with the alliance to date, and if not, why not. Any problems can thus be put right, or minimised as soon as possible. Thus direct and continuous follow-up during your alliance is an essential part of successfully selling yourself.

PRIORITISATION OF EFFORT AND IMPACT

One of the toughest challenges facing sales executives today is to make every hour of the day count for more. Difficult economic conditions and a highly competitive commercial environment have made efficient and profitable use of time essential for survival.

Working harder and longer is not necessarily the answer. What is needed is a good hard look at where you are spending your time and whether or not you are getting maximum payback for your efforts. Too much of your time may be spent on associating with marginal or non-productive contacts, time that could be spent developing and maintaining the more profitable clients—your allies. This is just good business sense. Remember that in selling yourself and developing your influence you are managing your own business and you must keep one eye on the results, without rushing, pressuring or alienating any of your clients.

By far the best way of ensuring that your time is spent efficiently and profitably, while interacting with your clients properly, is to plan. Time management and planning is essential to your personal success, but is often ignored in favour of the 'hit and miss' approach. Planning takes time, but if undertaken in the evening or at weekends it need not eat into your personal selling and business time. How and where do you get started?

A common pitfall in selling yourself is to devote far too much time to low-potential clients and insufficient time to high-potential clients. If all of this time can be recouped, it often improves personal selling efficiency by one-third or more. A close analysis of how you spend your time should point out where your plan may need some restructuring. In order to do this, you will need to complete a classification of your existing and prospective clients, and one way to do this is by a 'I, II, III Analysis'.

In this analysis 'Is' are the high-yield/high-potential clients (existing and potential clients) and you may find they represent 20% of your clients, yet 80% of your alliance and influence potential. Devote maximum time and attention to each 'I' client. 'IIs' are the mid-yield/mid-potential clients. They may represent 30% of your contacts and 15% of your alliance and influence potential. Devote some time and attention to each 'II' client. 'IIIs' are the low-yield/low-potential clients. They may represent as many as 50% of your clients, yet only offer alliance and influence potential of 5%. Devote minimal time and attention to each 'III' client and consider referring them to someone else in your organisation or dropping them altogether.

The first step should be to gradually discontinue your low-yield/low-potential clients. The time saved can be used to increase the results from your existing, high-yield clients, as well as to cultivate those prospective clients with a high-yield potential. In submitting your existing and prospective contacts to the 'I, II, III Analysis', don't be too hasty in rejecting current low-yield clients, particularly if you have some reason to believe that the yield will improve dramatically in the future. But as the manager of your own personal selling and influence development business, you should dedicate the major portion of your time and effort to those clients who yield the greatest return on your time, efforts and expense.

DEVELOPING CLIENTS

Generating new clients—allies—is a prerequisite for sales success. If you have a strong network of clients and contacts externally who think well of you, this will enhance your reputation, which will be referred to others who matter in other organisations. This in turn strengthens your position and future.

Generating new external contacts is the very first step in extending your external network of clients. Indeed, your success in this is directly proportional to the number of people you contact (everything else being equal). As such, the importance of generating new external contacts cannot be over-emphasised.

First, let us define exactly what we mean by some terms: 'contacts', 'leads', 'alliance' and 'prospects'. A 'contact' is just about anyone you know or seek to know, or who may seek to know you! A 'lead' is a contact who *may* have an interest or need to develop an alliance with you. Leads can come from many sources, such as existing clients, newspaper announcements, social contacts, family and friends, and so forth. Keep in mind that since most leads will have neither definite interest in nor desire to develop an alliance with you, you may have to generate many leads to get the few who actually do have a need or interest. The term 'alliance' means ongoing client-supplier liaison and mutual support, as noted earlier.

Once a lead has demonstrated or acknowledged a definite interest or need to develop an alliance with you, the lead becomes a 'prospect'. However, before expending considerable time and effort in trying to form an alliance with a prospect, you should first qualify the prospect, for which there are three main steps:

➤ Determine which factors you feel are important and should be used in your qualification. Some typical factors for analysing organisational prospects might be: the type of business and area of expertise of the prospect; the level of seniority and influence of the prospect; and, range of contacts accessible through the prospect.

➤ Determine whether or not the prospect possesses these qualifications. It may be that the prospect doesn't need to pass every test—some factors will be more important than others, and you must decide if the prospect possesses enough of the important variables to qualify.

➤ Decide whether or not it will be worthwhile pursuing the prospect. This should really be an economic decision. Some prospects may qualify very well, but should not be pursued because to do so would be unprofitable. The main example is the marginal prospect who requires a high proportion of time in relation to the benefits derived. Your decision not to pursue such a prospect should be balanced by a consideration of whether or not the benefits will be likely to increase sufficiently in the future.

By effectively qualifying prospects, you can save a lot of time and frustration chasing after people who, for one reason or another, are not worth forming an alliance with. Once a prospect has been qualified, effective selling skills will hopefully result in an alliance being formed, and turn the qualified prospect into a 'client'—someone with whom you will continue to do business and with whom there is some form of mutual support.

Forming the alliance is not the final step. Appropriate follow-up and a satisfied client produces an ongoing profitable alliance, and this should be the final goal of all your prospecting efforts. Systematic, well-planned prospecting will allow you to 'get the jump' on the competition, by aiming your efforts at individuals and organisations who will produce the best results for your efforts. Very often, effective continuous prospecting is what separates the high performers from the low performers in successful selling.

There are numerous sources of external leads available. We will address several of these sources here, but no list is ever complete. To be good at selling, you should be flexible and experiment with a wide variety of potential sources. Some of these will be exhausted in a short space of time, while others may continue to be fruitful for years. We will now consider some of the more common sources of leads:

➤ *Your existing prospects.* Your own current list of prospects can be a good source of leads. This source can be tapped by asking a few simple questions during your liaison with prospects, for example: 'Do you know of anyone else who may be interested in discussing this?' or 'Is anyone else in your company experiencing similar problems?'

Some people in selling make it a common practice to try to get one or two leads for every person with whom they are in contact. This is known as the 'endless chain' method of generating leads, and if handled tactfully, it can be very effective.

➤ *Clients for referrals*. Satisfied clients provide the best single source of leads. If they are pleased with their alliance with you, they may tend to mention your name to others in casual conversation. This gives you a personal endorsement which increases your credibility and makes your networking job that much easier.

You can also ask your clients directly if they know of anyone who may be interested in what you would like to discuss or if they will introduce or recommend you to new prospects. This is known as the 'direct referral' method and is very productive since it reduces the time spent on prospecting and qualifying. It also increases the possibility of receiving a positive response to the subsequent contact made.

In seeking leads from clients, try using the following system. The best time is when you have just concluded a fruitful discussion or meeting with them. Give them a focus—'Do you belong to any professional associations?' 'Is there anyone you know of with expertise in this area …?' Based on the above focus, ask them for the names of people who might be interested in meeting you. Then ask qualifying questions, and the contact details. Even ask your client to make a call on your behalf and introduce you or help you to arrange an appointment. If your client's reaction is not too positive in this, ask if you can use their name, when you make contact yourself.

➤ *Internal sources*. Other people and areas within your own organisation can be a valuable source of leads.

➤ *Social contacts*. Because of their close association with you, family, friends and social acquaintances can also be helpful in providing leads. Here the 'direct referral' method can be used.

Another method is to use your social contacts to reach the 'centres of influence' in the community—people who, because of their positions within business and professional groups, exert a lot of influence with certain types of prospects.

➤ *Clubs and organisations.* Professional clubs and service organisations can provide an excellent source of leads, but be careful not to join for this sole purpose. Avoid obnoxious 'lead chasing' and make sure you believe in the philosophy and goals of the organisation, and that you can contribute something to it—keeping things relaxed and in perspective will usually result in some prospects materialising anyway.

➤ *Public records, newspapers, magazines and the Internet.* Publications such as newspapers, magazines, trade journals and related publications should be scanned regularly for leads, as well as of course the Internet. Professional appointments, new business and office openings are just some examples of potential prospects to be followed up.

➤ *Conventions and trade shows.* Participation in professional conferences, conventions, trade shows and exhibitions is a very good way to identify prospects. In fact, in the professional selling idiom, prospecting is very often the main reason for taking part in such shows and get togethers.

COMMUNICATION

Selling yourself, finding clients and negotiating your way to sales success comprise basically a communication process. Selling yourself successfully depends on your communication skills. These skills can be learned and improved upon, so as to upgrade the quality of communication and all subsequent contacts with your target audience.

What do we mean by communication? According to the common definition: 'Communication is a process by which meanings are exchanged between individuals, through a common set of symbols.' The symbols take the form of speech, written messages, facial expressions, gestures and actions. Effective communication requires both a transmitter and a receiver. Simply 'explaining something' to a contact does not guarantee that communication has taken place. Refer to 'Communication' in Chapter 10.

PREPARATION

In professional selling, approach planning is the preparation for sales calls on specific prospects or clients. The approach itself is actually opening the discussion and setting the stage for the meeting. How you handle these steps, and their main purpose, will depend on the current status of the other party.

When you are calling on qualified prospects (and they really should be qualified prospects if you are going to take the time to call on them), your approach will be crucial in building confidence and respect. We all know the importance of first impressions. Make this work for you rather then against you, by becoming familiar with these initial steps of the personal selling sequence.

The main elements in approach planning are: meeting content, focus on the other party, discussion technique and obtaining the meeting.

➤ *Meeting content*. In deciding the actual content of the meeting, or what you are going to say, keep in mind that all the other party really wants to hear is how you can satisfy and discuss their particular interests, needs or wants.

Obviously in order to do this effectively, you must do some preparation by learning something about the contact's organisation, processes, products and problems. Once this has been done, the next step is to translate the features of what you want to discuss into benefits which will coincide with their interests or needs.

➤ *Focus on the other party*. Once you have reviewed the content of your upcoming meeting, you will need to focus on the other party in order to decide on the most appropriate technique to use in this particular situation. Who you are calling on will affect what you are going to say, and how you will say it, as well as the topics and benefits on which to focus at your meeting. For example, a meeting to discuss computer systems with a senior executive (who may have little 'hands-on' contact with such systems, but who may be concerned with how such systems can increase company efficiency and profitability) will differ from a meeting with the company's information technology managers and staff.

➤ *Discussion technique*. Achieving success in personal selling depends just as much on the technique you use as on your knowledge and extent of preparation. You should tailor your technique and behaviour to fit the other party, not expect them to adjust to your own particular operating style. This is the concept of 'flexible behaviour'. The operating style you plan to use is best decided before you approach the other person, from information obtained during your preparation.

However, this style may have to be adjusted, depending on the other person's mood at the time of the meeting, or on whether other key people are present. Commonsense and flexibility should be the rule, which is why you should steer clear of 'canned presentations'.

Tailoring your degree of 'proactiveness' and 'receptiveness' to the other party, and to the situation at hand, will increase your chances of success. Of course, if in doubt about the other person's operating style, observe them carefully and adapt to or even 'mirror' their style.

➤ *Obtaining the meeting.* Make sure the person you are going after is the most appropriate person, unless you want to waste a lot of time. A little checking ahead of time should help you to establish this. Once established, there are several techniques for obtaining the meeting: *cold calling in person*; *cold calling by telephone*; *third party introductions*; and, *letter writing*.

When *cold calling on people in person*, it is essential that you identify yourself and state the purpose of your call. Don't try to deceive or trick your prospects just to get a meeting, as it will inevitably backfire on you. The main problem in using this method is that it can waste a lot of your time, if the other party is unavailable for a while.

Cold calling by telephone can save you a lot of time, but remember the purpose of such telephone calls is ideally to obtain an appointment, not just to conduct a discussion, if you seek to develop a close alliance with the prospect. Again, identify yourself immediately to the prospect and state why you are calling.

Be flexible in arranging appointments—let prospects fit you into their schedules, not the other way around. Keep the initial telephone call brief, positive and general, so that there is no opportunity for a turndown at this stage—concentrate solely on getting in to see the prospect.

When *being introduced by a third party*, ideally you will need something tangible, such as a letter of introduction, a telephone call to the prospect by the third party, or even a business card with a note scribbled on it. This is usually very effective in getting an appointment, as it gives you some credibility.

Writing letters to prospects asking for appointments can save you time, if done well. You don't have to compose each letter individually—have one or two standard letter formats which you need to personalise by name and opening statements. This method has the advantage of getting through to the prospect directly, but needs to be followed up with a telephone call anyway.

Only you can decide which methods work best for you. If you are just starting out in professional selling, try them all, and then evaluate the response you get in relation to the time and effort spent.

Refer to 'Meetings' in Chapter 10 for the six steps to conducting an effective meeting.

Structured versus personalised approach

There has been a lot of controversy over the best type of approach to use in selling meetings—structured, personalised or balanced.

Structured

In the structured, or 'canned' approach, you have total control, since the whole meeting has been worked out ahead of time, right down to the exact wording to use. All possible objections which may be raised are anticipated and responses are prepared. With this approach, you know that all key points will be covered, and nothing will be missed. The advantage of this type of approach is that it can provide the new, inexperienced personal salesperson with confidence. It also simplifies personal selling self-development efforts, since one basic approach is developed, potentially to be used in all meetings.

The obvious disadvantage is that is does not allow for the differing needs, interests or behaviour of the other party. Also, it can sound very stilted and unnatural and the other party may resent being treated 'just like the others'. We all like to think we are special, and this goes for prospects, too. The totally structured meeting can also be a problem if the same person is visited several times.

Personalised

On the other hand, the problem with the completely *personalised* approach is that a different one must be prepared for each situation, and this can get pretty unwieldy and time-consuming. It can also be confusing if you handle more than one or two personal sales meetings a day.

Balanced

It has generally been found that *a balanced* approach is best, where some kind of framework or meeting outline is prepared which ensures that nothing important is overlooked—sample statements and questions can be written down. In this way, you can retain some control over the meeting. However there is some flexibility, in that decisions on the exact wording to use, information to add, or what to omit, are left to your discretion at the time of the meeting. This leaves room for questions from the other party, as well as interaction in the process—essential ingredients in most successful meetings.

VISUALS

This brings us to an effective way to elicit participation by the other party—the use of visuals. Visuals can help you develop a better discussion, and are often used by the more experienced salesperson. They include brochures, presentation manuals, slides, overheads, videos and testimonials. In using visuals, you can often present more in a crisp and timely fashion (bearing in mind you have only 15–20 minutes to retain the other party's attention and interest).

Visuals can be used in 'structured', 'personalised' or 'balanced' meetings—you can either stick rigidly to them, or orientate the main benefits in the visual to the specific needs of the other person. In using visuals, make sure your prospect is seated in a way that they can see the visuals, and you can see their reactions.

Whether you use presentation manuals, slides or overheads, it is recommended that you have one set relating to each topic you wish to address. Topics they might address can include an introduction to yourself and to your organisation, information relating to what you or the organisation has accomplished or undertaken in the past and which is relevant to the meeting, and information relating to what you or your organisation can do for the other party—all related in the form of benefits.

In using such visuals you need to be fully conversant with their contents. Point with a pen for emphasis, and look at the visuals yourself and then at the other party for reactions—this will keep them looking at your visuals, and then at you, intermittently. With regard to brochures, underline or circle key points, and leave the material with the other person.

CLOSING

'Closing' is the ultimate goal of your meeting, it assists your prospect or client in making the right decision, in other words to accommodate what you are seeking. If you cannot close, then you cannot accomplish this, no matter how good you are at planning, prospecting, approaching, questioning and overcoming concerns or objections. A football team might have all the moves, speed and techniques needed to get the ball near the goal, but it won't win if it doesn't score! Over the long term, success in closing determines the extent of your network of clients and influence, the achievement of your goals, and even your level of income.

In spite of the importance of closing, many executives engaged in selling fail to learn and practise closing techniques, and thus limit themselves to a network of clients, influence and income level much smaller than they could attain with a little extra knowledge and skill in closing.

There are certain times during the meeting when attempting to close may be appropriate—the trick is to learn how to recognise these opportunities. Closing doesn't have to wait until the end of the meeting; if the other party is ready, it can come very early in the selling process—sometimes right after the approach. Take the case of the football team where goals can be scored in the last and *first* few minutes of play.

How do you recognise when the other party is ready to accommodate what you seek? There are certain 'closing signals' which you must watch for. Those who learn to identify these signals will be more successful in closing than those who try to close indiscriminately throughout the selling process. Closing signals can be classified as either *verbal* or *physical*. Some examples:

➤ *Verbal:*

'Yes, I guess that would solve our problem.'

'Did you say you would consider providing some ongoing input?'

'How soon can you get involved?'

Verbal closing signals are also when the other party asks more questions about the topic being addressed, or when they apparently start to slow down—both may indicate a high level of interest.

➤ *Physical:*

The other person nods in agreement. They re-examine the visuals more closely. They check something in the files or on their computer. Verbal and physical clues are numerous—you can probably come up with many more from your own experience. Practice will improve your ability to recognise these signals of interest and readiness to form an alliance with you or accommodate your other needs.

Once you have determined an opportune moment for closing, there are several methods which may be used, and they can be built into the following sequence:

➤ Display a full understanding of the other party's requirements, motives, preferences and any objections (which should have been overcome).

➤ Portray sincerity, empathy and a confidence that you are able to address their interests or meet their precise needs.

➤ Recognise closing signals.

➤ Apply a test close.

➤ Apply one or more closing techniques.

➤ Be silent after you have asked the closing question. Don't say another word until the other person has responded.

Two popular closing techniques are assuming a close and direct close.

➤ *Assuming a close.* Here you proceed as if the other party is ready to accommodate what you seek, whether or not they have indicated as such. With this type of close, the onus is on the other person to stop you if they are not ready. The sequence is to pause, smile and ask such questions as: 'Incidentally, which is the best date for our commencing?' 'Incidentally, which of your colleagues should I meet at our start-up meeting?'

➤ *Direct close.* Here, you ask the other person directly, for example, whether they would like to do business with you. Obviously, the risk is that they will decline, so don't use this method unless they have somehow indicated a definite readiness to do business with you.

A powerful analogy is the fly fisherman. Such people go to great lengths to equip themselves and to venture forth to cast and hopefully make a catch. In the final analysis, however, unless they get within range of the fish, and unless they cast the right type of fly across a patch of water the size of a table top, they will fail to attain their objective. Closing is like this. You have to be equipped and prepared. You have to have tracked down leads to find prospects. And you have to find the right moment and place to cast that all-important fly with accuracy—the close—in order to attain your objectives.

MEETING THE NEEDS OF YOUR CLIENTS

Many people consider 'closing' to be the final step in the selling sequence. However, selling doesn't really have a final step. For the person engaged in professional consultative selling who wants to build a solid base of satisfied clients, and wants to constantly expand on that base, selling should be viewed as a cycle, without a definite beginning or end.

Closing with a prospect is merely the beginning of an ongoing relationship, which must be maintained with effective follow-up and service where necessary. There are several ways in which new clients can become established ones, and established clients maintained and developed effectively. This is all about building loyalty, which requires taking care of the interests of your clients. Stay in touch with them by planning and scheduling your calls and visits.

Some sales executives keep a daily 'reminder' file, so that they call their clients or visit them at predetermined times. There is no 'right' number of times to keep in touch, or 'right' amount of time to wait between making contact again. This will depend on each client, the types of topics addressed with them, and their importance to you as individuals. The main point to remember is to schedule callbacks and visits into your planning—this will ensure that each client receives adequate attention.

Meeting the needs of your clients is not just a cliché or an attitude for the professional sales executive, it is a blueprint for action. It should be more than winning one-off meetings and ensuring the meeting is successfully concluded. Effective 'servicing' of your clients encompasses every contact point with not only yourself, but with your company or organisation also.

Corporate notifications, mail-outs or invitations, although not necessarily your direct responsibility, should be of your concern, in order to ensure that each of your clients is properly serviced. Good service can help to maintain your existing base of clients—your network of supporters.

Handling difficulties is one of the most challenging aspects of ensuring ongoing liaison with existing clients. If a client has a concern about you or your organisation and the concern is serious, it will probably affect your client's preparedness to continue to do business with you in future. Therefore, to build long-term relationships means that any difficulties need to be handled properly.

The best way to do this is obviously to try and reduce the possibility of their occurrence as much as possible. A difficulty represents a failure of some kind—whether in you or your organisation—in meeting your client's expectations. Your performance, or that of your organisation, may be below par, or their expectations may be too high. In either case, you may not have fulfilled the responsibility of ensuring that your client understands just how well you or your organisation can match up to their genuine interests, needs and expectations, and where there may be limitations. This illustrates, once again, the importance of acquiring thorough knowledge relating to the reason for your alliance and the topics you wish to address.

If you have done everything possible to avoid difficulties and they still occur, the first thing to find out is whether or not the concern is valid. One way or another, amends must be made. The extra time and effort involved in ensuring that this situation does not arise in the first place will be well worth it.

Clients sometimes make special requests, over and above the normal servicing give-and-take. If a special request is made, this may command extra time or resources—be aware of your organisation's policy here. If your client expects the organisation to deliver, you have to make a decision—should this be accepted and the costs absorbed, or should you decline the request, and risk losing an ongoing association?

Be very careful to treat all special requests consistently if you want to avoid problems of comparison cropping up later—clients do tend to talk to each other!

Simply maintaining your current network of clients is not enough if you want to be really successful. It is the consistent growth in the size of your network of support which distinguishes the mediocre sales executive from the outstanding one. There are basically three ways to increase the potency of your network: increase dealings with current clients; develop new clients; and win back lost clients.

➤ *Increase dealings with current clients.* Your best chance to develop your influence is to deal more with your existing clients, as they have already been won over to you. How much easier it is to build on this existing goodwill than to search out and win over new ones.

Dealing more with existing clients can mean either developing your relationship more on the current lines, or meeting more of your client's needs by addressing a wider range of needs. Also, as your know-how is being upgraded and improved constantly, there is a great opportunity to make your clients aware of this increased knowledge and how this can apply to their interests and needs.

EXAMPLE

Let us take a professional consultative selling example of increasing sales to existing clients. The prospect has been closed on a car insurance quote. The astute insurance agent then asks a raft of questions that supposedly

relate to information needed to complete the application process, so that the car insurance policy can be issued. In fact, that insurance agent is certainly doing that, but more besides. They are finding out about potential additional insurance needs. When their new client drops by to collect the policy, the agent will be ready with alternatives for him for home insurance and other forms of cover.

This example illustrates clearly a technique for developing your existing clients. Adapt it and in the process, 'buy ownership' of your own adaptation!

➤ *Develop new clients.* Existing, satisfied clients are an excellent source of leads for new clients. They can usually provide you with several names of good prospects, as well as offer suggestions as to how to meet the prospect's interests or needs. Clues picked up in this way are one of your best methods of developing new clients. Remember, elitist executive and managerial networkers acquire up to half a dozen referrals for every alliance developed. Elitist sales professionals also dedicate more than 90% of their selling time to referrals.

➤ *Win back lost clients.* Because selling to established clients forms the basis of successful selling, losing clients can greatly erode your current and future sales scope. If you lose a client other than through them moving away or going out of business, then something has happened to upset the status quo. If you value the client, it is important to find out what happened. Either their views about you have deteriorated, their interests and needs have changed, the effort entailed in your alliance has become too great, or others have done a better selling job. For whatever reason, if the loss of your client comes as a complete surprise, you have not been doing your job in staying in touch with your client, or keeping up to date with developments in this field.

Once clients are lost, you may be able to win them back if you find out the real reasons, and do your best to rectify the situation. Spend as much time and effort on trying to win back the client as you feel is justified, considering the value of your alliance, and your chances of being successful. Otherwise, you'll have to let the client go, but learn from the experience, in order to prevent such a loss happening again.

MAJOR CLIENT MANAGEMENT

Major clients—your best allies—are those, perhaps no more than 20% of your total clients, who represent, or have the propensity to represent 80% of your potential for developing your profitable sales volume. This 80/20 rule (Pareto's Principle) is found to apply time and time again. But in order to generate that 80%, these clients have to be 'managed'—management often being defined as getting superior results through or from people.

CASE STUDY

Here is a real life example of major client management. The case study relates to a major commercial bank where I undertook some preliminary research and analysis of their major client management capabilities in business banking. I found that their major business clients had fairly wide-ranging needs in terms of bank services, and of their expectations of bank officers, as summarised below.

The following distills the essence of a series of interviews I had conducted with bank clients:

'I want to deal directly with someone who:

… knows what they are talking about in terms of:

finance and lending

business management

the economy

bank products and services.

… can make decisions, who can respond rapidly, who can respond positively, and who will make suggestions for alternatives rather than simply turn me down.

… is on my side, who can recognise and understand my needs, and who can offer a range of financial solutions.

… has demonstrable expertise in main-line business lending, and who can source and introduce me to the specialists for specialist banking areas.

… is a peer—a business manager. Not a salesperson. Not a bureaucrat.

… is approachable, professional and trustworthy.'

Based on my initial findings, I felt that at that time there was an excellent opportunity for the business banking operation to differentiate itself against its competition. At the same time it could generate superior results by adopting a 'major client management' orientation with its major business clients. In fact, this was the orientation these clients were seeking, and this orientation needed to embrace:

➤ *exceptional customer service.*

➤ *a consultative approach rather than an obvious 'selling' approach.*

➤ *less selling of bank products and services and more selling of the impact that the bank and its offerings might have on the major client's business operations and performance.*

➤ *concern for the profitable growth of the client, generating enhanced bank earnings as a result.*

➤ *the seeking out of profit-making/cost-reducing opportunities for major clients.*

➤ *the development of a 'win-win' and 'partners in profit' relationship.*

➤ *genuine interest and as far as possible, immersion in the business interests and affairs of major clients.*

➤ *development of client relations and loyalty which make them hard to break by competing banks.*

➤ *development of service excellence, where cost becomes secondary to service.*

➤ *effective management of bank expertise and resources on behalf of the major client.*

Major client management also requires the development of superior management skills, in other words getting desired and superior results through people. Such people include the major clients themselves, and on behalf of such clients, other bank personnel. Managing people in your own organisation, as well as outside—that is the major client—is the cornerstone of any major client management philosophy.

PROMOTIONAL TECHNIQUES

There is a wide range of promotional techniques executives, professionals and managers can use.

Over the years I have written a wide variety of papers and contributed to many other forms of publications, and have found that the following considerations are important in the context of promotional impact:

➤ Publishing material that is targeted to specific business sectors, rather than general business audiences.

➤ Taking into consideration the direct mail 'time-bomb' when designing a publication or mail-out. A typical response by the receiver of a mail-out:

First few seconds: 'Shall I throw it out or keep it?'

Next few seconds: 'Shall I examine it now or later?'

Next few seconds: 'Is it pertinent or interesting?'

Next few seconds: 'Is there a specific benefit in it for me?'

Next few seconds: 'Where shall I start reading?'

Next few seconds: 'Shall I continue reading?'

Next few seconds: 'Bang! This is interesting'—you have had the desired effect!

➤ Taking a reader orientation rather than a sender orientation: in both language and content.

➤ Minimising text and maximising graphics: the busy executive needs all the help available in time management!

➤ Using quality paper stock and covers.

➤ Using colour in print and text.

➤ Publishing quarterly newsletters (one of the fastest growing sectors of periodicals), again on a business sector basis, but calling them something other than a newsletter.

➤ On a targeted basis, circulating transcripts of professional speaking engagements—try cassette tapes rather than transcripts.

➤ Developing comprehensive handouts to go with seminar presentations, briefings and conferences in which the executive or manager presents or participates.

➤ Attaching a compliments slip (bearing an executive's name that is known to the recipient) to all publications that are sent out.

Research, as well as trial and error, have shown that the following elements are important, in developing *corporate brochures*:

➤ One brochure theme and heading has more impact than a multiple theme/heading: this requires a series of targeted brochures, rather than one general brochure.

➤ The orientation of the brochure must be the reader's needs, objectives and benefits first, and the sender's capabilities second.

➤ Use of sub-headings and minimisation of text enhances reading conduciveness.

➤ Soft 'pledges' from the organisation have impact: 'We will undertake whatever is necessary in an attempt to ensure your complete satisfaction.'

➤ Starring (*) some of the benefits, and adding this copy line can be very effective: 'Starred services include tested, innovative approaches unavailable from others in our industry.'

➤ Include a section in which you attempt to quantify the benefits of dealing with the organisation or the costs of not dealing with the organisation.

➤ In such quantification, use charts and graphics for credibility and substance.

➤ Encourage feedback from clients and prospects about their reaction to corporate brochures.

In preparing *brochure copy*, the following criteria are important:

➤ Who is the target audience and why should they listen to you?

➤ How will they benefit?

➤ Be specific, for example, describe a technique that was developed in August 1999 (rather than 'recently'), which improves productivity by as much as 38% (rather than 'greatly'). Every vague phrase risks losing credibility and readership.

➤ Enumerate whenever it makes sense ('The five steps are: 1..., 2..., 3..., etc.') as this makes for more logical, easier reading.

➤ Use words and phrases rather than lengthy sentences in order to get more descriptive copy in less space, which generates livelier, more compact, faster to read material.

➤ Stress uniqueness: the different, the startling, the unknown, the new. Avoid the old hat, the stereotype, the obvious.

➤ Write in a lively, powerful, exciting style. Start by taping an oral presentation of the subject and then typing a transcript (spoken words are often more exciting than written ones).

➤ After the first written draft (based on the transcript), edit, rewrite and polish. Test it on colleagues. Read every word asking ... 'Will the average prospect be interested in this?'

➤ Eliminate 99% of the 'soft' copy: history, introduction, background and so forth. Contacts seek up-to-date, hard-hitting, practical information and solutions to their problems.

Other promotional materials which I have found to be successful include:

➤ Using 'tickler' advertisements and mail-outs, which tease and engender curiosity on the part of the reader, and are geared to developing response and leads.

➤ Sending out regular media releases with industry information and comment on topics of current interest—but these releases have to be newsworthy so that you become acknowledged by the media as a source of expertise and knowledge.

➤ Developing information packages for media representatives attending seminars and conferences.

➤ Writing articles for publication in newspapers and periodicals, always enclosing a photograph of the writer and brief information on the organisation.

➤ Becoming known as an authority on a certain subject, with resultant periodic radio and television interviews, at which brief written information about the organisation is always provided for accurate newscast introduction purposes.

➤ Developing low-budget video movies, demonstrating capabilities, for use at open houses in the organisation's offices, and at other events. Make sure you are in them!

➤ Circulating information packages on the organisation and yourself to prospective clients attending seminars and conferences.

➤ Using invitation cards, rather than conventional letters or mail-outs, for invitations to special events sponsored by the organisation, and hosting 'free lunches' or breakfasts at such gatherings (usually generating greater response).

➤ Using telemarketing for a variety of market research and direct mail follow-up purposes.

➤ Envelope 'stuffing'—taking the opportunity of introducing or reinforcing specific topics, by appending special write-ups to normal everyday correspondence.

DEVELOPING WRITING EFFECTIVENESS

Writing has no other goal than to help readers understand and comply with your propositions, requests and ideas. The reader should never experience problems working out what you are trying to say. The first rule of any written information is to assist the reader to follow and understand what you are trying to communicate, and the guidelines below will help you attain this.

Giving your document 'person-appeal'. Check out these two statements:

➤ 'The package will be shipped express courier on Tuesday.'
➤ 'I will send you the package via express courier on Tuesday.'

The first sentence suggests a production line. The second expresses more person-appeal, as it tells you who will be involved. Include person-appeal wherever you can in your writing. Compare the following statements to see the effect of the person-appeal approach:

➤ 'An error was found when your invoice was compiled.'
➤ 'I found an error when I was compiling your invoice.'

Emphasise reader first, sender second. When you write, place yourself in the shoes of your audience. What might their first question be? How might the reader react to the write-up? What extra information might the reader seek? What information might raise doubts in the reader's mind? For example, a marketing manager reviewing a brief for the latest promotional campaign may be less concerned with costs and other financial matters, if the writer emphasises the creativity of the promotions.

Be factual. Minimise unnecessary vagaries in your text. Listen to these two statements and assess which might be more effective in persuading you to accept the new approach.

➤ 'This latest approach can increase production and enhance your bottomline.'
➤ 'This latest approach can increase output by 15% without any extra staff expense, adding $90 000 to your margin in six months, according to our preliminary assessment.'

Write like a 'video camera'. Try to visualise your subject while you write, just as though you were looking through the viewfinder of a video camera. Also help your reader see your ideas, not just read your words. For example, 'Your restaurants are seas of happy faces' creates a graphic and realistic impression. 'You have a lot of customers in your restaurants' is an oblique and easily forgotten statement.

Simplify the reading. 'Signpost' statements act as guidelines for your readers. They guide them to where your text is going. These statements are known as signposts because they reveal what is about to follow. They simplify reading, so your readers do not have to work out what you are trying to say. For example: 'Next I will summarise some possible disadvantages to our program and then why I believe you should accept it.'

Effective writing techniques. Some key techniques for communicating written messages effectively are:

➤ *Anecdotes*: 'Across the board we experienced great savings. For example, the technical division saved 15% against forecast by improved filing systems; dispatch saved 10% by recycling.'
➤ *Benchmarking*: 'Although personnel expenses increased 8% last year, in our business sector a 12% rise was more often reported.'
➤ *Metaphysics*: 'Our approach to monitoring operations follows the principle of the temperature gauge. It alerts the need for action if labour costs exceed expectations.'

Structure. Formal correspondence should never deviate from the theme that is being addressed at any one place in the text. For example, in a proposal for public relations, costs relating to investor relations might be addressed. In that same section, do not deviate by introducing an idea for better newsletters, unless this directly relates to the subject of those costs.

Structure relates to the sections of your reports and needs proposals; paragraphs and sentences. All the paragraphs in one particular section should relate directly to the same subject. A paragraph needs to address just one topic. A sentence needs to include one single notion, not a range of concepts.

Establishing certainty. Writers strengthen their cases by establishing certainty in their texts. The best text is assertive and sounds credible. It makes direct assumptions rather than clouds the reader with uncertainties or ambiguities. Compare the following ambiguous statements with the more credible statements:

➤ 'Our process may perhaps cause minor irritation.'
➤ 'Our process will cause some minor yet tolerable irritation, bearing in mind the benefits.'

Clarification. Probably the most annoying question for the reader to have to ask is:

➤ 'What are you referring to?' Here is an anecdote demonstrating this: 'Our parts were sent in different packages without approved labelling and delivered by truck. We did not expect this.'

➤ What does 'this' refer to? Was the person writing the report concerned about the packaging, the labelling, the mode of delivery, or all three?

Statements which are unclear give the impression of muddled thinking. Whereas some mistakes are mere hindrances to easily digested communication, failure to be accurate about what you are referring to can cause confusion.

CONTINUING AND CONCLUDING THE TYPICAL COACHING PROCESS

Clearly, role play and video critiquing represent powerful media for improving selling style. Also, joining the coachee on sales calls and critiquing their performance greatly enhances the coaching process and outcome.

Other than that, the core coaching processes of coaching meetings, progress reporting and closure all continue to play vital roles in this high impact coaching intervention, which invariably generates tangible and highly beneficial outcomes, both for the sponsoring organisation and the individual.

KEYNOTE

➤ Sales training is only the starting point in the journey to sales proficiency, let alone excellence.

➤ Building and applying new skills as if they are habits requires sustained effort and input over quite a timeframe.

➤ Executive coaching does this, by including pre-brief, role play, test and debrief.

➤ Leading to continuous improvement under the watchful eye and supportive attention of the appropriately experienced and trained senior coach.

Chapter 16

A Typical Coaching Process for Professional Presentations and Public Speaking

> 66 Presentation delivery is 80% of the group communication success formula 99

INTRODUCTION

It is interesting how far we have developed in communications. We can speak to people around the world and in space, and we can receive and project images over huge distances. We all treat long distance telephone calls as a natural part of our business and personal lives.

However, what happens when you have to stand up in front of an audience and make a speech or presentation? Do you get a knot in your stomach? Does your voice rise an octave? Do you forget your words? How do you start? How do you perform as you get underway? How do you end your presentation? Here are some speaker traits you need to try to avoid!

➤ *Rambling on and on and going off in many different directions.* This speaker is not usually prepared and he often loses himself, as well as the audience, by moving from one subject to another without apparently noticing. The effect is disastrous as he fails to make his point successfully and the audience turns off completely.

➤ *Pacing backwards and forwards, like a lion in a cage.* This trait gives the speaker a thoroughly bored appearance. It is almost as though the time will pass more quickly if he walks to and fro.

➤ *'I...I...I...'* This speaker is constantly saying, '*I* did this, and *I* believe in that and *I* must tell you about the other thing that happened ...' She is pompous, sometimes arrogant and certainly has a good opinion of herself. She puts the audience off quite early in her speech.

➤ *Lack of animation.* This presenter is expressionless, statuesque, blank-faced and has a remarkable ability to put people to sleep after a good lunch.

➤ *Lack of sincerity.* This speaker is too contrived and too much of an actor to be convincing. She goes to the other extreme and tries to appeal to the audience's emotions, but without sincerity. She assumes that the audience will be fully behind her as she play-acts her role. The only trouble is, the audience senses that this is a well-rehearsed sham and they switch off.

➤ *Forced funniness.* How many funny presenters really are funny? One in 20 perhaps. The funny presenter often assumes he has to make his audience laugh and so he tells a joke, often resulting in laughter out of sympathy. Forced funniness can turn an audience off.

➤ *Difficult to hear.* The presenter who cannot be heard fails to realise she is speaking to an audience, and she rambles on with her dissertation in a one-to-one affair with the lectern!

Most executives, professionals and managers suffer from some or all of these symptoms, occasionally or every time they make a presentation to a group. Such apprehension and traits are often caused by concerns about not being able to remember your lines, or making a fool of yourself, or making a poor presentation, or failing to meet your objectives, but mainly from inadequate training and preparation.

Stand back from all this for a moment, and do some 'imagineering'. Dream a little! Suppose you were flying across the Pacific and the pilot asked you to take over the controls, how would you react? Suppose you attended a symphony concert and the conductor handed you the baton, how would you react? Suppose your were in an operating theatre and the surgeon asked you to take over an operation, how would you react?

You would likely get a knot in your stomach, you would get that tight sensation around your collar, and you would not know how or where to start. You would definitely portray some strange and atypical traits as you tried to grasp the fundamentals of your new and strange role! This is because you are neither trained nor prepared to fly a plane, conduct an orchestra, or perform surgery! If you had been trained or prepared, how would you have reacted? No problems, hand me the controls, music maestro please, hand me the scalpel, nurse!

Yes, the secret to making successful speeches or presentations is to be both *trained* and *prepared*, particularly in the art of delivery which is 80% of the group communication success formula.

Most executives and managers, on the other hand, can find group presentations quite difficult, as did Demosthenes in ancient Greece, who was afflicted with a terrible speech impediment which caused him great difficulty early in his career. However, he persevered to overcome his impediment and practised his speeches by shouting at the surf and talking with small stones in his mouth; in this way, he coached himself to become the greatest orator of his time. His presentation 'delivery' became outstanding!

And through coaching in executive or professional presentations and public speaking, the presentation delivery of coachees can become outstanding.

EXAMPLE

A technically/functionally brilliant partner in another well-known professional services firm found it very difficult to communicate with groups of people. By using my proprietary methodology in presentations and public speaking, she became more comfortable, confident and effective as a presenter. Video-taped and critiqued rehearsals always add outstanding value in such coaching assignments.

A TYPICAL COACHING PROCESS IN MORE DETAIL

Rather than become overly repetitive, the core coaching processes described in Chapter 6, and discussed further in terms of their application in the professional consultative selling context in Chapter 15—'A typical coaching process for professional consultative selling', can all be used to good effect in the case of coaching in presentations and public speaking.

As noted in Chapter 15, the coach needs to explore previous training provided and use and leverage off any such previous investment in it. Invariably, however, little if any such training has been provided, in which case we use my guidelines. An extract from which now follows.

EXTRACTS FROM MY PROFESSIONAL PRESENTATIONS AND PUBLIC SPEAKING GUIDELINES

In developing your delivery to maestro standards, you first need to be clear about speaker styles, in fact, your own speaking style. By way of reminder (refer to Chapter 7—'A typical executive coaching process' for more details), your operating style is likely to be one or more of the following:

➤ *Commander/doer*: usually directs other people and works energetically to get results.

➤ *Responder/initiator*: seeks to understand others, communicates very well and leads enthusiastically.

➤ *Empathiser/humanist*: the people, rather than production-orientated individual, with an amicable style.

➤ *Evaluator/detailer*: the analytical, logical and meticulous planner and organiser.

➤ *Idea generator*: the conceptual and creative thinker who can see endless possibilities and show extremes in behaviour.

➤ *All-rounder*: the balanced individual, who has a flexible style, yet does not show extremes in behaviour.

FIRST IMPRESSIONS COUNT

What happens to the audience, when the speaker stands up or goes to the speaker's lectern? They stop, look, listen and form first impressions.

Here are some examples of first impressions. The first speaker immediately searches for a glass of water and gulps it down, while eyeing the audience nervously. He coughs and loosens his collar. He has trouble getting out his notes and overheads, and drops something on the floor. His hands are shaking, and as if to stop them he grasps the lectern with both hands and stares at the back of the room. He is obviously so nervous that the audience feels embarrassed or turns off completely.

The second speaker starts by not being sure where she should position herself for the speech—where she is sitting, at the table, or at the overhead projector.

She scratches her head and looks blank or somewhat baffled. She 'ums' and 'ahs' and starts her speech by saying that she really cannot add much to the previous speakers. She is obviously unprepared and can turn the audience against her. Why should they bother to listen if she is unprepared? She is wasting their time.

The third speaker walks very slowly, even slinks up to the lectern, looking very serious indeed, and very *unhappy*. He scowls at the audience and starts off by saying they will have to bear with him as he does not normally speak in public. He seems as though he is about to take on a task he would far rather avoid. The audience can react by being reluctant too—reluctant to listen to him!

The fourth speaker has problems getting up off her chair—it is too close to the table. As she rises, she staggers forward as she gets her thigh caught against the table. Her glass of water rocks perilously and she makes a lunge to save it! A shaky start like this does not bode well for the rest of the speech, and the audience knows it.

The correct way to start and to create a good impression is to slide back your chair from the table and walk over to the lectern (if there is one) as though you are walking over to greet an acquaintance whom you have not seen for a while. Then pause, look at the audience, smile and then start your presentation. Your audience is there to hear your speech. Make sure that your first impressions count and help them concentrate on your speech.

HOW TO DEVELOP SUCCESSFUL PRESENTATIONS AND SPEECHES

There are several elements to be reviewed, including administration, objectives, fact-finding, assembling content, and format.

ADMINISTRATION

Review the following:

➤ Date, time and location of speech.
➤ Duration of speech and whether there will be time for audience questions.
➤ Room size, shape and layout and whether it will allow the use of visual aids.
➤ Availability of visual aid equipment.
➤ Speech subject and orientation—you may know the subject but are you aware of any preferred orientation? For example, theory versus practice or personal experience versus second-hand experience.

➤ The make-up of the audience in terms of age, sex, background, interests and reasons for attending the presentation.
➤ Who the other speakers are and why you were chosen.

OBJECTIVES

Consider the following:

➤ What information is to be imparted to the audience, and how can it best be imparted? Through a straight lecture? Using a 'Socratic' approach (questioning the audience)? Through stories or anecdotes? Through audience involvement in case studies, group discussion, individual exercise or simulation?
➤ How are you to excite the audience and provoke thought and possibly action? By being enthusiastic yourself? By demonstrating a knowledge of relevant facts and figures? By demonstrating conviction? By being short and to the point? By asking the audience for response or action?
➤ How are you going to amuse the audience? Through limited use of humour? By keeping the speech short and easygoing? By appealing to their specific interests? By orientating your presentation to the specific event?
➤ How are you going to be convincing? By being logical? By appealing to their emotions? By quoting facts and figures authoritatively? By being precise? By quoting with accuracy? By articulating audience advantages?
➤ Delivering information, exciting the audience, amusing them and being convincing are all important ingredients for successful speech-making.

FACT-FINDING

Being asked to speak on a selected subject or subjects requires the acquisition of information or facts. Fact-finding can be conducted in many ways:

➤ *Through desk research*: use of publications, books, periodicals and files at the office or at home.
➤ *Through library research*: similarly, at the public library. Main branches can provide information on virtually any topic.
➤ *Through computer databases*: you can access a wide variety of information on the Internet and other databases. By using key words you can source abstracts and summaries from a wide range of data sources.

➤ *By contacting people with the necessary knowledge*: informal or formal interviews, either over the telephone or in person, can provide very useful judgemental information which may be able to amplify some of the bare bones or facts derived from other forms of non-personal research.

➤ *Through careful analysis of all acquired information*: the 'raw' information derived from all these sources needs to be 'refined' through careful analysis in the context of audience needs and appeal.

ASSEMBLING CONTENT

Once the fact-finding is refined and oriented towards the audience, the material has to be assembled in an order and format that can be presented. In terms of order, the following is offered as a guide and is somewhat similar to the steps for successful one-on-one meetings:

➤ How shall I start in a way which grasps audience *attention*?

➤ How shall I continue in a way which develops their *curiosity*?

➤ How can I continue in a way which enhances their *trust* of me and my presentation?

➤ How can I develop the *main thrust* of my speech?

➤ How can I end with *impact*?

FORMAT

Some of the key points here are:

➤ The information provided must be to the point and relevant to the audience.

➤ The speech must progress logically form one part to the next.

➤ Time must be allocated suitably to each part of the presentation. For example: 'attention' 10%; 'curiosity' 10%; 'trust' 10%; 'main thrust' 60%; and, 'ending impact' 10%. However, in planning your time allocation, remember set-up time and allow five minutes for this, and also allocate for questions, which depending on the length and style of your presentation, may account for 10 to 20 minutes.

HOW TO GRASP THE AUDIENCE'S ATTENTION

You may have heard the expression: 'You win or lose the sale in the first 30 seconds!'

The same can be the case with making a speech or presentation—you can win or lose your audience in the first 30 seconds. In order to improve the chances of successfully winning your audience in the first 30 seconds, you must, as stressed earlier, have done your homework and know who comprises your audience and what they are expecting, both as a group and as individuals. Also, in order to attain and retain audience attention, the way in which you 'open' the speech is vital. Some of the do's and don'ts are:

Don't:

➤ Waver. Once you have taken your place at the lectern, taken a few seconds to get yourself organised and to allow the audience to become quiet, move forward boldly to your opening.

➤ Start negatively by using such phrases as 'Public speaking is not my forte', 'I have not had time to prepare', 'Please bear with me', 'I am not very knowledgeable about this subject', 'I have been asked to speak against my will' or 'I am afraid you will find this topic unpalatable'.

Do:

➤ Deep breathe well in advance of your speech.

➤ Move your chair away from the table before being introduced.

➤ Make sure you have approached the lectern or stood up at the table in a positive, business-like fashion.

➤ Organise your notes, visual aids and microphone before you start speaking.

How to build curiosity and trust

Having grasped the audience's attention, the speaker's job is now to develop the audience's curiosity and trust. As noted before:

➤ '*Attention*' will only last so long, and relates to the audience's sub-conscious question, 'Is this interesting?'

➤ '*Curiosity*' is the next phase in the sequence and relates to the audience's sub-conscious question, 'Might I learn something here? What has the speaker got up their sleeve?'

➤ '*Trust*' is the next phase in the sequence and is likened to the audience's sub-conscious question, 'Can I trust what the speaker says? Are they someone of integrity?'

The sequence of the speech can be likened to the ebb and flow of surf on the beach as the tide comes in. That tide has got to work its way up the beach, but in so doing the surf comes and goes, always moving higher up the beach. This is similar to audience interest: as the sequence of the speech unfolds, their interest ebbs and flows, but it must progress not only through the opening, curiosity and trust phases, but also through the key issue and ending phases.

It is your job as speaker to control the audience's interest, just as it is the job of some divine right or power to control the tides of the ocean! You have to get them up the beach. To do this, we will now concentrate on the 'curiosity' phase—the phase immediately following the opening of the speech, when the audience's attention has been grasped by your wonderful approach and opening statement! Here are some techniques:

➤ *Positive reactions.* It is often said that closing the sale is the culmination of a series of 'yes' responses from buyers. Get them and keep them in a positive frame of mind and they will close! This also applies to speakers and audiences, particularly during the early portion of the speech—you simply cannot afford to turn the audience off by provoking negative reactions.

➤ *'Confidential' information.* So-called 'confidential information—don't quote me' has an excellent effect on the audience and arouses considerable curiosity. Watch what information you give the audience, however. They are almost certain to quote you!

➤ *Visual aids.* We will review these later, but they are useful tools for arousing curiosity and for use later in the speech.

➤ *Audience interests.* Whenever possible, relate to the personal interests of your audience, be this social, domestic, business or career. Work out in advance how your subject matter can relate to the personal interests of the audience, leaving your own interests until last, if you include them at all. 'You' followed by 'we' appeal is the name of the game.

In order for your audience to develop trust in you the speaker and in what you are saying, the following aspects need careful consideration:

➤ You must appear to be sincere and to be telling the truth.

➤ You must not appear to over-exaggerate; whatever you say must be believable.

➤ You must appear to show respect for the audience, by being punctual, by dressing suitably for the occasion and by making an effort in terms of content, delivery and manner.

➤ Verify your presentation with quantifiable evidence or support such as statistics and factual accounts, wherever possible.

➤ Try to demonstrate your own expertise and experience, whether this be qualifications, career, research studies, other speaking engagements or practical experience. This is best managed by the person introducing you, detailing your relevant experience in their introduction. You should then enlarge on certain aspects of your background, which enhance the credibility of your presentation, as and when applicable. Keep these brief and to the point.

➤ Talk at the audience's level—never over the top of them, and never down to them.

➤ Incorporate all the positive elements of voice, word, breath and eye control.

HOW TO DELIVER THE MAIN THRUST OF YOUR SPEECH

Speech-making and presentations are a communication process—presenting effectively very often depends on the communication skills of the presenter, just as it is the case with professional and personal selling. These skills can be learned and improved upon, so as to upgrade the quality of personal presentations and communicating with groups.

Effective presenters know that they must vary their approach and operating style, depending on their audience. This is quite natural. We don't act the same way with different kinds of people we meet or different family members; we are constantly adjusting our style, depending on the response we get. By understanding different operating styles, professional presenters adjust their presentations and overall style to elicit the most positive response. Audiences tend to prefer professional presenters whom they perceive to be most like themselves.

We all have enough facets to our personalities to downplay some traits and emphasise others in a particular situation, without appearing phoney. By identifying the operating styles of the majority or main members of the audience, you can adapt your own style in order to gain the most favourable reaction and response. The research for this is best undertaken in advance.

As a group, there can and will be differences. For example, a group of business directors will be a very different audience to that of a group of supervisors or shop floor workers. As individuals, you need to assess who the key people are in the audience and their individual operating styles (see Chapter 7).

Clearly, a natural question is how to cope with different operating styles in the audience, as some of these styles seem to conflict. First, you need to identify who the key members of the audience are in terms of decision-making, politics, power and influence. Secondly, when developing eye contact with them, engage in an appropriate style of delivery which coincides with their own operating style. If you have not been able to identify who the critical members of the audience are, or their operating styles, then the main thrust of your speech can be enhanced by ensuring, just like the salesperson, that you concentrate on presenting benefits (rather than features) along with verification.

Features are things that are important to you, the presenter. Benefits are things that are important to the audience. For example, in making a case about why the audience—a group of prospective customers—should do business with your firm, features you may care to consider using may include: oldest firm in the business sector; most experienced staff; and, most technologically advanced products and services.

Converting these to benefits, they become 'We represent your "least risk" purchase decision, as we have been in business for 15 years'. 'Our highly experienced staff have the greatest capacity to understand and meet your precise needs.' 'Our products and services are designed to be cost-effective and quality assured as a result of our state-of-the-art technology in production.'

Verification in the case of your group presentations relates to providing validation, evidence or proof in the form of independent reports, testimonials, competitor comparisons, facts, statistics, case studies, demonstrations, anecdotes and examples. By building in such verifiers during the main thrust of your speech, you will become much more believable in the eyes of your audience.

ENDING WITH IMPACT

The football team starts the game with style. Their footwork, passing and team coordination is inspirational. They fail to score, however! This is the analogy of ending your speech or presentation with no impact. No matter how good the speech has been up to the end, if you don't end with impact, you won't have won over your audience. The ending needs to leave the audience inspired, motivated and above all, in full accordance with what you have been saying. Ending with impact can be accomplished with the following techniques:

➤ *'Act now'*. This technique asks the audience to do something right way, to act. In fact, the audience is likely to act sooner rather than later after your speech if you ask them to do so. If you ask them to do something the following week, they will more than likely forget or procrastinate. 'Act now' creates an excellent climax. Example: ' Register today and be assured of a place on the program!'

➤ *'Questioning'*. Ending by asking the audience a question can also have excellent impact. The question best relates to the main thrust of your speech, or to your opening statements. The question should be phrased so that the audience focuses on the main issues you have raised. Example: 'What will you do about drinking and driving now?'

➤ *'Saying'*. By quoting a better-known saying as an ending statement, one that directly relates to the main thrust of your speech or important elements of it, some speakers can have good ending impact. Be careful not to use a saying which is neither less than totally relevant to your speech nor which goes over the head of the audience. A better-known saying from an authoritative and well-known source is by far the best. Example: 'All work and no play makes Jack a dull boy.'

➤ *'Based on my experience'*. This technique summarises a third-party factual experience that directly relates to the main thrust of your speech. Example: 'In England as far back as in the 1930s with their Special Areas Act they attempted to diversify industry away from the major cities. They failed and in the main have continued to do so. It simply does not work.' With a factual example, the credibility of your speech and impact at the end are enhanced.

➤ The *'accountant's ending'*. You literally develop a balance sheet by summarising the pluses and minuses of your argument—the pluses far exceeding the minuses. Example: 'On the plus side, you have better prices, greater choice, better parking and higher levels of service. On the minus side, it will take you a few more minutes to get there. Isn't the choice obvious?'

In summary, ending with impact is important if you are to leave the audience in a favourable frame of mind or motivated to follow your advice. The ending must leave them 'on a high'.

SPEECH AIDS

There are several different kinds of speech aids which can be used in group presentations according to specific requirements. The main ones are fully typed scripts and prompter cards.

FULLY TYPED SCRIPT

This is best used for formal occasions, or for when you are 'going on record'. It can also be used when you have very tight time constraints—a typed script will allow for an average of double the content compared to speaking from prompter cards.

When preparing a script, simply follow the sequence suggested earlier: developing the speech, the start of the speech, curiosity and trust, the main thrust and end with impact.

Double-spaced typing and plenty of paragraphs are suggested, along with wide margins for making necessary notes regarding first impressions, speaking style, and voice, eye and word control.

The most important delivery criterion is to regularly eyeball the audience. This will require a slower delivery than if you were simply reading a book out loud. Not only must you regularly scrutinise the audience, but you must also be animated—use hands, facial expressions and supporting language. The reason for this, is that the audience may switch off if they simply see a statue read a text they could have read themselves at home in half the time.

What in fact you are doing is acting out the text for them. Be animated. Also don't *turn pages*—*slide* them across from one side of the lectern to the other when you have finished reading them, or slide them under your pad of pages if you are not using a lectern.

The advantages of the fully typed script relate to confidence that you are not going to forget your lines and that the intended content will be delivered accurately. The disadvantages relate to audience acceptance. You can appear to be too formal, stilted or boring and the audience can react negatively: 'I could have read that—I did not need him to read it to me.'

PROMPTER CARDS

Prompter cards can be used for any speech or presentation, providing you have the necessary notice to be able to develop them. The best prompter cards are of a size that fit comfortably in your hand—approximately 14 cm by 9 cm. They should be postcard weight for durability and ease of handling. Write on only one side of the card and each card should contain enough information to relate to one important element of your speech. So the first step will be to break down your speech into separate elements—each element addressing one idea or topic in full.

At the top of the card, you should write down the main lead-in sentence that addresses the element. Bold letters are needed to enhance legibility. Lower case often works best, but you can use upper case if you feel this is easier to read. Below this lead-in, note the various sub-elements that support or expand on the lead-in sentence. Again, in bold writing—felt tip pens are ideal. Each sub-element should be in point or bullet form, to make it stand out from the rest.

On the left-hand margin of the card you can note, as and when you need to show a visual aid, with a letter A, B, C etc., which is cross-indexed to the visual aids. Also, number the cards in sequence in the top right-hand corner in case you drop them. Use colour for highlighting key points.

For delivery purposes, just glance at your cards from time to time—don't read them. They are prompters only, not full scripts. They can be used at a lectern or at a table when standing or seated. Either lay them in front of you and slide them across as each one is finished with, or do the same in the palm of your hand, tucking each one behind the last one, when it is finished with.

There is no need to hide the prompter cards—indeed it would be wrong to do so—but don't rely on them to the extent that you are reading from them. Generally prompter cards are designed to be a brief synopsis of your speech, and are a marvellous prompting device to remind you what to say at any given time. Their advantages are far-reaching:

➤ They give you confidence that you will not forget your lines and that you will deliver all your intended content.
➤ They enhance your eye contact with the audience, allowing you to speak to them rather than just read a text.
➤ They allow you freedom to talk animatedly rather than having to hold a typewritten speech, or to walk about and 'mix it' with the audience.

➤ They can be carried in a pocket or purse, and handled unobtrusively in the palm of the hand.

➤ They may be re-used often, as they are durable.

➤ They can be used in front of both large and small audiences.

The disadvantage of prompter cards is that they do take time to prepare and are more effective if you also take time to practise with them.

USE OF VISUALS IN PRESENTATIONS

Visual aids can help you make a better speech or presentation. The most popular alternatives include: overhead transparencies and computer graphics, flipcharts and whiteboards. Use of visuals is recommended whenever practicable because they increase audience retention rates, in other words the amount they remember of your presentation, from 20–30% with just words to 40–50% with words and visuals. These retention rates are increased to between 60–70% if you use words, visuals and also get the audience involved through discussions, questions, case studies and simulations. Naturally visuals are not always appropriate, for example with an after dinner speech.

Visuals provide for greater impact, emphasis, clarity, understanding and interest. They assist the audience grasp more complex issues, concepts and relationships more readily. They help you, the speaker, stay organised, be more confident and help to ensure that you do not leave out important items.

OVERHEAD TRANSPARENCIES AND COMPUTER GRAPHICS

There are many commercial firms that produce overhead transparencies—in colour too, although these can be quite expensive. The alternative is to produce them yourself using a computer, graphics software and a colour printer. Transparent overlays can also be used to build up more complex charts and diagrams. For example, you could start with a map of China, then overlay it with the provincial borders, then overlay that with the provincial capitals and so on.

To point with transparencies, use a piece of paper to gradually uncover your transparency revealing an unfolding story, diagram or series of bullet points. Also you can use a pen or pencil to point to particular items on your transparency or you can purchase special arrows for this. Never face the screen and talk at the same time, as this detracts from 'eyeball rapport' with the audience.

In developing content for an overhead, make sure the text is bold and large—a standard font is usually too small—it has to be visible at the back of the room. Keep the overhead simple and precise, don't write too much on each one. Handwritten overheads have to be legible and have a balanced format—using graph paper behind them when you write them up helps vertical and horizontal consistency. Number the overheads as this helps to keep them in order and you can reference the number in your speech notes. Turn off the overhead projector when you aren't using it to cut out the glare from the blank screen which can be distracting.

Increasingly presenters are replacing overhead transparencies with computer graphics which through an adaptor, can be projected onto a screen. This makes for a highly professional presentation with great impact, but the impact can be created by the technology rather than by the presenter, which can be the major strength or weakness of computer graphics—you be the judge!

FLIP CHARTS AND WHITEBOARDS

Flip charts are usually large pads of paper on an easel or stand at the speaker's side. They offer a marvellous way to record key points or features of your presentation, or audience comments, questions or replies. They can be written during your speech or presentation, or prepared beforehand.

One useful way to write them during the speech and to remember what to include, is to pencil in the content in the top corner of the flip chart which is closest to you and to copy it when and as appropriate in full size on the flip chart. With complex diagrams you can pre-prepare them in pencil (which will not be visible to the audience), then use felt-tip pen to trace over the pencil guide—very impressive!

The same rules for content apply here as for overhead transparencies and computer graphics: boldness, clarity, simplicity and not too much verbiage. Use consistent letter styles and sizes and vary the colour occasionally for effect or emphasis. Felt-tip pens stand out most effectively. When writing on flip charts during your speech or presentation, avoid turning your back to the audience and don't talk to the chart as you write!

If you decide to prepare them before the speech, use a blank sheet to cover the first chart, or intersperse blanks whenever you aren't referring to the flip chart. The height of the letters should be approximately 4 cm for every 12 m of maximum distance from the audience. If it is necessary to refer to more than one flip chart page at a time, you can tear them off the pad and attach them to the walls of the room using masking tape or 'blue-tack'.

An alternative to the flip chart is the wipeable whiteboard with special erasable markers, which again provides for impact, professionalism and ease of operation. Electronic whiteboards are particularly effective if you need a copy of what you have written.

In continuing and concluding a typical presentations and public speaking coaching process, as always the coach conducts coaching meetings, progress reporting and closure—our trusty core coaching processes from Chapter 6!

EXAMPLE

A senior executive charged with corporate strategic marketing responsibilities was felt to be rare talent by some of his colleagues, while others found it hard to understand him or accept his thinking 'outside the square'. Through executive coaching I was able to help him and the organisation ascertain that he indeed had much to offer, but that his problem lay in communication. Coaching over time helped him significantly improve his personal selling and group presentation capabilities and performance.

KEYNOTE

➤ Preparation, preparation, preparation is the key to presentation success.
➤ The above, coupled with proven techniques which can be learned and applied with the help of an appropriately experienced and trained coach and entailing plenty of video-taped and critiqued rehearsals.
➤ Here is yet another example of an effectiveness area which can be dramatically improved through coaching.

Chapter 17

OVERALL SUMMARY AND CONCLUSIONS

66 Time to walk the talk! 99

I have had more than two decades' work experience spanning four continents in such diverse roles as teacher, sports coach, purchasing agent, salesperson, production manager, HR specialist, marketing manager, general manager, CEO, company director, business owner, consultant and executive coach.

I can categorically say that what differentiates successful from less or unsuccessful organisations, be they public, private or not for profit, is the way they lead and manage their most vital and variable resource, their people.

And I can also confirm that the vast majority of organisations, large and small, do not do this very well. As one managing director said, who came to see me the day before writing this last chapter: 'You know I believe business is fundamentally quite simple. What complicates it, is the people!'

And what can make business fly is the people through their galvanisation into a cohesive, unified force who know where they are headed, are appropriately equipped, trained and coached to get there, and who are amply rewarded (extrinsically *and* intrinsically) for their efforts.

This has to start at the top and continue at the top. For unless the investment, energy and time is put into senior people in any organisation, their motivation and performance will neither be maximised nor sustained. This will have sub-optimal consequences on leverage through their staff, their teams and the financial and other resources for which they are responsible.

I am not talking here about management fads or mirages. I am talking about sustained one-on-one individual input to ensure continuous improvement in human endeavour at the top, and indeed throughout organisations. This is the opportunity that coaching provides. Coaching also provides a vehicle by which talent can be better attracted, retained, grown and developed. Talent management represents a key factor for organisations to compete successfully in the future and becomes a 'boiling' organisational imperative for many.

And coaching adds value in so many other ways, whether it is fast-tracking the assimilation of newly appointed people, further developing the effectiveness of key people, lifting team performance and output to new levels, bedding down major change faster and more surely, resolving square-peg-in-round-hole issues, or turning around performance.

The economic benefits of attaining such outcomes, through coaching, can be huge. Time and again at my organisation, we find the return on investment on coaching processes exceeds 20-fold within 18 months. Where else can you get a better return?

And although coaching can cover a great spectrum of applications, coaching efficiency can be enhanced through the use of core coaching processes, which can be applied effectively to many different circumstances, particularly in the hands of well-trained and highly experienced top practitioners of coaching. But for coaching to be truly effective, its variants of executive coaching, career consulting and mentoring, along with counselling, all need to be well researched, well understood and carefully applied as and when appropriate.

And so as you come to the end of this book, which I hope you have enjoyed and found stimulating, just think about where you might apply this reinforced or new-found knowledge:

➤ Would you coach that new hire to assimilate faster and more surely into the organisation?
➤ Do you know of a gifted technical or functional specialist who needs to develop their collaborative 360° leadership skills?
➤ Are you worried about losing a talented key person?

➤ Are you, or your organisation, seeking to groom someone or some people for the top?

➤ Is your organisation about to go through major change?

➤ Are you wondering how to help someone implement new-found knowledge or use, practically, new self-awareness from performance review or 360° surveys?

➤ Do you know of a mature executive or crucial person who will benefit from, and where the organisation will also gain, from unravelling how they spend the last chapters of their careers with the organisation and thereafter?

➤ Or, do you know of a key person who lets themselves down when they have to speak in public, make a presentation, or sell themselves (personally or professionally)?

If so, try 'executive coaching!' Or if the assignment is too tough, or time too short, call us in to provide it from The Stephenson Partnership!

Further reading

BOOKS

Bridges, W. (1997) *Creating You & Co.: Learn to Think like the CEO of Your Own Career*, Addison-Wesley, Reading, Mass.

Catalyst, inc. (1998) *Advancing Women in Business – The Catalyst Guide: Best Practices from the Corporate Leaders*, Jossey-Bass, San Francisco.

Fortgang, L.B. (1999) *Take Yourself to the Top: How the Secrets of a Leading Life Coach will Help You Achieve Success*, Thorsons, London.

Fritts, P.J. (1998) *The New Managerial Mentor: Becoming a Learning Leader to Build Communities of Purpose*, Davies-Black, Palo Alto.

Grigg, J. (1997), *Portfolio Working: A Practical Guide to Thriving in the Changing Workplace*, Centre for Worklife Counselling, London.

Letcher, M. (1997), *Making Your Future Work*, Pan Macmillan, Sydney.

Moses, B. (1997), *Career Intelligence: Mastering the New Work and Personal Realities*, Stoddard, Don Mills, Ontario.

Quick, J. and Tice, L. (1997) *Personal Coaching for Results: How to Mentor and Inspire Others to Amazing Growth*, Thomas Nelson, Nashville.

Vandevelde, H. (1997), *Beyond the CV: Securing a Lifetime of Work in the Global Market*, Butterworth-Heinemann, Oxford.

Whitworth, L. et al. (1998) *Co-active Coaching: New Skills for Coaching People Toward Success in Work and Life*, Davies-Black, Palo Alto.

Witherspoon, R. and White, R.P. (1997) *Four Essential Ways that Coaching Can Help Executives*, Center for Creative Leadership, Greensboro.

ARTICLES

Ballati, J., Edwards, J. and Andrew, P. (1997) 'Mentoring structures within a professional development program', *Training and Development in Australia*, Vol. 24, no. 5, pp. 8-14.

Davis, G.E. (1999) 'CEO succession crisis: lessons learned', *Management Review*, Vol. 88, no. 4, p. 62.

Ewart, J. (1997) 'Fill your skill gap', *Management* (NZ), July, pp. 50-52, 54, 57.

Goldstein, L. (1999) 'A career coach tries to make a leader out of me', *Fortune*, Vol. 140, no. 5, p. 290ff.

Grossman, R.J. (1999) 'Ensuring a fast start', *HRMagazine*, Vol. 44, no. 7, pp. 32-38.

Hall, D.T., Otazo, K.L. and Hollenbeck, G.P. (1999) 'Behind closed doors: what really happens in executive coaching', *Organizational Dynamics*, Vol. 27, no. 3, pp. 39-53.

Hyatt, J. (1997) 'The zero-defect CEO', *Inc.*, Vol. 19, June, p. 46-48.

Kiser, K. (1999) 'Executive coach', *Training*, Vol. 36, no. 8, pp. 34-35.

Laabs, J.J. (1998) 'Career help on the Internet' *Workforce*, Vol. 77, March, supp. pp. 21-22.

Masciarelli, J.P. (1999) 'Less lonely at the top', *Management Review*, Vol. 88, no. 4, pp. 58-61.

McColl, G. (1999) 'Engendering good management', *Management Today* (AIM), May, pp. 15-19.

McKenzie, B.C. (1997) 'Facilitating learning in organisations', *Management* (AIM), April, pp. 20-21.

Ragins, B.R. and Mattis, M. (1998) 'Gender gap in the executive suite: CEOs and female executives report on breaking the glass ceiling', *Academy of Management Executive*, Vol. 12, Feb., pp. 28-42.

Tapsell, S. (1999) 'With a little help from my friend', *Management* (NZ), Vol. 46, no. 2, pp. 45-47.

Thach, L. and Heinselman, T. (1999) 'Executive coaching defined', *Training and Development*, Vol. 53, no. 3, pp. 34-39.

Index